VIDEO RECORDING TECHNOLOGY:

Its Impact on Media
and Home Entertainment

COMMUNICATION TEXTBOOK SERIES
Jennings Bryant—Editor

Broadcasting
James Fletcher—Advisor

BEVILLE • Audience Ratings: Radio,
Television, Cable
(Revised Student Edition)
ADAMS • Social Survey Research
Methods for Mass Media
Research
NMUNGWUN • Video Recording
Technology: Its Impact
on Media and Home Entertainment

VIDEO RECORDING TECHNOLOGY:
Its Impact on Media and Home Entertainment

Aaron Foisi Nmungwun

 LAWRENCE ERLBAUM ASSOCIATES, PUBLISHERS
1989   Hillsdale, New Jersey   Hove and London

Grateful acknowledgment is made for permission to reprint the following copyrighted material: Excerpted from: "Teething Rings," from *The Media Lab*, by Stewart Brand. Copyright © 1987 by Stewart Brand.

Lawrence Erlbaum Associates, Inc., Publishers
365 Broadway
Hillsdale, New Jersey 07642

Library of Congress Cataloging-in-Publication Data
Nmungwun, Aaron Foisi.
   Video recording technology : its impact on media and home entertainment / Aaron Foisi Nmungwun.
      p.   cm. — (Communication textbook series)
   Bibliography: p.
   Includes index.
   ISBN 0-8058-0360-2
   ISBN 0-8058-0622-9
   1. Video tape recorders and recording—History.   2. Magnetic recorders and recording—History.   I. Title.   II. Series.
TK6655.V5N65   1989
621.388'34—dc19   88-31281
                                                       CIP

Printed in the United States of America
10 9 8 7 6 5 4 3 2 1

Contents

This book is dedicated to my father, Aaron Nmungwun, Sr. and to my best friend Ekeoche Awajiogak, whose untimely deaths dealt a serious blow, yet presented a challenge; to my mother Ruth; and to Kim, Ante, Ntente, Emma, Jiller, Lola, and Isomgboawaji. Finally, thank you Joan for the last minute inspiration.

Preface

*T*his book is the result of several readings on the growing interest of an emerging new technology in the media. Curiosity, as well as interest, prompted my quest to document the history of video recording technology and the factors that contributed to such changes in new technologies. During my research for the PhD Comprehensive Examination in Media Theory, I came to realize that although video recording technology has made a great impact on the media, and more recently on consumers, little was known about its origin. Understanding its relationship to film and television technologies, I was also curious to explore not only its history, which I discovered was buried deep in magnetic recording history, but also what factors brought about such technological changes. During the 4-year period that followed, this curiosity led to intensive research culminating in the birth of this text.

The basis of this study is twofold: First, the influence of two pioneers in the field of video recording technology, Ampex Corporation and RCA, is imminent in this study. Of the primary research materials collected, those from these two organizations (especially Ampex) form the bulk of this study. For the first time in their history, Ampex opened their archives to the extent required by this study (which not only deals with video recording but also includes audio magnetic recording technology). Peter Hammar's (curator and consultant at the Ampex Museum) relentless input, provided through several meetings, telephone calls, and recorded interviews, served as an integral part of this study. Wendy Chu's contribution at the David Sarnoff RCA Research Laboratory Library in Princeton, New Jersey, was also valuable. The second part of this study deals with the determining factors resulting in changes of such new technologies. Dr. Janet Staiger, an authority on the subject of film technology with several publications and a dissertation to her credit, has made a great impact on this aspect of my text. I thank each of these individuals.

During the 4-year period it took to complete this research, several other individuals have contributed generously. For their assistance in obtaining those materials that are not available in any public library, I am particularly indebted to Judy Friedman of the NBC Library and Doris Katz of the Research Department at NBC in New York, Edana McCaffery of the Television Information Center in New York, and also to Mark Schubin.

Considering how important various periodicals, technical journals, and government publications were to this study, it would not have been possible to accomplish my task without the assistance of The New York Public Library's Science, Performing Arts, and Patent Divisions and the Theatre Arts Library.

I am particularly indebted to Professor William K. Everson, my mentor, whose advice and guidance were invaluable throughout my doctorate program at New York University.

Aaron F. Nmungwun

Prologue

*T*he video recording industry is one of the most economically viable industries today. Its popularity has culminated in the continual expansion of the consumer market for videocassette recorders. However, all along, its history has taken a backseat. Contributing to this ignorance is the lack of adequate text that attempts to trace the origin of magnetic audio/video recording. This book shows that the concept of magnetic recording was seriously considered by the mid-1800s, resulting in its ultimate practical use in the early 1900s. Initially developed in Europe, audio magnetic recording, although seen by many as a potential success, failed due to factors including mismanagement, blackmail, and inferior technology. The revival of this technology came in the 1930s when a market was imminent for it in the broadcast industry. Europeans, especially Germans, pioneered an intensive development, signalling the appearance of a new and superior audio magnetic technology during the World War II years.

The transfer of this technology to the United States after the war resulted in another evolution in the industry. By the early 1950s, audio magnetic recording had established a firm root in the broadcast industry in America which had earlier rejected to transcription.

By the mid-1950s it was evident that the principle of magnetic recording could be extended to include videotape recording of television programs. Thus, network television companies were assured of a permanent resolution to their long problem involving television recording. Amidst an intensive competition culminating in developments and improvements on various video recording equipment, the industry has expanded into the home with the introduction of videocassette recording. This text has attributed the continued growth in the industry to economic, scientific (technological), sociological, and ideological factors. The impact of video recording technology has been felt in many other related industries including television and advertising, cable television and theatrical movies. So far, video recording has found its applications in a wide variety of areas including educational and commercial industries (especially television recording) and finally home entertainment.

Chapter 1

Introduction

*T*elevision has developed enormously since the days of the Nipkow disc. In the same manner, since its inception in 1956, the videotape recorder has also undergone considerable development, and it is now an essential element in the video environment.

The invention of the videotape recording process was made possible by both the prior knowledge of magnetic audio recording techniques, and the needs of television. The general concensual view of this history has magnetic recording inscribed as a post-World War II innovation that was pioneered in the Third Reich, whereas videotape recording is seen as its off shoot invented in the United States, and a little over a decade old. There is little validity in this.

The technique of audio magnetic recording has been understood ever since the late 1800s, and the essentials of the design problem was understood by the early 1900s. The technology underwent a lengthy developmental period. During the 1920s and 1930s, efforts were made not only to improve on the magnetic recording technique but, even more significantly, to find uses for it. Suggestions for uses included its utility as a stenographic machine; a message recorder; a medium for teaching in schools; and a means of improving sound on talking pictures. These potentials and the prototypes created to exploit them were practically unknown in the United States, with the result that the principles of magnetic recording attained an advanced stage in Europe especially in Germany by the early 1930s.

Television, on the other hand, was in a mechanical prototype stage in the mid 1920s, nevertheless, this period also saw the initial efforts to record television images. Shortly after John L. Baird introduced his mechanically scanning television, he began a series of experiments researching, among other subjects, stereoscopic, color, long-distance transmission, low light cameras, and "the act of recording television pictures," which he called "phonovision." He recorded a television signal on a phonograph disc using a "Phonoscope." However he soon abandoned such electronic recording systems, although successive attempts at recording television images were made in Europe by others in the 1920s and early 1930s. Instead, film became the preferred medium, the first postwar film recordings of television images being made in 1946 at the Naval Air Station at Anacostia, DC.

Film allowed the emerging television networks in the United States to compensate for time differentials and, it also permitted stations not connected by radio relay or coaxial cable to utilize network services. Television personnel could attend to other duties when a film program was telecast or avoid working nights with considerable savings in labor costs. Recorded programs also provided a reserve program for emergency or contingency purposes, but film was itself costly and slow.

In April 1956, the first commercial videotape recorder was introduced, and with it came the contemporary system of recording the television image. The videotape recorder, a device that recorded, on a strip of magnetic tape, the electrical signals emerging from a television camera system, was very similar in principle to the audiotape recorder, which also recorded, on a narrow strip of magnetic tape, the electrical signal that emerged from a microphone system. But unlike the audiotape recorder, the videotape recorder recorded both sound and picture, with instant replay, but without visible deterioration.

Videotape's many advantages, including its immediate playback functions, elimination of development (chemical processing), and the capability of being re-used made it an invaluable asset to the television industry. This was in fact a new technology that cut costs by saving time or physical capital, and improved the quality of the product by making the results of the work more predictable. The increase in videotaped programs and advertising commercials were prompted by similar economic motivations as well as by the industry's awareness of videotape's quality. By the late 1950s, the physical attributes and economic gains that resulted from the videotape recorder were felt throughout television and affiliated industries.

The videotape recorder has reached into the home. The popularity of the videocassette recorder (VCR), at present, can only be compared to that of color television in the 1960s. As of the first quarter of 1988, almost 52 million VCRs have been sold in the United States accounting for 58% penetration in American homes with a thriving software business. Furthermore, the consumers' interest in VCRs has been boosted at home by accessibility to such services as cable and pay television.

This book is centered on the technology of the videotape recorder, tracing its roots into the early 1900s and before. The eventual conjunction between audio magnetic recording and television that resulted in videotape recording is the central focus of this study, which utilizes both primary and secondary sources in recovering this history.

This chapter, an introduction that apart from providing an insight into topics discussed in the following chapters, includes a brief suggestion toward a theoretical model of technological change that this study could illustrate.

Chapter 2 examines attempts to reproduce sound in the prephonograph era. The evolution of magnetism and electricity leading to the development of the first authentic recording devices is recorded in chapter 2.

Chapter 3 examines the early development of magnetic recording through various scientific and trade debates over the theories and applications of the different aspects of magnetic recording technology through the late 1800s. This early history is critical in shaping the development of magnetic recording. (In fact, when Valdemar Poulsen of Sweden invented the "Telegraphone," its main uses were for telephony and telegraphy purposes, contrary to the major uses of audiotape recorders today.) As advances were made in the field, Germany became the center for the magnetic recording industry, with a remarkable level of technical and commercial achievement in the 1920s and 1930s.

The fourth chapter examines the German advances in magnetic recording in the immediate prewar and World War II period as two industrial giants—Allgemeine Electricitaets Gesellschaft (AEG) or General Electric Company, and IG Farben, a chemical conglomerate—introduced magnetic tape recording technology to German radio and other users. A series of postwar studies organized by the victorious Allies in Germany and some private initiatives were instrumental in transferring this expertise from Germany to the United States and elsewhere as the basis for present-day audio magnetic recording industry worldwide. This chapter thus examines the introduction of magnetic tape recording via these means into the United States. Ampex Corporation became the first successful company to produce a commercially viable audio magnetic tape recorder in the United States in 1947. A general hostility to broadcasting of any "canned" materials existed within the American broadcasting industry before the introduction of magnetic tape in 1947; therefore, the development of magnetic tape recording as well as Ampex Corporation's ultimate success and public acceptance of the medium are emphasized.

The fifth chapter surveys the various nonmagnetic method of television recording in use before the introduction of videotape recording technology. Particular emphasis is placed on the kinescope, which was the primary system that sustained television recording until the advent of videotape recorders and beyond.

In chapter 6 the "marriage" between audio magnetic recorder and television, which leads to videotape recording techniques, is examined. Videotape recording is compared with audio magnetic and efforts made by the Crosby Enterprises are analyzed. The breakthrough by Ampex Corporation heralding the advent of videotape recorder paved the way for the participation of other companies interested in the field. Ampex's technological advances in both black-and-white and color videotape recorders, in the mid-1950s is also discussed. RCA's contribution to videotape recording technology is also surveyed. RCA's research efforts in the early 1950s resulted in the demonstration of a videotape recorder as early as 1953. Although the technology did not effectively compete with Ampex's at the time, its contribution was not unnoticed. RCA's reappearance in the videotape recording market after the development of the first commercial recorder encouraged competition, which contributed to the growth of the industry. The BBC's development of vision electronic recording apparatus (VERA) is also discussed.

Chapter 7 explores the developments from industrial videotape recording equipment to home video. This history is traced from its start in Helical-scan experiments of Toshiba and Ampex, through the introduction of the U-matic by Sony, to the expansion of videorecording technology into the consumer market. The competing consumer systems such as electronic video recording (EVR) and Telcan, which failed in the marketplace, are also described. Latest amateur portables (camcorders) are also discussed.

Chapter 8 analyzes the current VCR market situation, chronologically comparing the present VCR market growth with those of cable, and broadcast television. Penetration in various markets is also examined.

The ninth chapter examines videodisc technology. The early history of videodiscs is traced, and some early models are discussed. The presence of the videodisc as a consumer product in the mid- to late 1970s is the focus of chapter 9. Corporations such as RCA, North American Philips, MCA, and Pioneer, whose contributions to videodisc technology were instrumental, are examined.

Miniaturization has been a significant factor in all of these developments and therefore portability in the industry and home is examined in chapter 10. Early portable equipment, manufactured by Sony, Ampex, and Machtronics, and the development of electronic news gathering (ENG) are examined.

The significance of all these technologies is described in chapter 11, which examines the impact of magnetic wire recording on the telephone and phonograph in the 1900s, and the impacts of videocassette recording on television, pay cable, and Hollywood. Regulation (or lack of it) is examined. Attention is given to the Supreme Court decision on *The Motion Picture of America Association versus Sony Betamax* (January 17, 1984).

Finally, an epilogue which reviews the consumer electronic industry from its inception and establishes the importance of video technology in the industry. Concern for advancement in the industry led to several research efforts that are now in progress. This progress is destined to integrate various aspects of the communication industry.

The continued process that has occurred in the magnetic recording industry beginning in the late 1800s until the present, has been overwhelming. Technological change is not brought about by a single compelling factor; rather it is necessitated by a combination of factors that interact to make such changes possible. A survey of any particular technology's development would necessitate a parallel explanation of significant economic factors involved in such ventures. In videotape recording for example, economic demand does promote the actual technology, but the technology form as well as its economic foundation are conditioned by an encompassing ideological demand: quality, to reproduce the world "as it is," and to produce ("the effect of reality").

Various phases of the development and implementation of magnetic audio and video recording could be explained in terms of the interplay between economics and ideology. However, economics and ideology cannot explain the various developmental phases of magnetic recording between 1900 and 1930, but jointly they can explain the process' lack of development during the period. Magnetic recording, with its initial primary objective of recording various telephone conversations was simply a technology with little purpose, given the ways in which the telephone was being used at the turn of the century. The primary use of magnetic recording was found in a shift to sound and music recording; but magnetic recording with its sound quality inferior to that of the phonograph at the time, was a step away from the basic ideological aim of increased audio realism. Nevertheless, sufficient economic demand for magnetic recording encouraged some organizations to produce and market the recording device both in Europe and in the United States. A similar interplay is seen in the limited application of magnetic techniques in the film sound recording. By the mid-1930s, magnetic recording was superior to optical systems, the industry norms. Both the technological determinist and the ideological determinist would be at a loss to explain why the magnetic system did not then supercede the optical. For the technological determinist, the superior technology should have been enough, for the ideological determinist, the greatest "realism" should have been sufficient to compel acceptance. Obviously these drives were balanced and checked by economic factors.

In the magnetic recording industry, as elsewhere, the technological changes that occurred in the 1930s and 1940s could best be explained by the serious interplay of economic and ideological demands. I.G. Farben (BASF) and AEG's arrival on the magnetic recording scene was solely for economic reasons. Traditional German chemical industry approaches seem to offer an opportunity for a unique product. Their management acumen coupled with strong financial investment set the stage for latter improvements in the industry. However, although not yet a commercial music product, in Germany as well as all Europe, music lovers who were exposed to the equipment were dissatisfied with the poor quality of sound as produced by the early D.C. biasing recorders. This led to a quest for superior sound quality, which resulted in the creation of the "realistic" sound quality in the A.C. biasing Magnetophon machine produced by these firms—the first effective standard tape recorder. Nationalism and other necessities, including the military, played parts in this development.

Similarly, Ampex became involved in the magnetic recording market when it was evident that the end of World War II meant the expiration of the Navy contracts, which was the firm's *raison d'etre*. There was a dire need for new product development. The pay off that resulted from Ampex's efforts in the production of magnetic audio and videorecording equipment was outstanding. As discussed in chapter 4, the appropriation by American and British industries of what was essentially a German technology is an important economic determinant in technical and commercial development of magnetic recording for Ampex and others in the United States and United Kingdom. Historically, such an outstanding technological transfer could have been handled through international licensing agreements, trade cartels, or similar channels, which in effect guarantees a regulated, orderly assimilation of particular technology, as well as a fair share of profit maximization for the original developers of that technology. However, this was not the case here: Refined German magnetic recording techniques were quickly diffused in the American industry, disseminated for little or no cost by the federal government. Small companies like Ampex, as well as larger corporations such as Western Electric and RCA, benefited from this mass confiscation of German technology. This economic base is complimented by ideological determining factors; for instance the on-going attitude of the American broadcasting industry up to 1947 when the first magnetic tape recording equipment was demonstrated. American radio stations would not utilize any recorded "canned" materials on air because of poor quality. A brief encounter with the German magnetic tape recorder demonstrated by AEG at Schenectady before World War II was far from convincing the Americans. It took several days of demonstrations by John Mullin to convince Bing Crosby, his technicians, and subsequently the broadcast industry to accept the magnetic recording equipment as their main recording medium.

This same interplay of economic as well as ideological factors were responsible for the videotape recorder that was introduced in 1956. Due to the series of problems encountered from the 3-hour differential between the East and West coast, the numerous operational problems caused by kinescope (film recordings) and the costs involved, videotape recording was made popular in the television industry. The current technological changes that have resulted in the development and expansion of the videocassette recording industry has been extensive. About 44 corporations are involved in the manufacturing of videocassette recorders, whereas about 23 manufacture the blank tapes used in this hardware. A variety of organizations are also involved in the production of prerecorded cassettes. All these organizations supply the economic "backbone" of this young industry. For consumers, there is an increased variety of programs, the ability to record any program at will, either on network, independent, or cable television, to play back at a convenient time (time-shifting) and to record when absent.

The sequence of development in each of these cases, audio recording, broadcast standard videotape recording, and home videotape recording can only be understood in terms of an interplay between economics, ideology (including social factors), and technology.

Reproducing the Sound of the Living World

Communication in modern day society has been greatly enhanced by mans ability to reproduce sound. The advancement in today's broadcasting exemplifies the deep-rooted antecedent established by the ability to simulate sounds in general, and that of the human voice in particular. Inventions such as telegraph, telephone, phonograph, gramophone, radio, and later, television have benefited from the basic concept of reproduction and preservation of the human voice. The act of recording therefore is best comprehended within the context of broadcasting, telecommunication, and entertainment.

Although the medium of recording has undergone drastic changes over the past century as a result of technological advancement, it has continued to rely on two components that have been the very essence of the recording technology—*magnetism* and *electricity*. Whereas tape filament replaced the once popular copper or steel wire, and digitization rendered the century-old mechanical technique an anachronism, elements of magnetism and electricity still dominate the core of recording technology.

The evolution of recording is as essential in modern communication as it is controversial—be it audio recording versus telephone in the early 1900s or video recording versus television in the 1980s. VCRs have been centerpieces in most American households. They are compatible with almost every household, commercial and industrial entertainment, and communication component. They have been referred to as a "prima-donnas" in some quarters and sabotage in others. It is this compatibility that makes the video recording technology such a fascinating subject that it cannot be dealt with in this book single handedly. It is therefore addressed in the company of other existing technologies such as broadcast television, cable television, audio-recording equipment, satellites, computers, telephone, laser, and so on. Understanding video-recording technology in terms of these second-generation technologies then sets a precedent for the study of the subject.

EARLY ATTEMPTS TO SIMULATE THE HUMAN VOICE

Man's longing for miracles has from time immemorial driven him through the sphere of the supernatural; through the pages of the Holy Scriptures, and through the fables of antiquity.

From the beginning of time, man has tried to reproduce by mechanical means, every conceivable sound surrounding him in his environment. Many proofs exist of mankind's mimetic disparity with various antiquity of musical instruments. However, the first recorded attempt to simulate the human voice is the legendary statue of Memnon at Thebes, which dates back to the 18th Egyptian Dynasty, in 1490 B.C. It was claimed that one of the two remaining statues located on the west bank of the Nile made sounds at dawn. These sounds were interpreted to be Memnon's morning salute to his mother, Eos, the Goddess of Dawn. Easily dismissed as myth, most visitors to the statues were convinced otherwise by the cuneiform writing inscribed on the base of the statue by famous early travelers.

An earthquake tumbled the statue in 27 B.C. Several notable travelers who visited it gave conflicting accounts of their witness. In 7 A.D., Strabo, who by all accounts was one of the earliest visitors, cautiously dismissed the sound as a noise. Tacitus, in the entourage of Germanicus, a Roman general in 79 A.D., described the sound as "musical." Other dignitaries whose visits to the statue were recorded included Titus Petronius, a Roman Prefect in 82 A.D.; Emperors Hadrian in 140 A.D.; and Septimius Severus in 194 A.D. Most described Memnon's sound as a song. One of the inscriptions regarded as the earliest, dating back to 65 A.D., refers to the fact that Memnon at its prime could speak in languages, but only reduced to producing inarticulate sounds due to damage done to it. One of the best expressions was offered by a Roman imperial Procurator, Asklepiodotus:

> Know, O sea-born Thetis, that Memnon could not die. When the hot rays shed by his mother [EOS] fell brightly upon him, his clear song rings out while the Spreading Nile parts the Lybian hills from hundred gated Thebis.[1]

This statue, which seems to be valuable to ancient historians, was restored by Septimius Severus soon after his visit in 196 A.D., however, its ability to utter those sounds was gone. It has been generally concurred that Memnon's ability to produce sounds was due to some architectural artifice.

SOUND RECORDING DURING THE MEDIEVAL ERA

The next 10 centuries witnessed a tremendous effort by individuals who clearly devised talking automation mechanical units that were expected during their days. The modus operandi for such instruments however were trickery as they always involved echos produced by concealed individuals. Some notable exhibitors during this era was a German Monk, Gerber, who constructed a head that talked. Another individual, Albertus Magnus, developed an identical unit during this period. Both were dismissed as legendary. However, what was considered the first authentic talking device was invented in the 13th century by an English Philosopher, Friar Roger Bacon. His was a generally constructed machine resembling the mythical Speaking Head of Orpheus, said to be an inspirational enigma of early Greeks. Cases of priests playing pranks on audiences with "talking devices" were rampant. Ironically, Bacon's talking head was confused with such devices as the colossal statue of Silva, the Destroyer, an Indian God. This device involved a priest who was seated and concealed under the supposed talking head. Bacon's head is considered as the first talking machine according to various testimonies.

Little was chronicled between Friar Bacon's 13th-century talking head and the 19th century, except for the 1740 construction of a device known as the duck of Vaucanson, referred to as one of the mechanical wonders of the century. It was claimed that this "duck" quacked, waved its wings, plumed its feathers, ate grains, and could even digest its food.[2] However, the invention that stimulated much thinking into the act of modern day authentic recording was simply called the "talking man" and built by an experimenter, Herr Faber, in 1860. With an oval mouth whose size was ingeniously controlled and operated by a sliding section, and a keyboard, it was equipped with rubber lips and tongue that expertly controlled both vowels and consonants.

A miniature fan was inserted in its throat on which the letter "r" was rolled. Its vocal cords were made of ivory reed. In order for it to speak French, a tube was attached to its nose to improve on its phonology. Mr. Faber's device was considered extremely complicated, even by Thomas Edison's 1877 or the late-perfected phonograph standard.

Every sound reproduction equipment created, intentionally or otherwise, contributed to the fact that there was a dire need for a genuine sound recording and reproducing system. The Andonis (a group among the Ijaw tribe, inhabiting the Atlantic coast of Eastern Nigeria) have for centuries treasured the sounds made by one of their primary sacred cults, Ofiokpo, keeping the sounds a secret for ages. An invisible force with Supernatural Power, Ofiokpo can only be heard, but can not be seen. For centuries, twice each year (when it leaves its home in the sacred forest, to fish in the sea; and when it returns) the "Ofiokpo" festival is celebrated in the dead of night, when no one but *Ofiokpo* club members (a highly secretive male-only group) are allowed to roam the streets. Responding to its caller who leads it either from its sacred forest to the shore or back after 3 weeks, it responds with a sharp penetrating voice that chills the whole town and the environs. Ironically, for almost a century, missionaries and young native intellectuals have unsuccessfully tried to analyze its tone with preposterous hypotheses. Reproducing its sounds has always proved unsuccessful and embarrassing. Even recently, as its membership is almost extinct, the author and some friends observed one of their festivities. All members were closely observed for 3 weeks until the final day of festivities culminating in the grand finale. Every member apparently lost his voice due to excessive drinking of local gin. However, at night, the sacred "Ofiokpo" maintained its voice as it has always for over 500 years. The mystery still remains.

EARLY RECORDING HYPOTHESES

Faber and preceding inventors were aware of the problem involved in recording and reproducing human sound. However, they approached it by investigating the "cause." Most equipment was made in the form of a head, duck, or a whole human frame, therefore attempting to recreate human voice from its very physical source. On the other hand, Thomas Edison saw an effect from all these attempts, thereby ignoring the old idea of reproducing the "causes" of the vibrations that resulted in articulate speech. Instead, he resorted to obtaining the mechanical "effects" of such vibrations, recording them on magnetic materials and reproducing them. Whereas Faber was interested in copying the movement of the vocal organs, Edison studied the vibrating diaphragm and reproduced the ear drum's action when acted upon by the vibration caused by the vocal organ.

IMPORTANCE OF MAGNETISM
AND ELECTRICITY IN RECORDING TECHNOLOGY

In his patent application for "improvement in phonograph or speaking machines" dated December 15, 1877, Thomas Edison discussed some method of constructing the cylinder upon which recording could be made. He strongly recommended the use of "thick metallic foil." Even when paper was suggested as a possible substitute, Edison recommended that a magnet be used to indent it.

It was not surprising then, that when Valdemar Poulsen patented the first practical magnetic recorder, the Telegraphone in 1898, that a major component of his recording device was a magnetized steel wire or ribbon. Other experimenters on the subject of recording such as Wilhelm Hedic of Holland and Oberlin Smith of the United States had professed that thorough understanding of the subject depended on one's understanding of the field of magnetism as well as electricity.

Magnetism

The history of the magnet could be traced back to antiquity when it was commonly believed that its unique characteristic was simply embedded in occultism. Natural magnet, commonly referred to as lodestone, is found in the form of mineral magnetite, $Fe3O4$. Intriguing observations by early experimenters and sailors alike always had as their focal point the reaction of iron in the presence of natural magnet. Magnetite being a mineral form of black iron oxide, it is wise to believe that contact with magnet was made prior to or during an era popularly known as the iron age. This era is believed to have occurred around the 14th century B.C. along the Mediterranean. Homer, the great Greek epic poet of the ninth century B.C. mentioned iron in his work, referring to it as a luxury, thereby roughly placing the advent of the era around 1000 B.C.[3]

Some of the first research on magnetism was done by Petrus Peregrinus of Maricourt who recorded his results in his *Epistle to Sygerus of Foncaucourt* in 1269. Referring to the magnet as occult in nature, Peregrinus described its characteristics in terms of color, homogeneity, weight, and virtue. He also referred to it as "bearing in itself the similitude of the heavens."[4] Undoubtedly, little was known of this metal then, even among intellectuals.

It is said that the magnet was discovered by a shepherd who marvelled as the iron on the crook of his staff was attracted to magnet on the rock beneath which he was grazing his sheep on Mount Ida in Greece. Magnet was known to the Greeks by various names. It was called *Lithos Herakleia* or Heraclean stone, either named after the town of Heraclea on the boundary of Lydia, or named after the mythological Heracles. It was also called *Lithos Magnetis*, probably named after the city of Magnesia, a part of ancient Lydia, in Greece. This name is the one that was preferred in the English language. *Lithos Sideritis* was given to it because it attracted iron; and *Lapis Nauticus* because of its use in navigation.[5]

The earliest mention of magnet was by Aristotle, the Greek Philosopher (384–322 B.C.) who quoted Thabes of Miletus (624–548 or later) as saying that the driving force behind magnet's motive force was its soul. In the orient, there was evidence that the Chinese were exposed to magnet at an early date. However, in modern history is Kuo Puo's writing on magnet in 4th century A.D.

On the whole, these early scholars agreed on certain benefits of the magnet. It was, among other things, widely used in magical practices; it was also used for medical purposes (it would be covered up and attached to the affected area of the anatomy); it was used for occult purposes. Magnet's attraction was far beyond its reaction with iron, for it piqued the curiosity of Greek and Roman intellectuals such as Pythagoras, Plato, Lucretius, Cicero, and Pliny. Pliny did considerable studies on magnets, and his compilation of "natural history" helped to structure most schools of thought in the western world. Some famous muslim intellects were also involved from the 7th century in the study of magnetism. Jabir ibn Haiyan (c.776) was considered the most famous of these Islamic scientists on the subject. The delusion surrounding magnet has since been eliminated. It has also been put to use in a variety of ways. Modern science and technology owes a great deal to this iron ore that has such a long and ambiguous past. However, by the late 1800s the cloud that surrounded magnet was beginning to fade when scientists prying into the art of recording discovered its usefulness in various applications. One such application was the introduction of magnetized steel wire to the instrument that later became the Telegraphone, the first magnetic recorder. When the Germans discovered a better substitute for the steel wire (L-coated tape) in the 1930s, it was nevertheless magnetized to make it possible to record sound.

Electricity

The definition of electricity as we know it today, the "physical action made up of charged particles which produces light, heat, chemical decomposition and other physical characteristic" is a far cry from what was known of it in the 17th century. By the end of the 1600s, the scientific community or philosophers (as they were commonly called), were still ignorant of the true concept of electricity. Granted, the ancient greeks were aware of some attraction and repulsion to light pieces of straw, chaff, hair, and feathers by amber when rubbed. The word "electricity" originated from the Greek word *elecktron* for amber. Added to the ignorance that existed in the comprehension of the phenomenon was the fact that most philosophers regarded the force possessed by amber and magnet to be alike. Earliest mention of the attractive characteristic of amber is accorded Thales who lived in the 6th century B.C., however, serious examination of this phenomenon is credited to Theophrastus (372–287 B.C.). The confusion heightened when it was discovered that diamond possessed identical property possessed by amber. William Gilbert of Colchester (1540–1603), Queen Elizabeth's physician was a respected philosopher whose work *De Magnete* set a stage for more dialogues in the fields of electricity and magnetism. He differentiated the properties of both amber and natural magnet, noting that most writers confused both metals and ignored further observation into their properties. Gilbert noted that amber's attraction was similar to those of other substances such as diamond, sapphire, carbuncle, iris gem, opal, amethyst to mention a few, but not magnet. Because his study was written in Latin, he used the word "electrum" for amber. He categorized those substances that had similar attractions like amber as electrica (electrics) and those that attracted differently as anelectrica (nonelectrics). He introduced such terms as *electrified state, magnetic pole, electric attraction,* and *changed body,* which set up a new school of thought in electricity.

Although Gilbert's work has been considered a foundation in the fields of electricity and magnetism, others have attacked various aspects of it. Galileo (1564–1642), who was more interested in Gilbert's theories on magnet, deployed his lack of mathematical insight, whereas another Italian, a Jesuit, Niccoto Cabeo (1585–1650) attacked the very nucleus of Gilbert's treatise. The field of electricity gradually became a center of attraction as the 1700s progressed. The first phase of the study of electricity, was over, while the second stage, marked by the construction of electric charge generating machines, was introduced. Otto van Guericke, Sir Isaac Newton, DuFay of France, Dr. Benjamin Franklin, Sir Humphrey Davy, Michael Faraday, and Stephen Gray were few among many whose contribution brought electricity to the present day standard.

Electromagnetism

Up to the end of the 1700s, scientists had fruitlessly worked to establish a relationship between electricity and magnetism. Most even doubted that any such relationship existed. In 1820, Hans Christian Oersted, a professor at Copenhagen, discovered that when an electric current is passed through a wire held horizontally above a magnetic needle that is parallel to it, the needle is deflected, positioning itself at right angles with the conducting wire to the end of the positive pole of the magnet. Simply stated, a wire that has a constant source of electricity passed through it becomes practically a magnet. From Oersted's study, scientists such as Ampere, Arago of France, and Sir Humphrey Davy of England concluded their individual studies that concurred in their finding that current electricity magnetized small pieces of iron and steel. An individual whose contribution to the theory of electromagnets was astounding, but who never received much recognition for his work was Professor Joseph Henry (1797–1878), a professor of physics at Albany Institute and later curator of the Smithsonian Institution. Professor Henry's work integrated the principles that are so much inevitable in modern day electronics including phonographs, radio, television and hi-fi in relation to electricity, magnetism, and mechanical energy. In essence, his theory was the basis for Morse's telegraph, Bell's telephone, and other modern sound-producing mechanisms. It was this principle that enabled Valdemar Poulsen to record the first sound on a magnetized steel wire. This principle also paved the way for modern-day audio and video recording technology.

BEFORE THE PHONOGRAPH

A rough anticipation of an instrument like the phonograph was earlier suggested by a Briton, John Wilkins, Bishop of Chester. In his work titled *Mathematic Magick* (1651) he envisioned a method of preserving the human voice or spoken word in a hollow trunk or pipe that would be opened at a later date. He somehow was inclined to believe that the voice would be released in the same way it was spoken. This however, was only a thought, and was far from being a reality. In the 1700s and 1800s several attempts were made to record sound, but most, although absolute failure, were nevertheless material prophecies leading to the advent of a practical recording idea.

One of the attempts was made in the early 1700s by Duhamel who tried to trace sound curves on his lamp-blacked revolving cylinder. Surprisingly, Edison's first generation phonograph would later assume this cylinder format. In 1747, Reverend J. Creed proposed to make a machine capable of recording tempore piano-forte organ voluntaries. As a follow-up on the same idea, Hohlfeld of Berlin teaming up with a mathematician colleague Euler, constructed a crude music recorder in 1752 called the Melograph. Almost simultaneously, another German mechanic, J.F. Unger, was building a similar instrument and proved priority of conception as he dated his idea, from 1745. In 1836, an English patent was given to Eisenmanger of Paris for an apparatus that recorded piano music, using a depressed stylus and carbonized paper. Similar equipment was invented in 1840 by M. De Tressog of Paris, and in 1856 by Merzelo, an Italian.

The importance of music during this era was well understood, therefore it was only proper that the objective of these efforts in developing a recording device centered on the recording of music, especially the piano or organ extemporizations. The driving force behind these attempts was literally based on the fact that the quality of the piano had reached its saturation point, having evolutionized from the clavier and the clavichord. This excellence in the quality of the piano was evidenced in the amount of work produced by great German composers such as Bach and Handel in the early 1700s, Hayden, Mozart, and Beethoven toward the end of the century, and Spohr, Chopin, Mendelssohn, Meyerbeer, and Liszt in the 1800s. All these musical activities culminated in a desire to create a device that would permanently record the quality work of all those great artists and composers for future generations. In this way, the arts of music would later foster the science of the recording device.

Expanding on the directives set by Duhamel in his experiment, Leon Scott, working with Konig in 1856, perfected a device called the Phonautograph. This was simply an instrument that recorded graphic traces of sound vibrations with winding scratches on a lamp-blacked coated paper wrapped around a revolving cylinder.

Scott's invention was patented in France in 1857. Scott's device recorded sound vibration on a cylinder cranked by hand and positioned forward by a screw. The cylinder was covered with smoked paper on which sound vibration would be traced by a stylus attached to the center of the diaphragm as words were spoken into a large barrel-like mouthpiece. One of Scott's concerns was to amplify the resulting vibration, therefore, he introduced an animal membrane for his diaphragm. This was an attachment called a subdivider, which became a prototype of the dampers in Edison's phonograph. Although considered the closest instrument to the phonograph, there were elements of similarities and dissimilarities between them. For instance, both recorded on cylinders rotated by a screw. However, the contrast was in the movement of the stylus in both equipment. In Scott's Phonautograph the stylus movement was lateral, whereas that of the phonograph was vertical.

In 1863, F.B. Fenby of Worchester, Massachusetts was granted a patent on a device he called "the electromagnetic phonograph." He thereby became the first to coin the name "phonograph"—although his instrument was not exactly practical for an exact recording and even left much to be desired as far as reproducing sound was concerned. What is considered closest in style and function to Edison's phonograph to a lesser degree, and Berliner's gramophone to a greater degree, was M. Charles Cros' idea that he deposited in April 1877 (7 months before the date of Edison's patent) with the Academie des Sciences des France in a sealed package. This package was opened as the Academy convened at its December 1877 sitting. Its content was a general description of a device, which was similar to the phonograph and gramophone.

At this point in time, a generation of "trials and errors" was coming to an end culminating at the same time in a genuine configuration of a recording device that suddenly was acceptable due to its superiority over all others. The events of the two centuries preceding the advent of the phonograph point to the strange trend of human invention and endeavors. Such efforts have been witnessed in every scientific field, be it aviation, electricity, chemistry, or geology. Many strive but fail, but one would achieve perfection, learning from past endeavors.

THE TELEPHONE

America had just celebrated its centennial anniversary, and to many scientists, despite the uproar of religion versus science that seemed to divide the society, the final years of that century was regarded as progressive in terms of scientific achievements. Scientists were now able to measure the advancements made especially in the field of electricity and acoustics (transmission of speech electrically, and of recording and reproducing sound mechanically).

In 1854, an idea was advanced by a French man, Charles Bourseuil, which entailed two diaphragms operated by electricity and electromagnet respectively, used for transmitting speech over telegraphic distances. Bourseuil suggested that when spoken into one diaphragm, each vibration produced would make "electric contact." The resulting pulsations set the other diaphragm vibrating and enabled it to reproduce the transmitted sound. Although hailed as ingenious in many countries, this theory was considered misleading to some colleagues, especially Bourseuil's suggestion for a movable or flexible diaphragm. Alexander Graham Bell had worked on the premise of utilizing a flexible diaphragm for his invention, but failed in many attempts. The idea was borrowed from the flexible tympanum membrane of the human ear, but neither Bourseuil nor Bell considered the drastic modifications that vibrations undergo before reaching the auditory nerve by the various muscular hinges in which the tiny bones of the ear are mounted, and which cushion the tympanum membrane.

The Didaskalia, a prominent German semi-weekly newspaper, published a reprint of Bourseuil's idea under the heading Electrical Telephony on September 28, 1854 calling Bourseuil's idea an "ingenious and wonderful conception." As with any important concept of the time, Bourseuil's was well regarded in Germany especially in Frankfurt, which boasted a physics society. One member of this organization, Phillip Reis, a teacher, actually began experimenting on Bourseuil's idea, and 5 years later built an equipment simply known as the "Reis telephone." Reis, however, died before analyzing his work.

The key practical players in experiments that led to the invention of the telephone however were Bell, Elisha Gray, and Edison. These individuals were working independently on tedious experimentations that ironically were not related to the telephone. They were each researching means of transmitting multiple messages through a single wire that otherwise was known as harmonic telegraph. However, the idea of transmitting sound itself over wire rather than codes as used in telegraphs was a superimposed objective for these three as well as other notable scientists both in the United States and in Europe. Telephone, therefore, required an extra effort of developing a transducer capable of receiving sound, turning it into electric current, and back to sound again through a simple wire. As Bell invented the telephone in 1876, it could be argued that he did not realize the intensity of his invention. Perhaps this accounted for some of the controversies surrounding his announcement of his invention. Contributing to this confusion was Bell's definition of his invention, referring to it in terms of the harmonic telegraph he was experimenting with at the time. In his patent granted March 7, 1876, he referred to it simply as "telegraphy." No wonder then that there were initial doubts as to the authentic "first" inventor of the telephone. The Germans for instance, saw nothing new about it from the Reis telephone. Specifically, it was argued that Bourseuil/Reis' electromagnet became Bell's transmitter. Initial controversies were put to rest by the United States Supreme Court's unanimous decision in favor of Bell so far as the Bourseuil/Reis device was concerned. Ironically, although Edison had made remarkable advances on telephony before Bell's patent, and continued to improve on it thereafter, he never challenged Bell's invention.

THE EDISON PHONOGRAPH

It is commonly known that the tin-foil phonograph was discovered accidentally by Edison. While busy experimenting on a telegraphic machine (intended to repeat Morse characters recorded on paper by indentations that transferred messages to another circuit automatically), he stumbled upon the idea that resulted in the phonograph. In examining the indented paper, Edison noticed the speed at which it moved, and a humming noise that emanated from the indentation. This sound was a severe rhythm almost identical to human speech heard faintly (see Fig. 2.1).

In order to decipher this sound, Edison fitted a diaphragm to the machine. This also acted to amplify the sound. It was then obvious that the problem of recording human speeches and reproducing them by mechanical means was solved.

Edison proceeded to develop a machine exclusively for capturing the vibrations of the human voice as well as repeating them at a latter time. The machine was christened the "phonograph" (see Fig. 2.2). In November 1877, Edison officially announced his invention and on December 24, 1877, he filed a patent application for the phonograph with the U.S. Patent Office. This was duly approved as patent number 200,521, issued on February 19, 1878. (See Fig. 2.3 and 2.4.)

The tin-foil phonograph was built by John Kruesi, who had worked with Edison for several years. Edison had only given a rough sketch of the phonograph to Kruesi, explaining what its functions were to be. It was a cylinder machine, with the cylinder covered with tin-foil for recording

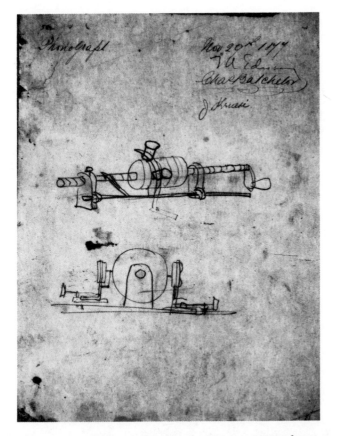

FIG. 2.1.   Sketch of original phonograph, Nov. 29, 1877. Edison's assistant, John Kruesi, made the working tin-foil phonograph from this Edison sketch. In most of his inventions, Edison would provide sketches (sometimes complicated) and Kruesi would translate them into working models. (*Source*: U.S. Department of the Interior, National Park Service, Edison National Historic Site, West Orange, NJ.)

purposes. When Kruesi concluded work on the machine and brought it to Edison, he set it in motion and spoke into it:

Mary had a little lamb,
It's fleece was white as snow,
And everywhere that Mary went,
The lamb was sure to go.[6]

When rewound, his exact words in clear tones was repeated, contrary to the hoarse murmur that he anticipated, Edison was baffled at the performance of the little machine. (See Fig. 2.5.)

FIG. 2.2. The first phonograph. The photograph shows the first phonograph invented by Thomas Edison. This phonograph used tin-foil as its
recording medium. (*Source*: U.S. Department of the Interior, National Park
Service, Edison National Historic Site, West Orange, NJ.)

FIG. 2.4.   Edison with improved phonograph, June 16, 1888. Edison is shown at 5 a.m. after working for 72 hours to get the "bug" out of this phonograph before shipping it to England for publicized demonstrations. (*Source:* U.S. Department of the Interior, National Park Service, Edison National Historic Site, West Orange, NJ.)

FIG. 2.3.   Edison and his assistants. Edison and his assistants posed with the improved phonograph after working 72 hours before sending it to England for public demonstration. (*Source:* U.S. Department of the Interior, National Park Service, Edison National Historic Site, West Orange, NJ.)

FIG. 2.5. Edison "fireside" phonograph. The Edison "fireside" phonograph was one of the cylinder systems. (*Source:* U.S. Department of the
Interior, National Park Service, National Historic Site, West Orange, NJ.)

THE EDISON PHONOGRAPH

The first sound reproducing device was an Edison Phonograph, invented by Thomas A. Edison in 1877, at Men'o Park, N. J., where he
then had his laboratory. In 1887 Mr. Edison took up his residence and his laboratory work at Orange, N. J., and here, under his personal
direction, the Phonograph has been developed into the wonderful musical instrument it is, known and enjoyed in the homes of every nation.

FIG. 2.6. Publicity release for Edison Phonograph. (*Source:* Clark Collection, Smithsonian Institution, Washington, DC.)

FIG. 2.7. Publicity release for Edison phonograph. (*Source:* Smithsonian Institution, Washington, DC.)

FIG. 2.8. Publicity release for Edison phonograph. (*Source:* Warshaw Collection, Smithsonian Institution, Washington, DC.)

Enormous publicity was accorded the phonograph once released. Promotional tools included newspaper and magazine advertising, and personal demonstrations (see Fig. 2.6, 2.7, and 2.8).

PHONOGRAPH AND GRAPHOPHONE

The Graphophone

The early relationship between Bell Telephone and the Edison Speaking Phonograph Company was cordial. In fact, both companies shared some backers, who included Gardener G. Hubbard, Alexander Graham Bell's father-in-law and the chief organizer of the Bell Telephone Company.

Two individuals, Charles A. Cheever and Hilbourne Roosevelt, were also principals of both companies. Of course, there was no competition between these two "little" companies at this point in time. In fact both shared office space and expenses at 203 Broadway in New York.

FIG. 2.9.   Edison's cylinder phonograph. Edison's cylinder phonograph powered by foot treadle. (*Source:* U.S. Department of the Interior, National Park Service, Edison National Historic Site, West Orange, NJ.)

FIG. 2.10.   Edison with tin-foil phonograph, April 18, 1878. This photograph was taken in Washington, DC, while Edison was visiting the city to demonstrate the phonograph to the American Academy of Science, the members of Congress, and to President Rutherford B. Hayes. (*Source:* U.S. Department of the Interior, National Park Service, Edison National Historic Site, West Orange, NJ.)

The personal relationship between the Bell and Edison families was initially also cordial. However, Edison made some business decisions that were regarded unpopular to Bell, which probably resulted in the seeming animosity between both inventors. First, Edison continued work on improving the telephone, patenting his inventions as he went along. In fact, subsequent to 1880, Edison had accumulated a minimum of 25 patents on telephony improvements. He sold his popular carbon transmitter patent to Western Union, Bell's major competitor. These moves probably influenced Bell's decision not to contribute to any improvement on the phonograph when such was much needed.

In 1880, the French Academy of Science awarded Bell the notable Volta prize in recognition for his work on his invention of the telephone. Bell established a Volta Laboratory with the $20,000 prize in Washington DC. He engaged the services of two assistants, his brother, Chichester Bell, and Professor Charles Sumner Tainter.

The research at the laboratory was to focus on electrical and acoustic studies. Documents later submitted to the Smithsonian Institute by the estates of Tainter revealed that the Volta Laboratory group almost entirely focused its attention on improving the phonograph. On February 28, 1880, Bell and Tainter deposited a sealed envelope with the Smithsonian Institute. In it was an "intent to invent," which sounded as more or less a warning or insurance against any competition. On October 20, 1881, the group deposited a wooden box containing notes and sketches representing an internal blueprint describing "a method of reproducing sound from a phonogram record by means of a jet of compressed air." This instrument was later described as the first "Graphophone."

FIG. 2.11. Edison with cylinder phonograph. By 1906, Edison was producing separate lines of business and entertainment phonographs. The phonograph shown in this picture is an entertainment model. (Source: U.S. Department of the Interior, National Park Service, Edison National Historic Site, West Orange, NJ.)

FIG. 2.12.   Edison listening to disc phonograph, 1921. (*Source:* U.S. Department of the Interior, National Park Service, Edison National Historic Site, West Orange, NJ.)

Major Research at Volta Laboratory

As far as the phonograph was concerned, experts acknowledged that it remained in an unsatisfactory and unfinished condition for 9 years after its invention. It was not surprising therefore that Alexander and Chichester Bell and Tainter of the Volta Laboratory Company would devote much of their time in researching further improvement on the phonograph. Realizing that in order to produce a perfect phonograph some major components of the old phonograph must be substituted, recommendations made by the Volta Laboratory Company after its 2-year study of the phonograph were therefore valuable.

The recommendation focused on three major components of the pho-

FIG. 2.13. The Columbia grand graphophone. (*Source:* Smithsonian Institution, Washington, DC.)

nograph, namely indentation, cylinder-coating process, and speaker system:

1. The incarting process would be discarded and replaced by an engraving process.
2. The best substance for the recording surface was considered to be beeswax hardened by a mixture of paraffin or similar wax-like substance.
3. Reduced volume would yield the best result, although this would in turn render reproduction only to the volume level of a good telephone conversation. The louder the volume, the less distinct it became as it is reproduced.

On May 4, 1886, Patent No. 341,214, was issued to Dr. Chichester A. Bell and Mr. C.S. Tainter. Among their claims were:

> The method of forming a record of sounds by impressing numerous vibrations upon a style, and thereby "cutting" in a solid body the record corresponding in form to the sound waves, in contradistinction to the formation of sound records by indenting a foil with a vibratory style, etc.

The vibratory 'cutting' style of a sound-recorder substantially as described.

A sound record consisting of a tablet, or other solid body, having its surface cut or engraved with narrow lines or irregular and varied form corresponding to sound waves, substantially as described.

The method of forming a sound or speech record, which consists in engraving or cutting the same in wax or a wax-like composition, substantially as described.

Compounding these findings, Bell and his associates introduced the Graphophone in Spring of 1887. It was the first reliable and practical device of the phonograph family.

FIG. 2.14.   Advertising sheet for Edison phonograph models. An assortment of phonograph models produced by Thomas Edison. This advertisement stresses compatibility. (*Source:* U.S. Department of the Interior, National Park Service, Edison National Historic Site, West Orange, NJ.)

FIG. 2.15. Phonograph parlor. Phonographs were available at public places. By inserting a nickel in the machine, one could listen to music through a set of earphones. (*Source:* U.S. Department of the Interior, National Park Service, Edison National Historic Site, West Orange, NJ.)

Berliner's Gramophone

It has been suggested that the gramophone took after Charles Cros' idea of reproducing original sound on a photo-engraved relief or intaglio phonautographic record through the reaction of a stylus on a diaphragm. However, Emile Berliner the inventor of the gramophone, had testified on vari-various occasions that his first contact with Cros' idea was on August 30, 1887, 3 months after he filed his patent application. Berliner claimed he first read of Cros' work in a German science magazine at his attorney, Joseph Lyon's office. Berliner immediately asked Lyon to investigate the extent of Cros' experiment. Cros, Berliner discovered, had never practically carried out his ideas. After close examination, Berliner concluded that Cros' idea, although correct in terms of their general principles, were impossible to achieve practically.[7]

Emile Berliner was a German immigrant who arrived in New York at the age of 19 in 1870. He moved to Washington DC, where he worked as a clerk in a dry-goods store for 3 years. He left his job, and during the interim, worked at various jobs in various cities throughout the United States. One such establishment that made an impact on Berliner's life was Constantine Fahlberg's (of the saccharin fame) laboratory, where he was responsible for

FIG. 2.16. Victor Talking Machine. A model of Victor Talking Machine, popularly known for its universal trademark "his master's voice." (*Source:* Warshaw Collection, Smithsonian Institution, Washington, DC.)

washing bottles. This environment instilled in him a special interest for science. In order to learn more about his new interest, he spent his evenings and spare time at the nearby New York's Cooper Union Institute library where he read basic chemistry and physics books. In 1876, he returned to Washington DC, at his former employers request, to take up a high-paying appointment. Despite his high salaried job, his interest was still in the scientific field. He dreamed of becoming an inventor, so he began conducting experiments in electricity and acoustics that required the knowledge he had accumulated through his readings so far.

Berliner was interested in Bell's newly invented telephone, so he was dedicated to improving the telephone transmitter system. He progressed exceedingly, and applied for a patent for his work. Almost simultaneously, Edison had perfected his carbon transmitter (a similar device to Berliner's), which he sold to Western Union, the up-and-coming competitor to Bell Telephone. Berliner contacted Bell Telephone with his new invention, which was welcomed in view of the ensuing competition between them and Western Union. He was paid a large sum for his invention in 1878 by Bell Telephone, and was retained as a consultant with monthly fees.

Berliner soon left Bell Telephone to pursue a more personal interest. He set up a company called the Telephone-Fabrik Berliner with his brother,

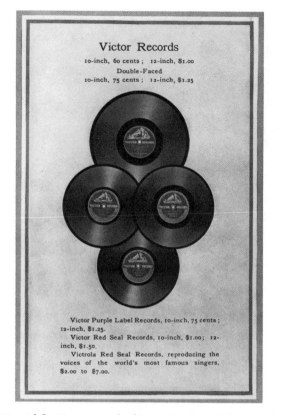

FIG. 2.17.   Ad for Victor records. (*Source*: Warshaw Collection, Smithsonian Institution, Washington, DC.)

Joseph in Hanover to manufacture telephone equipment for the German market. After 2 years, he returned to the United States, and continued experimenting independently. So far, all the major players in the invention and improvements thereof in telephony were also researching to improve the phonograph. Berliner was no exception.

Berliner was convinced that the phonograph, as invented by Edison, was crude and inferior. Improving it was then one of his priorities. He valued the progress and recommendations made by Bell and his associates at the Volta Laboratory Company. Being envious as to the simplicity of the telephone, he looked for a simpler way to achieve his goal in the production of a workable disc. Diverting from the well-known cylinder method, Berliner used a glass disc covered with greasy lampblack, which was made to revolve on a turntable. A stylus mounted on the feed screw rotated spirally on the disk. As it was incited with sound waves, the stylus vibrated laterally in a clockwise direction making visual tracing on the disc possible. After tracing, the disc was then varnished and photo-engraved. During playback, the original sound was reproduced via the stylus and diaphragm reproducer.

Demonstrating his invention at the Franklin Institute on May 16, 1888, Berliner promised a reproduction of sound in as little as 15 to 20 minutes. He also promised that these records could be "multiplied" in any quantity through the electrotype process. To eliminate the problem caused by dust or wax accumulated at the tip of the stylus as it dragged along the disc (thereby causing a blurring or indistinct sound), Berliner introduced commercial alcohol that he applied to the disc surface. The alcohol evaporates slowly but not entirely until the record is finished. The effect of the alcohol therefore kept the stylus point clean at all times.

It was far more difficult to duplicate recordings by the process Berliner had envisioned. In fact, this contributed to lack of progress experienced with the gramophone in succeeding years. Berliner soon discovered a more feasible way of duplicating the discs. Berliner was granted a patent for his invention of the gramophone. In modern terms, both the gramophone and phonograph are used interchangeably. However, during the 1880s, the

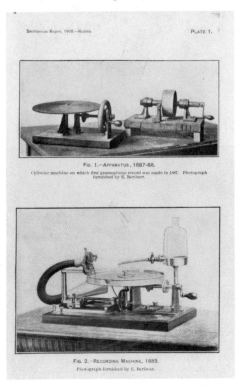

FIG. 2.18.   Emile Berliner's gramophone. (*Source:* Smithsonian Institution, Washington, DC.)

FIG. 2.19. Gramophone. (*Source:* Smithsonian Institution, Washington, DC.)

FIG. 2.20. Recording the Liberty Bell. The recording of the sound from the Liberty Bell in Philadelphia, Pennsylvania in early 20th century. The recorder is Roy Sooy. (*Source:* Smithsonian Institution, Washington, DC.)

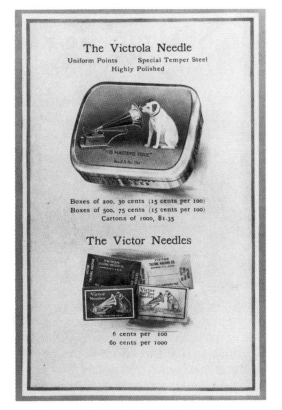

FIG. 2.21. Ad for victrola needle. (*Source:* Warshaw Collection, Smithsonian Institution, Washington, DC.)

gramophone was defined as that which recorded or reproduced "laterally" on discs, whereas the phonograph was known to record or reproduce vertically on cylinders. This is an important distinction, especially in the context of this text. Six years elapsed before the gramophone achieved any measure of commercial success in the United States. Its first taste of commercial success was in the German market.

Thereafter, improvements on recording equipment was universal. Individuals as well as companies were involved in various aspects of research to perfect the phonograph. Among such companies were Victor, which was later responsible for the Victor Talking Machine, and Columbia, which later put together its patents with Victor. Together, they controlled a large segment of the phonographic market.

The Origin of Magnetic Recording

Most historians date the modern history of magnetic recording with an article published September 8, 1888. The author, a metallurgist Oberlin Smith, described three possible methods of recording and reproducing sounds that were identical to later inventions in the magnetic field. Smith's apparatus was simple and mechanically easy to understand. The equipment consisted of a mouthpiece and diaphragm, with spring and indenting needles as in the Edison machine. But it differed in that it was equipped with two reels connected by a thin ribbon of iron, or steel, which served as the recording substance instead of Edison's wax disc. The ribbon was unwound from one reel onto another. A lamp would heat the ribbon, which then received an indentation as easily as tin foil. Heating the ribbon made it much harder and durable. This heated ribbon was the recording apparatus or transmitter. Smith saw the following advantages of his proposed device:

- The loudness of voice produced by the increased amplitude of vibration.
- The simplicity and cheapness of the machine.
- The cheap material of which the ribbon may be made.
- Durability of ribbon, even with repeated use.
- Convenience and freedom from injury in handling and transporting the ribbon-record when wound upon spools like thread.

Smith also proposed the impregnation of cotton threads with iron filings in conjunction with standard telephone hardware. He believed that the magnetic disposition of the thread's filing could be varied by an electric current modulated through the telephone equipment, thus converting the thread into a permanent magnet that was then able to hold a magnetized sound recording. The use of metal tape containing dispersed magnetizable dust to perform the same function was also suggested by Smith. Even this, however, was not the first time the idea surfaced. It was previously proposed in 1887 by Wilhelm Hedic, a Dutch engineer.

It is obvious that much work on the subject of magnetic recording had already been done before Smith's publication as he wrote: "There being nowadays throughout the scientific world great activity of thought regarding listening and talking machines. . . ." Although the concepts described by Smith were only referred to as "some possible forms of phonograph," they were in no way similar to the already existing phonograph. Most of the systematic operational frameworks analyzed by Smith were nonetheless similar to those found in modern recording devices. For the first time a reel, instead of a disc, was introduced: "To make the thread . . . 'talk back', it is after having been rewound onto reel . . . again drawing through a helix . . . in whose circuit is the 'talking' telephone . . . probably a Bell receiver."[1]

Although Smith's concepts clearly suggest the design of modern tape recording devices, they were nevertheless lacking in many areas. Although some of his theoretical proposals were scientifically valid, he lacked the technical background to realize his ideas in the field of magnetism. His knowledge of magnetizable media and electricity (which were vital to magnetic recording) was very limited. He confirmed:

> The writer confesses to a good deal of ignorance upon the subject, but he was somewhat surprised to find an equal amount in several well known electricians whom he consulted, and also to find that none of the books he had at hand gave any definite data regarding their best proportions for permanent magnets or their actual strength (when saturated) in pulling power.[2]

Audio historians seldom place much emphasis on Smith's contributions, although his efforts did generate some inspiration in the magnetic recording research community at the time. This, of course, was the very reason for his making public his concepts:

> The writer has not time, to say nothing of a properly equipped laboratory to carry the ideas suggested to their logical conclusion of success or failure and, therefore, makes them public hoping that some of the numerous experimenters now working in this field may find in them a germ of good from which something useful may grow. Should this be the case, he will doubtless get due credit for his share in the matter; but if, on the other hand, these suggestions prove worthless, they will still have served a purpose, on the principle that a

demonstration of what "can't be" done is often a pertinent hint as to what "can be."[3]

Ten years after Smith's publication, the Danish government would grant a patent to a young physicist, Valdemar Poulsen, thereby making public a complete description of Poulsen's magnetic recording device.

Although frequently ignored, Smith's work can be seen as the framework on which Poulsen's magnetic recording theory was based.

WIRE RECORDING—THE INVENTION
OF VALDEMAR POULSEN'S TELEGRAPHONE

The practical history of magnetically recording and reproducing sound begins with Poulsen. Poulsen is believed to have produced a working model of a recording device as early as 1894, but the quest for a marketable device took him another 4 years. On December 1, 1898, Poulsen was granted his original Danish patent for a recording machine, which he named "Telegraphone." The patent fully described a magnetic wire recording device.

Poulsen was an electrical engineering student at the University of Copenhagen, and by the time he graduated in 1894, he had already begun work that he believed would improve the efficiency of telephone operation. Despite his contribution in early telephony, being responsible for developing the "Poulsen Radio Arc" oscillator for telephone and telegraph systems, he would later be known mainly for his achievement in the development of early magnetic recording systems.

After graduation, Poulsen was employed by the Copenhagen Telephone Company as a mechanic. It was here that he conceived most of his ideas. During this period, a telephone line was only capable of handling one conversation at a time; this caused many delays in services. Poulsen's solution was to develop a machine that was capable of recording a message and then transmitting it over the cable at much higher speed than it was originally recorded. The message was then re-recorded at the other end with a similar machine and played back at the original speed. To guarantee secrecy while using the system, Poulsen's device rendered all messages unintelligible during transmission, making it impossible for interception by unauthorized persons; besides, the capacity of the phone lines was increased by speeding transmission time, but the whole scheme denied the phone's most important advantage—simultaneity.

A popular experiment at the time involved a magnetic pen used to write on a uniformly magnetic steel plate, making strong and weak impressions on the surface, and when iron filings were spread on the magnetized plate, the letters or words written by the magnetic pen immediately became visible. It was on this simple principle of variable magnetization that Poulsen's "Telegraphone" was based. Instead of a steel plate, Poulsen used a steel wire or ribbon, which he passed between the poles of an electromagnet and permanently, although uniformly, magnetized by the variable electric currents generated by the vibrations produced in the diaphragm of a telephone transmitter by acoustic impulses. The magnetized record was then reproduced at a telephone transmitter by passing the same wire or ribbon through the electromagnetic poles, so that variable electric currents were produced in the circuit to affect the diaphragm of the receiver. The Telegraphone was a break away from conventional and fundamental conceptions of mechanical recording by physical indentation such as in Edison's phonograph. Poulsen thought of replacing disc and cylinders as recording and reproducing media with magnetic wires. Most surprising, especially in view of modern techniques, was his suggestion of tape or a strip of some suitable material covered with a magnetizable metallic dust, also proving that it was possible to erase a recording and in its place record another piece of sound over and over again. Poulsen's invention, among other things, demonstrated that "commonplace physical phenomena, so commonplace, in fact, that they were no longer remarked, when studied and fully grasped by a mastermind, may be applied to ends little dreamt of."[4]

The first public demonstration of Poulsen's "Telegraphone" occurred at the World Exhibition in Vienna in 1898. Although the equipment did not have an amplifier or bias, its recording and sound quality were unquestionably overwhelming, so much that the original recording of the voice of Emperor Franz Josef I of Austria, paying tribute to the machine at the World Exhibition in 1898, can still be heard today. Even now, "one can hear the reverberation of the exhibition hall in which the recording was made." The Telegraphone received more publicity in 1900 at the Paris Universal Exhibition where it was very successful, winning a Grand Prix. Between 1898 and 1899, Poulsen filed applications for patents in 15 countries, including the United States. His U.S. patent was approved on November 13, 1900. In it, he concisely described his invention as "a certain new and useful improvement in methods and apparatus for effecting the storing up of speech or signals by magnetically influencing Magnetizable Bodies."[5]

Poulsen envisioned two basic functions for his invention. First, and foremost, was the telephonic role it was to play, helping to simplify telephone communication. Second, Poulsen intended to replace the phonograph with the Telegraphone, which he thought was much simpler and of better quality.

Two reasons for such a claim was that the phonograph operated mechanically in such a way that one of its mechanical parts striking against a receptive body made notches, and at the same time, transmitted air vibrations to a membrane. These notches caused the vibration to be repeated on a membrane. Because it was operated mechanically, the resulting noise was irritating. The Telegraphone, however, was a device that would be less expensive, and was of better listening quality.

Poulsen's first published comments about his invention were in The Electrician in November 1900. Here he gave a simplified description of the Telegraphone, having succeeded in making a considerable amount of adjustments as well as improvements on his invention. He had also found other uses for this equipment. His title read "The Telegraphone: A Magnetic Speech Recorder." The improvements and adjustments had made his equipment portable so that now it was not confined only to professional telephone and telegraph, but could also be extended to consumer and office use.[6] By the end of 1900, several changes had been made to the Telegraphone. The reason was obvious, only 50 seconds playing time. The original model gave way to a phonograph-like horizontal version with a 15-inch long by 5-inch diameter cylinder with 380 windings of wire, 0.1 inch in diameter wound around its helix. The cylinder, driven by a ⅙ -H.P. electric motor, in turn, energized the magnetic properties in the recording/reproducing head: the electromagnet, set into a carriage ran above the length of the cylinder, straddled the wire turnings and moved by the turning of the cylinder. The successor to the model displayed at the Paris Exhibition was produced in commercial quantities, and by 1902, this new magnetic wire Telegraphone could provide a magnetic sound record 45 minutes long.

On November 18, 1899, Poulsen's compatriot George Kirkegaard applied for, and was later granted, a U.S. patent for his device the "Telephonograph," which utilized similar principles. The German inventors Mix and Genest also announced their "short-duration recorder" and later a steel-tape machine with a 20-minute recording/reproducing duration, in 1900. The most interesting work after the Telegraphone was Peder O. Pedersen's invention that involved multiplex techniques. Two messages could then be recorded on the same wire simultaneously with the possibility of reproducing them independently. Pedersen later collaborated with Poulsen to produce Telegraphones for commercial purposes. Initially, they were responsible for two models: a wire-reel machine with a playing time of 20 minutes, with an attachment of a tiny electric motor fixed at the base of a compact console to energize three sets of electromagnets (two sets of erasure and one for recording/playback) driving also the two small wire reels. The improvement this machine represented was obvious as it could record at an impressive rate of 3 meters per second, and provide a 45-minute playing time. The second model used a disk 5 inches in diameter equipped with a pointed needle magnet and coil, contained in a carrier-arm that gradually moved to the center of the disk by a screw drive assembly. This

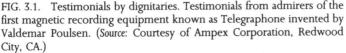

FIG. 3.1. Testimonials by dignitaries. Testimonials from admirers of the first magnetic recording equipment known as Telegraphone invented by Valdemar Poulsen. (*Source:* Courtesy of Ampex Corporation, Redwood City, CA.)

machine was popular in the United States, where it was regarded as the predecessor of the Brush Development Company's model known as "Mail-A-Voice" (a recorded disk that could be mailed anywhere for playback), and in Britain, it was the basis for EMI's "Emidicta" machine."

Up to this point, the Telegraphone and other recording devices were plagued by serious problems ranging from poor quality recording/reproducing to distortion. Of all the developments in the field of electronics at the time, progress in magnetic recording was small. The direct combination of the phonograph with the telephone, which seems so simple in theory, presented practical difficulties in practice which up to that point had not been successfully overcome, and the phonograph, over 20 years since its invention, remains little more than a scientific toy, whereas its contemporary, the telephone, has become almost indispensable adjunct on civilization.[7]

One of the principal drawbacks in magnetic recording devices of the period was the high speed at which the equipment had to be run to record the required frequency range for satisfactory reproduction. This, more than any other factor, was the principal cause of failure in various attempts to design machines for commercial use. For instance, a speed of 10 feet per second was needed to record a maximum signal frequency of 2,000 cycles per second satisfactorily. For fast and more efficient recording, it was possible to extend this to 30 feet per second for a further capacity of up to 6,000 cycles. At 6,000 cycles, it was reasoned that over 100,000 feet of wire would be necessary for an hour recording.

The necessity for high record speed under certain conditions is due to the fact that an excessive longitudinal section of the medium is required to properly register each individual cycle of any given signal frequency. The flux surrounding the polepiece of the recording magnet has a tendency to spread and influence a larger portion of the medium than would be the case if the field could be confined to the dimensions of the contacting portion of the pole tip. By making the latter very thin, it was possible to minimize the spreading effect but not to a sufficient extent to permit a material reduction of record speed without loss of higher frequencies.

Most experiments on the Telegraphone and subsequent devices were therefore centered around the control of speed and noise distortion. Realistically, a device had to be driven at a sufficient rate to move each recorded impulse far enough away from the pole tip to allow the proper amount of space for registration of the one immediately following, in order to avoid signal patterns overlapping and causing distortion or frequency loss. Besides speed, irritating background noise during playback had always been a disturbing factor in magnetic recorders. Noise identical to "metallic clicks or fluttering sounds" were the result of mechanical vibrations caused by the rapidly moving magnetic record passing the polepiece of the reproducing coil.

Furthermore, the early models of Telegraphone produced a transverse, "bipolar" recording, as a result of the polepieces of the record head arranged to be diametrically opposite to each other, on each side of the wire or tape. The recording process was therefore produced in areas of magnetization within the material that could be described as being transverse and having both N and S pole across the thickness of the wire.[8]

Working together, Poulsen and Pedersen soon discovered the disadvantages of these magnetic characteristics especially in relation to the small wire diameters and high speeds called for by the device, when self-magnetization resulted in a considerable loss in sensitivity. Improvement in performance was therefore achieved by adjusting the two polepieces. Besides, the absence of amplifiers in magnetic recording machines had been a major contributor to the crude method of recordings so far. The mass production of phonograph records completely overshadowed magnetic recordings. However, in 1902, Poulsen and Pedersen discovered the principle of direct current (D.C.) bias that when applied to the recording head during recording, drastically reduced distortion and improved sensitivity in the resulting record. Describing this important feature in their British patent application, Poulsen and Pedersen reported:

> For rendering the speech more distinct and clear, a continuous polarization current is employed which is led around the writing magnet so as to produce a vibration of the molecular magnets of the speech-carrying wire at the moment when they store the speech whereby the clearness thereof is increased.[9]

Although D.C. biasing when coupled with powered iron wires yielded reasonable performance, a considerable amount of distortion and noise levels still existed that magnetic recording enthusiasts had to live with until the advent of the A.C. bias system in 1940. Poulsen and Pedersen were granted patents for the D.C. bias in 1907.

Poulsen wrote in *The Electrician* about "an elegant method of compensation being invented by engineer P. O. Pedersen which allowed several speeches to be intermingled, so that they can afterwards be reproduced separately." Poulsen and Pedersen's relationship developed into a partnership, reflected in the combination of their names appearing in most of their subsequent patents. He also recognized the contributions he received from E. S. Hagemann toward the development of the Telegraphone.

The cooperative efforts that existed between Poulsen and Pedersen prompted them to form a joint venture partnership. Corporate organizations were formed simultaneously to exploit the commercial potential of the invention. In Denmark, the Dansk Telegrafonen Fabrick A/S (a manufacturing division) and the A/S Telegrafonen Patent Poulsen (a patent-holding corporation) were established in 1903. Dansk Telegrafonen Fabrick A/S produced about 200 machines, selling just a few. The wire-reel machine that was manufactured proved unreliable and the disk machine was a complete failure.

At the same time in November 1903, Poulsen formed The American Telegraphone Company, a U.S. patent-holding Telegraphone corporation. Also a manufacturing organization, it was located in the District of Columbia. By 1905, plagued by unacceptable and unneeded products, the Danish organizations were sold to the American Telegraphone Corporation.

THE AMERICAN TELEGRAPHONE COMPANY

Having been granted a U.S. patent for the Telegraphone, Poulsen thus established a corporation in the United States that would be responsible for the manufacturing and marketing of this new device. The American Telegraphone Company was incorporated with a capital of $5 million in the District of Columbia in November, 1903. Initially, Poulsen held the majority of stocks in exchange for his patent rights and their subsequent improvements. His stocks later resold to the public. The remaining shares were sold to 16,000 investors all over the United States. The company experienced a "zero growth" until 1908 when a factory was completed at Wheeling, West Virginia, with an impressive engineering unit. Not a single recording machine had been produced until then. The company was drained financially, having completed the factory, so it was forced into raising additional capital. Poulsen had by then left the organization and returned to Denmark.

Judge Lindley, the president of American Telegraphone Company, received two offers for financial assistance. The first was from a syndicate in the Board of Directors, who offered to finance the whole production of the Telegraphone. The second offer came from Charles Dexter Rood, who was then the president of the Hamilton Watch Company of Lancaster, Pennsylvania. Lindley convinced the Board of Directors to accept the second offer that included the sale of 94,000 shares at 20% of face value for $188,000; the difference between Rood's purchase price and the value per share at par was to be compensated for by Rood's services. The logic was that if Rood was so successful in the manufacturing of a delicate instrument such as a watch, no one would be more qualified to supervise the manufacture of the less sophisticated Telegraphone.

On July 30, 1908, Rood was confirmed as the President, General Manager and board member of The American Telegraphone Company. Rood was a respected salesman. A Springfield, Massachusetts, farm boy who went to New York to work for a jeweler for a handsome salary of $500 per year as a salesman, later taking over as owner, he once persuaded the railroads to equip all of their motormen and conductors with Hamilton watches and to recognize Hamilton as their official timepiece. Acting along the same lines, when on December 30, 1911, President Taft was scheduled to speak at the opening ceremony of a new department store in Philadelphia, Rood made sure that the Telegraphone was there to record the President's speech. Furthermore, when investigators in New York were finding it difficult to solve the highly publicized gambler Herman Rosenthal's murder case in 1912, Rood approached Detective William J. Burns who later used the Telegraphone to obtain the much-needed evidence that led to the conviction. But these publicity stunts marked the extent of Rood's positive actions at the American Telegraphone Company, for most of his efforts seemed bent on, and indeed eventually led to the collapse of the company. For instance, 3 years earlier speculating on the interest the Telegraphone would have for the public, the Commissioner of Patents requested that the American Telegraphone Company loan him a Telegraphone intended for display at the Alaska-Yukon Pacific Exposition in Seattle, Washington, on June 1,

1909. Initially, Rood agreed to the Commissioner's request but later did not comply.

In April 1909, Rood had transferred the company's factory from Wheeling to a third floor loft in Springfield, Massachusetts. In his first annual report, released on January 21, 1909, Rood recommended that the company manufacture both the wire and disk Telegraphones. But again, he was reluctant to follow up on the plan that called for the production of these machines. Due to pressure from frustrated shareholders, 50 Telegraphones were produced, out of which 20 went to satisfy an order placed by E. I. DuPont de Nemours Company of Wilmington, Delaware, for their central dictation system. These 50 machines were far from satisfying orders placed through the five sales offices already established by the company in Washington, Boston, Chicago, Philadelphia, and New York. However, DuPont discarded their Telegraphone installation system in 1919, due to a series of defects in the new machines and delays in supplying spare parts and replacements. An American Telegraphone Company top level engineer H. E. Chipman had resigned in May 1916, after discovering that the new machines were being tampered with in the factory before shipment. This cover-up was effective because it was initiated from the top. Requests from several organizations desiring a demonstration of the Telegraphone in their various exhibits were received, but all were ignored. On June 2, 1914, an American Telegraphone Company stockholder, Frank A. Brittain, in a letter to Rood requested permission to exhibit a Telegraphone at the Panama-Pacific World Fair in 1915, but Rood failed to acknowledge Brittain's letter.

On February 12, 1915, H. P. O'Reilly of San Francisco asked Rood for the company's assistance in exhibiting a Telegraphone at the same Panama-Pacific World Fair. After a telegram and a letter, Rood finally replied, declining to help O'Reilly in any way. Ignoring Rood, O'Reilly secured a Telegraphone machine, exhibited it at the Fair, and won a gold medal. Several years later O'Reilly became a driving force behind the organization of the stockholders, determined to end Rood's dominance in The American Telegraphone Company. Their first effort ended in failure when their lawyer accepted a $2,000 bribe from Rood to drop the case. Their second effort finally brought the case before the Supreme Court of the District of Columbia on March 20, 1920. They were asking the court to dismiss Rood and his associates from the management of The American Telegraphone Company on the grounds that they constituted an incompetent management.

The American Telegraphone Company had in its possession a total of 30 patents beginning with the initial Poulsen patent and ending with one granted G. S. Tiffany in connection with improvements on transport mechanisms. Fighting to gain renewal status for this Tiffany patent after lengthy mismanagement litigation, the stockholders, with the aid of a bill (S. 1301) introduced by Senator Copper and represented by George Sullivan, a pa-

FIG. 3.2. Tonschreiber, FT-2 and American Telegraphone Model C. From left to right: Tonschreiber Model B. Manufacturer: AEG of Germany. Produced exclusively for German forces between 1939 and 1945 for propaganda in the field. FT-2. Manufacturer: AEG of Germany. Intended for dictation purposes, this machine was produced in 1936. American Telegraphone Model C. Manufacturer: American Telegraphone Corporation, Springfield, MA. This machine was produced by the ill-fated American Telegraphone Corp., from 1911, and designed for dictation purposes. These three machines are currently displayed in the Ampex Museum of Magnetic Recording at Redwood, CA. (*Source:* Courtesy of Ampex Corporation, Redwood City, CA.)

tent lawyer, brought their case before a congressional hearing of the U.S. Senate.

Sullivan argued that the renewal of this patent would not only enable the company to update the Telegraphone, thereby ensuring its marketability, but would also offer the frustrated stockholders a hope for some form of return that up until then none of them had received, finally giving the public the satisfaction of enjoying the unique equipment.

Further testimony before the hearing committee revealed that Rood was acting with other forces, such as The American Telegraph and Telephone Company (AT&T), to destroy The American Telegraphone Company. The evidence behind this argument was that Rood on several occasions had represented AT & T's interests. AT & T saw the Telegraphone whose main function was the recording of telephone conversations as a threat. The logic here was that the number of their clients would decrease once they were aware that their business deals or private conversations could be recorded. In addition, Sullivan claimed that Rood was used by authorities in the phonograph industry to suppress the development of the Telegraphone for fear that the Telegraphone would take over the phonograph market. Due to Rood's interest in both the telephone and the phonograph, he was therefore compelled to place an embargo on the Telegraphone. This he did by "blacking out" all technical information on the Telegraphone from the public. Sullivan emphasized that every theoretical and practical topic on electromagnetism or magnetic recording was completely eliminated from electrical education and in American schools in general.[10] As it turned out, Sullivan's evidence implicated Rood in sabotaging The American Telegraphone Company, discouraging any contract arrangements with the company's clients such as DuPont, and denying the public the use and knowledge of magnetic recording technology.

The most serious evidence presented by Sullivan implicating Rood accused him of treason against the United States. Rood had refused to authorize sales of Telegraphones to several organizations in the United States including the U.S. Signal Corps, although it was later confirmed that he had masterminded the sale of six Telegraphones to the German Navy in May 1914, just before World War I, without any prior knowledge by the Board of Trustees or stockholders of the company.[11]

The U.S. Signal Corps had contacted The American Telegraphone Company inquiring about the possibility of utilizing Telegraphones for recording messages. And, although the Secret Service was aware of the fact that the Germans had been using the machine successfully for the same purpose for the past 4 years, Rood replied that the Telegraphone was still in the experimental stage. Fully aware of the real facts, the Signal Corps insisted, and in September 1918, just 6 days before the signing of the Armistice, The American Telegraphone Company delivered four machines to the Signal Corps. Unsurprisingly, when the machines arrived, none of them was in working condition. Furthermore, Rood asked to know what type of data would be recorded on the machines, where the machines would be located, and under whose supervision. Sullivan's testimony also revealed that Rood was given information on the movement of the ship U.S.S. President Lincoln, which was assigned to carry troops to France from the Springfield, Massachusetts vicinity. This ship was torpedoed.

Unfortunately for the stockholders, their case before the Supreme Court of the District of Columbia dragged on for about 7 years, until Rood was finally enjoined from direct management of the company. But Rood had already fulfilled his objectives; magnetic recording was all but dead in the United States and would remain virtually unknown for the next 20 years.

The events that led to the fall of the American Telegraphone Company was a classic case of suppression of technological innovation, apparently entirely engineered by a supposedly threatened rival, the telephone company, and encouraged by the limited use of the device itself. But nevertheless, evidence of public interest in the Telegraphone had resurfaced as other uses (other than recording telephone conversation) such as recording speeches and music were demonstrated with the Telegraphone at trade shows. But Rood had done his work too well.

THE FORGOTTEN YEARS
OF MAGNETIC RECORDING 1920–1930

After the end of World War I, a period of stagnation in magnetic recording followed. Only passing references to magnetic recording in the literature occurred, and quite often the subject would be Poulsen's models or improvements on them.

Due to the poor quality of magnetic wire recording devices, it was almost written off by 1920 as a failure. Moreover, the increasing popularity of phonograph discs rendered Poulsen's device unnecessary. Therefore, in order to resusitate magnetic wire recording, its effectiveness had to be proved technologically and uses beyond the home market needed to be found. An effective use of the technology was still being sought and during 1920–1930, as this did not occur, therefore most of the efforts went unnoticed.

Two important patents fall under this heading becoming a subject of controversy over their validity in recent times. The first of these was Leonard F. Fuller's of 1918, which involved the use of high frequency alternating current for erasing purposes. Then in 1921, W. L. Carlson and G. W. Carpenter, both of the U.S. Navy, filed a patent application for the use of A.C. bias on a wire Telegraphone. Their patent was approved in 1927. Rediscovered by several individuals several years later, including Walter Weber of Germany (in 1938), the application of A.C. biasing would revolutionize magnetic recording by drastically reducing distortion that had been a major problem.

Lee de Forest, who invented the "Audion" triode (vacuum tube) had suggested the use of amplifiers with the Telegraphone for music reproduction. A year later a Minnesota inventor, Henry C. Bullis, applied for a U.S. patent for the use of synchronized magnetic recorders for film sound. Forest and Bullis' ideas were ignored until May 1922, when Kurt Stille, a German engineer, formed the Telegraphie G.M.B.H. "System Stille" to acquire the rights of various magnetic recording patents, originate its own patents, and license these patents out for commercial exploitation. From as early as 1903, Stille had experimented with the theoretical and practical aspects of magnetic recording; in 1920, he modified and marketed a version of The American Telegraphone Company machine for dictation purposes in Germany. After World War I, magnetic recording equipment was still severely handicapped by inferior quality and the low volume output the wire recording medium produced. Because of these limitations, magnetic recordings were limited to commercial use such as dictation (including headphones) and telephone-exchange recording by major telephone companies. However, due to improvement and application of de Forest's invention of the Audion tube that resulted in the production of complex amplifier circuits, all problems concerning output and volume were put to rest.

In the same manner, Max Krohl, another German, successfully devised an electronic amplifying circuit and mechanically adjusted Poulsen's Telegraphone to use steel disks instead of wire as a recording medium. This idea provided a viable means of bringing the magnetic recording medium to competitive and superior levels, compared to the already popular disk system and the newly developed optical sound recording system in the film industry. In April 1922, Stille applied for his first patent for a wire recorder. His invention was described as a form of Telegraphone that used steel tubes as the carrier, almost similar to the drum machines described in Poulsen's patent of 1903. Stille also developed two types of magnetic recording and reproducing equipment. One was a steel tape machine that used perforated tape (with a single line of sprocket holes) which was ideal for motion pictures,[12] because the sprockets made it possible for sound to be synchronized with the picture. Yet steel tape was not only heavy and difficult to handle, but also difficult to control. Broken steel tapes could only be repaired by hardsoldering or welding, at which point the heated spot would produce a distinct audio "dropout."

Also included in Stille's patent was the idea of a multi-track recording system and a second development—an updated version of the wire recorder that utilized finer wire, hence resulting in longer telephone and dictation recording. This last was a joint effort of Stille's and a syndicate licensee, Karl Bauer. The machine was of better quality than wire recorders produced by the defunct American Telegraphone Company. Stille's wire recorder was called "Dailygraph," and by the early 1920s, Echophon Company, a subsidiary of Stille Organization marketed this device primarily as a dictating machine. Fascinating as it was, Stille's dailygraph was doomed by the post-World War I inflationary economy in Germany. It was cheaper to hire a stenographer than to purchase a dailygraph machine. In 1932, Echophon Company later sold out to ITT Lorenz, a subsidiary of the International Telephone and Telegraph Company. The Dailygraph was redesigned by ITT's German associates and marketed under the product name "Textophone" in 1933.

The idea of synchronized magnetic recorders for film sound had been initially proposed by Bullis. Stille, nevertheless, capitalized on the idea and became the first to give a practically successful demonstration of the device. Before this invention, "talkies" were made with synchronized transcription disk recordings.

PRODUCTION OF WIRE MAGNETIC
RECORDING IN THE UNITED STATES

From the collapse of the American Telegraphone Company until 1937 when Brush Development Corporation of Cleveland introduced the "Sound Mirror" tape recorder, no magnetic recording equipment had been produced in the United States. Credit for the progress made at Brush Development Corporation was given to S. J. Begun, who had previously designed the C. Lorenz Stahltonbandmaschine in Germany. Begun immigrated to the United States in 1935, later making a significant contribution to the future progress of magnetic recording in the United States. Brush's magnetic recorder was originally intended for speech recording for study or rehearsal. It had a continuous steel tape which provided a recording time of about one minute, running at 3.5 feet per second. A subsequent model was a console unit with components of tape equipment, "crystal stylus" cutter and turntable for cutting 12-inch 78 RPM records.

Reversing its apparent early hostility toward the magnetic recording industry, AT&T joined in the quest for an acceptable recording device. Ongoing research was instituted at the AT&T Bell Laboratories in the early 1930s. Engineers at Bell Laboratories were engaged in developing experimental steel tape machines from a new material called vicalloy, a substance of superior magnetic property and resistance to high humidity considered to be better than previously used carbon or tungsten steel. This experiment resulted in the demonstration of a stereo machine (by AT&T) which used two vicalloy steel tapes wound on the same reel that separated and passed over two heads. By 1939, AT&T's Western Electric Division had introduced the Mirrophone, the first commercial magnetic recorder manufactured in the United States since the Telegraphone almost 25 years earlier.

Unlike the first two decades of the century, in the United States, magnetic recording generated much curiosity in the late 1930s, especially in academic circles, as three Bachelor of Science Theses were written on the subject at Massachusetts Institute of Technology in 1938 testify.[13] Clearly, the dictation office function was becoming more economically feasible and other uses in radio networking or film were also increasingly worth exploring. Uses now included dictation, rehearsals, and even the recording of corporate board meeting's minutes.

The possibility of war brought great advances in magnetic wire recording

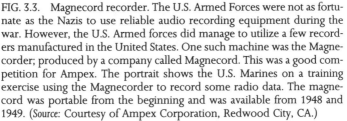

FIG. 3.3.   Magnecord recorder. The U.S. Armed Forces were not as fortu-
nate as the Nazis to use reliable audio recording equipment during the
war. However, the U.S. Armed forces did manage to utilize a few recorders manufactured in the United States. One such machine was the Magnecorder; produced by a company called Magnecord. This was a good competition for Ampex. The portrait shows the U.S. Marines on a training
exercise using the Magnecorder to record some radio data. The magnecord was portable from the beginning and was available from 1948 and
1949. (*Source:* Courtesy of Ampex Corporation, Redwood City, CA.)

in the United States as the emerging uses of the device were established. In
1940, Lockheed Aircraft Corporation was involved in recording various test
flight data with the "Planetest Magnagraph," a recorder manufactured by
the Heller Magnagraph Corporation of Los Angeles. A small microphone
leading to the Magnagraph machine was attached close to the pilot's mouth
during test flights. The pilot was therefore able to document as much data
as possible by commenting as much as he could on the details of the flight
without writing down anything in his log book or chart. The Magnagraph
used 1,800 feet of steel tape 7/32 inches wide. After a typical flight, the steel
tape was transcribed by stenographers. This form of record was adopted
because disc recording was too susceptible to vibration and acceleration
effects, whereas optical recording equipment was prohibitively expensive
and optical processing time lengthy; also Magnagraph could be adapted to
record electronically vibration, flutter, and strain measurement.[14]

The Magnagraph was developed by Herman S. Heller, a former chief sound engineer at Warner Brothers who was responsible for the development of the old vitaphone system.

WARTIME DEVELOPMENT
OF WIRE RECORDING IN AMERICA

With the war imminent, there was a necessity to develop adequate recording devices for the military at a more rapid rate. Marvin Camras, a student at Illinois Institute of Technology, was undertaking extensive research on magnetic recording that eventually led to his Master of Science Thesis in 1942. Camras, an associate of the Armour Research Foundation, applied for several patents that involved improvement on magnetic recording equipment and processes. As the Americans entered World War II, there was an urgent need for dependable and durable communications recorders. Camras had designed a prototype wire recorder, the Model 50 (later called the "Armour"), in 1942, which was accepted by the U.S. army and navy. Under a license from Armour, GE manufactured a new portable version of Amour's Model 50, known as GE's Model 20A.[15] This equipment was used by both the U.S. Air Force and British Royal Air Force, and its weight of less than 9 pounds was ideal for recording airborne reconnaisance missions. As the war continued, magnetic wire recorders found other applications including use by the public relations division of the Army and Navy to record invasion reports first hand for release to news wire services (such as the Marines' landing at Bougainville and Saipan in 1944 in the South Pacific) and the "off-the-air" recording of news programs and the "Army Hour" program weekly "time shift" for distribution to far-flung American troops.

Dr. S. J. Begun of ITT-Lorenz fame, confirmed that "recordings simulating landing operations transcribed onto steel wire did figure prominently in landings on Sicily and at Anzio." General Electric developed about four other wire recorder types by the end of the war. All the equipment was based on Armour's prototype as well as government sponsored research on magnetic recording (the 20B-2, 20N-1, 50A and 51 Models) done at Columbia University. GE utilized stainless steel with improved magnetic qualities for military recording equipment as opposed to ordinary wire used in Armour machines (tungsten steel) because the latter was vulnerable to rust in humid conditions, and because vicalloy was expensive and could not be quickly produced to meet the military needs.

In 1945, as the end of the war approached, GE envisioned commercializing their recording machines. At the same time, Camras and his associates at the Illinois Institute of Technology were researching more into the practical application of magnetic wire recording, as they introduced their system to the film industry in Hollywood. As the war ended, GE and Armour's dream of commercializing their products took priority. On April 1, 1945, Armour Research Foundation established a nonprofit organization called the Wire Recording Development Corporation to grant manufacturing licenses to interested companies—among them radio and phonograph manufacturers. By the end of 1945, a total of 19 licenses had been granted.

Brush Development Corporation was also manufacturing wire recording equipment for the military during the war. Brush's insight into magnetic recording extended beyond the use of wire, as they also used paper tape unlike Bell Labs that had experimented with this medium and were unable to produce a viable system.

In 1946, another company, Magnecord was formed to manufacture magnetic recording equipment.[16] Magnecord produced a professional wire recorder called the SD-1. From 1947 to 1948 Webcor (then Webster-Chicago), Sears-Roebuck, RCA, and others were manufacturing wire recorders for consumer use. But overall, a wire boom failed to materialize. Beyond comparatively specialized uses, there was still no fundamental and unique purpose served by the technology.

Back in 1944, Brush contacted Minnesota Minning and Manufacturing Company to investigate the possibility of developing a magnetic tape. Both companies agreed that if successful, tape might have some postwar applications. Early efforts failed as only poor quality tapes were made, and moreover there were no tape driven machines available to test them. In July 1946, Brush introduced a redesigned version of the "Sound Mirror" which used a paper-backed tape that had a black iron oxide coating. This was the way forward. By the end of the war, all signs were pointing toward a new era in magnetic recording in the United States, the magnetic tape era.

BLATTNERPHONE: INTRODUCTION OF MAGNETIC SOUND RECORDING IN RADIO BROADCASTING

An attempt to introduce magnetic sound recording to motion pictures failed as optical system was considered a better medium. However, the BBC capitalized on the new system, developed and later used it in its broadcasting activities. One of the objectives of the Stille Organization in Germany was to license patents out for subsequent exploitation. Telegraphie Patent Syndikat, the patent wing of the Stille Organization, sold the American and British rights to Stille's steel tape magnetic recording and reproducing machine to a British film producer, Louis Blattner for (25,000 pounds). Blattner, a German resident producer in Britain, had formed the Blattner Colour and Sound Studios at Elstree near London.

Blattner seemed to be pessimistic about the problems posed by disks and the often high cost of optical recording methods that was fast becoming the standard for the "talkies." Blattner produced his first machine and demonstrated it on October 18, 1929. *The Electrician* reported:

> A system of making and reproducing sound records, which seemed to be destined to supersede the old system employing discs or cylinders, was demonstrated last week to pressmen and others by Mr. Louis Blattner at the Blattner Colour and Sound Studios at Elstree. The nucleus of the new system, which is now ready for commercial exploitation, was discovered some 40 years ago; Dr. Kurt Stille began to work upon it 25 years ago, and the Ludwig Blattner Picture Corporation of London and the Telegraphie Patent Syndikat of Berlin have recently conducted laboratory and studio work which indicates that the invention will probably revolutionize present day practice . . . The items in the demonstration referred to include a reproduction of a monologue recited by Mr. Henry Ainley, whose enunciation was faithfully reproduced, and a "talkie" picture of Miss Ivy St. Helier, who sang to her own piano accompaniment, and concluded her performance with an amusing talk. This picture was very realistic, and the sound record was distinct and well synchronized.[17]

Blattner's was a multi-purpose machine that apart from its capability in film sound recording was also used for recording telephone conversations with instant playback and professional studio recordings. *The Electrician* described some of its uses as including utility as a dictating machine, a recorder of messages in the subscriber's absence, a "file" of conversation for use as evidence, and the teaching of languages and scientific and other lessons in schools.

Despite these praises the demonstration of the Blattnerphone in the Fall of 1929 was far from convincing to the film industry. The British Broadcasting Corporation, however, was impressed and was to play a significant part in promoting this device. Vice Admiral Sir Charles Caprendale of the BBC, and Noel Ashbridge, its chief engineer were at Blattner's demonstration. At this time, the BBC was seriously considering the provision of an Empire Broadcasting Service, which embraced five time-zoned services beamed to different parts of the world for 2 hours everyday. The necessity for the equipment to be compatible with the services to be provided was of utmost importance, because it was necessary to time the long distance transmissions to obtain reasonable hours of reception—usually early evening local time—broadcasts were beamed by using directional aerials, with the transmitters switched to each aerial at 2-hour intervals. Thus, to enable a program broadcast to Australia to be heard in Canada, the material had to be available for repeat. Disc recording had not been used in the BBC up to that time, and in any case, the playing time was rather limited. The Blattnerphone seemed to provide just the answer.

Throughout 1930, the BBC was using the Blattnerphone on an experimental basis after negotiating with Louis Blattner and Wilfred Dawson, Chairman of British Blattnerphone Ltd. (Stille System); the agreement resulted in a year's trial at a royalty of 5,000 pounds sterling. An experimental machine was installed at BBC Avenue House in September of 1930, and on November 12, it was used for recording and reproducing King George V's speech at the opening of the India Round Table Conference in London. Although the machine performed well for recording speech, it was not an ideal instrument for recording music. However, the BBC, impressed on the overall performance of the Blattnerphone, signed a contract with the British Blattnerphone Company in January 1931, thereby renting one machine at 500 pounds sterling for the first year, and 1,000 pounds per year thereafter, plus 250 pounds sterling a year for each additional machine. The Blattnerphone was installed at BBC's Savoy Hill facility and put into service in 1931. The first program of the Empire Service series was on air after the Christmas of 1931. By March 1932, a second machine was installed to aid in the busy schedule. Both machines used steel tape 6 millimeters and 0.08 millimeters thick, with a speed of 5 feet per second and a total playing time of 20 minutes.

The BBC research department pointed out some deficiencies in these machines, and a British Blattnerphone Company engineer, Von Heising, was advised to develop two entirely new prototypes. This he did in less than 3 months. But unexpectedly, in March 1933, the Marconi Wireless Telegraph Company purchased the rights in the Blattnerphone machines, and through a joint development program with BBC, (with Marconi being responsible for mechanical designs while BBC was in charge of electronics), a total of six improved models called "Marconi–Stille" machines were delivered to the BBC recording studio at Maida Vale in September, 1935. Marconi–Stille machines were also used in broadcasting in Canada and Australia. It was from this machine that C. Lorenz A. G. of Germany later developed the Lorenz Stahltonbandmaschine or "Steel Sound tape machine."

In July 1933, Blattner's company was liquidated, and his Elstree studio was reorganized, renamed "Anglo-American Studios" and equipped with Fidelitytone, an inexpensive variable-area optical sound recording system.

From what was a mere speculation by Oberlin Smith, came the invention of the Telegraphone by Poulsen. This invention was supposed to be a telephone recording instrument. However, major telephone interests, poor technical performance, lack of economic incentives, bad corporate management, and negative reaction from the public thwarted every effort for its growth. Therefore during the first three decades of the century, the demand for a recording medium was practically nonexistent, beyond playback units such as phonograph and disk. Then two prominent firms, Allgemeine Electricitaets Gesellschaft and I.G. Farbenindustrie A.G., were to dramatically change the history of magnetic recording for good between 1935 and 1945, thereby laying a solid foundation for what is now known as modern tape recording. The developments within these two companies marked the end of the magnetic wire recording era, and the advent of the magnetic tape recording in Europe.

Chapter 4

Introduction of Tape Development and the German Magnetophon

Ever since Poulsen's Telegraphone aroused curiosity among scientists and inventors all over the world, German scientists as well as their government, more than any other single group or nation, have encouraged further research on magnetic recording and reproducing and improvements thereon. Although American engineers, scientists, and the public were almost totally isolated from published information on magnetic recording theory and practice, due to Charles Rood's activities, the Germans had already mastered various aspects of the magnetic recording machines through their pre-World War I experiences with them, and their constant use during and after the war. One would have imagined that the publicity that resulted from the American Telegraphone case would produce massive interest in the American public, but the reverse was the case. The American public tended to accept the impression established by the American Telegraphone Company, that magnetic recording technology was a failure.

Initially, individual engineers and inventors, such as Kurt Stille, A. Nazarischarily, Karl Bauer, and Fritz Pfleumer, were responsible for keeping the magnetic recording industry alive in the face of a rigid competition from the phonograph industry. Until the late 1920s in Europe, wire was the main medium used in magnetic recording. But progress did not occur until the entrance of two industrial giants, the powerful chemical and plastic group, I.G. Farbenindustrie A.G. who under the supervision of its subsidiary BASF developed magnetic tape to an acceptable industry standard, and the electrical hardware manufacturer, Allgemeine Electricitaets Gesellschaft (AEG). Their collaboration would later form the groundwork for the modern magnetic tape recorder. The main interest in Germany was centered on

57

the broadcasting capabilities of the magnetic recording, the potential economic profits, and the quality, economic and technical advantages of magnetic tape. Intensifying their research efforts in the 1920s and 1930s, the Germans developed highly superior recording and reproducing equipment. But due to the events leading to the outbreak of World War II, and the war itself, these innovations remained practically unknown outside Germany.

This chapter documents the introduction of the magnetic tape recorder in Germany. The magnetophon is central—its various models and brands, the change from (direct current) D.C. to high frequency (alternate current) A.C. bias and the uses to which a history of the machine was put. The chapter ends with a history of the transfer of the magnetic tape technology to the United States and its early impact on American broadcasting.

THE MAGNETOPHON

Until the advent of the Magnetophon, the C. Lorenz A.G. Company dominated the magnetic recording industry in Germany. Lorenz manufactured the "Stahltonbandmaschine." The competition that ensued between this device and the Magnetophon conditioned the industry's entire research program.[1]

The most significant work was done by A.E.G. in conjunction with the Reichs-Rundfunk Gesellschaft (RRG; State Broadcasting Service) to develop a system of magnetic recording using plastic tape coated with microscopic particles of magnetic materials. Several recorders using this medium were produced in mid-1930. Although these prototypes were not outstanding in performance, the development of a supersonic recording and erasing process, coupled with considerable improvement in the recording tape, resulted in the production of commercial models that gave extremely high quality performance and made the machines extremely popular in Germany. Finally audio recording had discovered an economically significant function—radio broadcasting.

THE INVENTION AND MANUFACTURING
OF TAPE

Magnetic tape, as we know it today, was the work of a German engineer, Fritz Pfleumer, a consultant to the Universelle Company that produced cigarette manufacturing machines in Dresden, Germany. Among Pfleumer's previous discoveries were new forms of foam rubber and drinking straws made of plastic. At the turn of the century, Universelle developed a machine that designed cigarettes with a thin band of real gold around the mouthpiece; the use of real gold was expensive for the company, and sometimes would come off on the lips. Universelle also resorted to using bronze powder bands around the filters of cigarettes made by their machines. However, these bands came off on people's fingers and lips. Pfleumer was therefore assigned to develop a new coating process, one with smaller particles and a better glue or binder to hold the particles on the paper. From this work and from his hobby in audio, Pfleumer hit upon the idea of tape coated with a magnetizable powder such as carbonyl iron. Further development led to the solution that was a mixture of a bronze powder that he developed, and lacquer spread all over a strip of paper, cut into pieces and glued onto cigarette butts.

Pfleumer, like many Germans of his time, was knowledgeable in the functions of the Telegraphone, as well as being a music lover:

> Pfleumer was somewhat of an audiophile. He liked good quality radios and recording devices, and did much experimenting on his own. Of course, like most engineers, Pfleumer knew about the wire Telegraphone and the early experiments with steel-bond recording.[2]

In 1927, while sitting in a cafe in Paris on a business trip, he conceived the idea of utilizing the same coating process used for the cigarette mouthpiece label principle to produce cheap and durable magnetic sound recording media. He would mix iron powder with lacquer and spread them on paper, instead of the bronze powder used in the cigarette mouthpiece.

Combining his knowledge of paper tapes and his comprehension of magnetism and electro-acoustics, he developed the tape by initially mixing a compound of dissolved sugar or molasses, which he dried and "caramelized" by heating and ended up with a soft iron magnetic coating with an organic binder or tape. Pfleumer described his magnetizable powder backed with a nonmagnetic element as economical and an updated magnetic sound recording medium. Pfleumer's idea had been thought of by previous inventors who even took out patents (A. Nasarischarily of Germany in the early 1920s, Bullis and O'Neill of the United States in 1915 and 1926), but circumstances aided Pfleumer.

Due to limited funding, Pfleumer was unable immediately to pursue further development of his tape. More work was needed because the sound from the initial tape produced in 1928–1929 was characterized by distortion, wow, background noise, and flutter. Pfleumer then approached AEG for help. Fortunately, he managed to convince AEG. AEG was disturbed by cost, technical and operational drawbacks associated with the Swedish steel tape that was the industry standard. Also Pfleumer's system held the promise of chemical manufacturing, German's strong point. AEG bought out Pfleumer's patent and began to develop the tape. The company was fully aware of the amount of research that had to be done to bring Pfleumer's invention to perfection, and the chemical potentials so it contracted I.G. Farbenindustrie Aktiengesellschaft of Ludwigshaven. I.G. was a large company specializing in chemicals, and because of its prior experience in the research of iron compound production and its impressive facility at Wolfen, Germany, where films were manufactured, I.G. was considered the ideal company to handle the development of the new magnetic tape medium. I.G. commenced work on this project via its subsidiary Badische Anilin und Soda Fabrik (BASF) which conducted a series of tests with iron carbonyl powder coated on cellulose acetate tape throughout 1933. In 1934 the first 50,000 meters of coated tape were produced. A report issued by AEG on the subject in June 1934 endorsed the quality of the tape. Previously, many materials including paper were tried as a basefilm for tape. BASF initially used pure powdered carbonyl iron mixed with lacquer and spread on a cellulose acetate film, then cut into 5 millimeter-wide strips several hundred meters long. But by the mid-1940s, three basic types of tapes were widely used in Germany:

> Type C: This was the first tape introduced in 1936 by BASF following the joint venture research with AEG and I.G. Farbenindustrie. Although BASF had no trade name for this cellulose acetate basefilm, it was generally known as "Type C", the "C" standing for Cellit—a cellulose acetate.[3] Although noted for its high coercivity, Type C tape remained the standard tape for AEG machines during the World War II years, and was also commercially successful; but among its drawbacks was its ability to cause surface noise and most noticeably, its tendency to dry out and break easily unless stored in humid environments.[4]

> Type L: The trade name for this tape was Luvitherm—hence the "L"; it was a homogeneous tape/basefilm of polyvinyl chloride introduced by BASF in 1943. Type L was much tougher than Type C. It was made by rolling iron oxide into the polyvinyl chloride vat, and then extruding the mixture into solid film. The uniformity of materials and mechanical properties of Type L were excellent, and did not appear to deteriorate with age like the "C" tape. Type L tape gave excellent results especially with high frequency systems. Background noise was reduced considerably (see Fig. 4.1).

> Type LG: This tape was Luvitherm based with magnetic dispersion coating. Type LG was produced immediately after the war. It had a "Luvitherm" backing with a carefully controlled, uniform active surface of magnetite with adhesive. Initially, there were uncertainties in

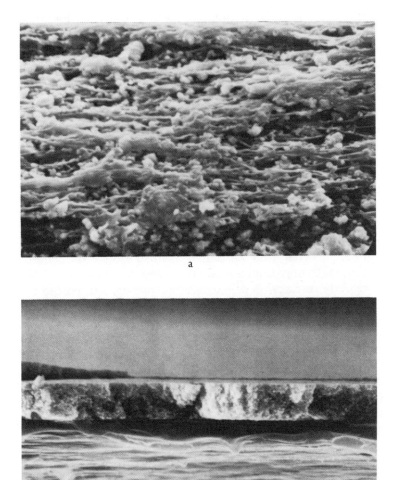

a

b

FIG. 4.1. (a) Type L (Luvitherm) tape. 2000 times blowup tape made at Ampex Museum of Type L (Luvitherm) plastic PVC backing. The oxide particle (visible as brownish lumps) were mixed right in with the PVC base film to create a homogeneous tape. There was no coating on this tape. (*Source:* Courtesy of Ampex Corporation, Redwood City, CA.) (b) Ampex 466 Digital Audio Tape. Particles not visible—and particles are much finer. Base film, binder, and oxide are separate layers. Compare this to the much older Type L. (*Source:* Courtesy of Ampex Corporation, Redwood City, CA.)

its quality, because of nonconformity of the base, but intensive research on particle size, permeability and layer dimensions led to the development of a layer size and composition which resulted in optimum performance.[5]

In the autumn of 1945, at the end of the war, BASF continued to manufacture Type LG at their plants in Wald Michelbach and Ludwigshafen even after the dissolution of I.G. Type C was also manufactured during and after the war by another I.G. Farben subsidiary, Agfa (Aktiengesellschaft fur Anilin) at Wolfen, a section of Germany controlled by the allied forces under the Russian supervision, while Type L was discontinued in 1946. Type LG was the closest to the tape model used in present day magnetic tape recorders. BASF and Agfa are still active in the manufacturing of tape.

Apart from magnetic tape, the most important part of any piece of recording equipment was the "head." Most failures in research pertaining to the magnetic recorder were attributed to frustrations experienced by experts' inabilities to fully realize what constituted a "perfect head." Poulsen, and other early researchers of magnetic recording, shaped the recording head very much like the stylus in a phonograph. This was a disadvantage for tape, because the stylus bit deep into the medium, destroying it as it recorded or played. The solution to the problems of the head came in 1932 when Edward Schueller, a research assistant with the Heinrich Hertz Institute in Berlin, designed a new ring head. This prompted AEG to hire him immediately to join their recorder development team. Schueller's "head," which became the industry standard, consisted of a split-ring made up of double columns of soft-iron laminations, and inserted to form a ring with nonmagnetic spacers that allowed an air-gap.[6]

AEG, with Pfleumer's tape medium that was entrusted to BASF for production, was ready to launch the prototype of their magnetic recording machine at the Berlin Radio Exhibition in August 1934. However, considerable doubt existed as to the reliability of the equipment after an internal demonstration to AEG and I.G. officials. One week before the Berlin Exhibition, this poor performance resulted in the withdrawal of the equipment although much publicity had already been made. Both companies absorbed the embarrassment that ensued. Two major problems existed with the prototype. It suffered from amplifier instability, and the overall performance did not measure up to the competitive steel-tape system. AEG engineers soon overcame the problems, and in August 1935, they unveiled the first complete system christened "Magnetophon K-1" at the Berlin Radio Exhibition.[7]

Contrary to the previous year's misfortune, the Magnetophon model K-1 was a great success.[8] Eight Magnetophons were shown, demonstrated, and immediately sold, justifying AEG's plan to embark upon production of 50 Magnetophons to meet the expected demand.

**Magnetophon-Koffergerät Mod. K 4
einschl. Zubehör**

FIG. 4.2. German-made Magnetophon Model K4. Manufactured by A.E.G. The model K4 was the first perfected Magnetophon suitable for broadcast in Germany. It had a frequency response of 50,000–60,000 cps ± 5 dB with a peak signal to ratio of 38 dB. (*Source*: Courtesy of Ampex Corporation, Redwood City, CA.)

The K-1 came with three cases, assigned for transportation, electronics, and holding the loudspeaker, respectively. AEG was also responsible for the production of the cabinet "FT" (Ferngesteuertes Truhe, or remote control cabinets) series Magnetophon. The Magnetophon K-1 was superseded by the Magnetophon K-2 introduced in 1936, followed by the K-3 in 1937. The K-3 was a portable machine that came in three parts: a deck, amplifier, and loudspeaker. The concentrated developmental effects of the AEG engineers paid off in 1938 when they finally perfected the Magnetophon K-4 machine, a 3-head recorder that was the first to offer confident playback while recording. (see Fig. 4.2) The K-4's frequency response was 50 Hz to 6000 Hz ± 5 db, with a peak signal to ratio of 38 db. While still poor, the K-4's audio reproduction quality qualified it as the new German broadcast recording standard. With extra production and the quality of the K-4 assured, came the first profits to AEG and I.G. Farben.

Meanwhile, beside the Magnetophon, the RRG was busy sampling the variety of recording equipment available on the market including the Stahltonbandmaschine, the Philips–Miller mechanographic-optical system, the "Selenophon" Optical System produced by Selenophon Licht und Tonbild GmbH, and Klangfilm's mobile optical recording equipment "Eurocord B" (including the portable version—the "Minicord T35") as well as the Magnetophon.

The progress made by the AEG engineers on the K-4 impressed RRG, and in January 1938, the RRG technical manager, Hans Joachim von Braunmühl, announced the adoption of Magnetophon by RRG. In fact, over the

next 4 years, all other equipment was completely displaced by the Magnetophon at RRG; even the previously supreme Stahltonbandmaschine was
discarded by 1939.

Just as the Germans deployed the Telegraphone to various assignments
during World War I, the Magnetophon was ready to go to war for the
Germans; this time, it would be an asset only the Germans would enjoy.

The national political situation in Germany was explosive and international relations were deteriorating fast, the dark years of World War II were
drawing in on the invention world. For those outside Germany, it was as if
the Magnetophon had never been; very few reports on the machine had
been written and fewer engineers had heard it demonstrated. The war was
to reduce information on the Magnetophon to nothing and it was not until
1945 that the audio engineering world was to be rocked by the progress
made during the war.[9]

A primary ideological advantage for the RRG was that the Magnetophon
obviated live broadcasting. It was of advantage for censorship so almost
none of the radio stations broadcast live. As a measure to promote strict
censorship, Magnetophon installation occurred in virtually all broadcast
stations in Germany. The Magnetophon was also later installed at radio
installations in German occupied France as well as in Luxembourg. In
addition, the Signal Unit of the German Army, the intelligence and to some
extent, the telephone company were using the Magnetophon. In Germany,
the machine's use ranged from entertainment, recording of speeches,
broadcasting, to an information data bank used by the military intelligence,
but first and foremost it was a censorship tool.

Magnetophon aided the Nazi leaders in achieving their political goals, as
the equipment was used to record speeches for later broadcast. At the
outbreak of World War II, Germans were instructed to produce goods
relevant to the war effort, be it tape recorders or coat buttons.[10] Therefore,
AEG produced a "tough" but portable model of the Magnetophon that was
accepted by the German Armed Forces for various uses. Named
"Tonschreiber," these machines were produced in various models that
included Tonschreiber B. Introduced in 1942, it was a portable field unit
used for signal recording, and fitted with a rotating pitch-restoring head that
made it possible for material recorded at high speed on one machine to be
"decoded" on another.[11] Tonschreiber C was a lightweight signals recorder, and Tonschreiber D was an adaptation of the Tonschreiber B for war
correspondents. The Tonschreiber F was used for dictating purposes. The
most popular of this series was definitely the Tonschreiber B. The German
naval communications unit was assigned another Magnetophon model
designated the A1000-L40, otherwise known as RE-3: a lesser unit called the
R-26, portable and spring-driven was used by war correspondents.

Because the radio was a major propaganda tool for the Nazis, the quest for broadcast quality was given a top priority by the German government, RRG, and manufacturers of magnetic recorders.

Introduction of High Frequency Magnetic Recording Systems

Thus, in 1935, the Germans had some level of quality for three of the four major ingredients that would constitute the basis for the modern tape recorder:

1. A stable transport system, pioneered by Lorenz's steel band recorders;
2. Acceptable tapes, which were developed by the researchers at BASF; and
3. The ring head, developed earlier by Schueller, an AEG engineer; it produced excellent magnetic properties and did not harm the fragile tape thus yielding excellent results.

The fourth and missing factor was the improved electronics that would result in magnetic "high-fidelity" recording. This would have to wait until the beginning of World War II when the Magnetophon electronics from 1935 were redesigned with A.C. bias for astonishingly good record/playback quality.[12]

No magnetic material would record properly in the absence of a bias current applied to the recording head, so every magnetic recording machine ever manufactured from Poulsen's Telegraphone to the latest Magnetophon K-4 developed in 1938 was equipped with direct current bias. Up to that point, direct current biasing was the only practical method of reducing distortion and noise, and increasing frequency response known to European recording engineers. Until 1939, the D.C. bias Magnetophon sounded as poorly as a 78 rpm transcription disc so much so that when in 1936 some AEG marketing representatives made a secret demonstration of the Magnetophon at General Electric in Schenectedy, New York, the Americans were uninterested with the resulting sound.[13] Describing the D.C. bias systems, Jack Mullin, the man credited with later introducing the Magnetophon to America, said "Once you hear D.C.-bias recording, you'll never want to hear tape again."

Because most of the magnetic recording equipment manufactured in Germany was designed for broadcasting purposes, it was absolutely necessary for AEG which manufactured the Magnetophon, to maintain a close relationship with its largest single client, the Berlin-based German radio monopoly (RRG). While AEG engineers were hard at work trying to eradicate and correct the D.C. bias problem, RRG was also concerned about the poor quality sound the Magnetophon produced. The engineering chief of RRG, von Braunmühl, went as far as purchasing some Magnetophons (all fitted, of course, with D.C. biasing) and instructed Walter Weber, his best engineer, to refine the equipment up to the point where they could be effectively used on air. Weber's initial task was to eliminate some of the irritating noise by "adding an inverted bridge circuit," which thereby resulted in a 180-degree phase shift and, in turn, reduced the tape noise to about 3 db. Weber, like all scientists, kept a log of his experiments, so as he listened to tapes made at different points of his work in 1939, he was astounded by what he heard on one of the tapes. Referring to his log, he traced the recording to a Magnetophon K-4 which used his new low noise reduction circuit, and whose audio amplifier had broken into high frequency oscillation, thereby becoming an A.C. bias oscillator.[14] The sound was unbelievably "pure" with extended frequency response, low noise, low distortion. Playing it over and over with von Baunmühl, Weber noticed that instead of deteriorating, the recording was indeed improving to an outstanding degree.[15] They were listening to "high-fidelity." Weber was then sure that the solution to hi-fi tape recording was A.C. recording bias. Weber and von Braunmühl proceeded to develop and equip all new models of RRG studio Magnetophons with appropriate supersonic oscillator circuits that in turn provided the heads with high frequency bias.

Throughout the course of World War II, no one on the Allied side seemed to have any knowledge about the hi-fi Magnetophons. It was even more surprising that this ignorance on the Allied side persisted despite a series of articles written by German engineers on German radio stations and equipment that appeared in popular German newspapers and magazines and sold in neighboring Switzerland, which was a neutral country in the war. It is an ironic possibility that if information concerning the A.C. bias Magnetophon was classified as "confidential" by the Nazis, the Allies might well have become aware of it.

As mentioned earlier, although von Braunmühl and Weber's brilliant research efforts resulted in the first high frequency recording in Germany in 1939–1940, the record indicates that others had thought about the possibility of A.C. biasing before then. The first reference concerns the use of a radio frequency erasing, combined with direct current premagnetization for the Telegraphone wire recorder proposed by a Californian, Leonard F. Fuller in 1918.[16] In 1927, two U.S. Navy Research Laboratories staff members were granted a U.S. patent for their invention, which involved the application of high frequency (A.C.) bias to steel wire to enhance sound reproduction.[17] Another Californian, James H. Alverson, proposed the use of radio frequency to saturate steel wire in magnetic recording. It was also apparent that research on A.C. bias, and its use, was done under Kenzo Nagai in Japan in the 1930s.[18]

The major difference between the A.C. bias suggested by the aforementioned individuals and the AEG/RRG high frequency was that although the early machines used steel wire as their recording medium, the latter used high quality tape that, in effect, allowed the advantages of A.C. bias to be fully deployed.

All pre-1938 Magnetophon K-4s were equipped with D.C. biasing; but subsequent to the introduction of A.C. biasing in 1941, most of these K-4s were updated to incorporate the A.C. biasing device. The broadcast version of the K-4, R-22, and R-22A were the first to be redesigned at RRG laboratory at Kosten near Berlin, and renamed R-122 and R-122A after being fitted with A.C. biasing. A special K-4 model designated H.T.S. (Hochfrequenz Truhe Speziell, or A.C.-bias cabinet special model), which was a high quality studio recorder was produced and used at RRG.

A complete unit of the R-22, R-122, or R-122A consisted of two mechanisms, R-22 or R-22A, consoles, two recording amplifiers, two playback amplifiers, two power supplies, one amplifier for line, one monitor amplifier, one mixer and fader panel, and one test jack panel.[19]

GERMAN POSTWAR IMPROVEMENTS IN MAGNETIC RECORDING

A more advanced Magnetophon, the K-7 studio machine, was developed in 1945 immediately after World War II. K-7 was almost entirely developed by AEG, and immediately following the end of the war, only a few prototype models were completed. In order to ensure its portability, it was built in units consisting of a tape unit, amplifier unit, and loud speaker for control and playback. The tape was driven by three motors with a fan blower attached to the bottom of the motor shaft to cool the reel motors. The 3-motor K-7 had a special frequency response of 50–10,000 Hz, a peak signal to noise ratio of 60 db, and a harmonic distortion of only 3%. Some of the special features in the K-7 were an indicator in the form of a clock, a marking system used to indicate specific locations on the tape, and an interlock for synchronizing two or more machines for continuous recording. A reel of tape on this system ran for about 22 minutes at 77 cm per second.

Although the Germans involved subsequently claimed that it was not intentional on their part, the Magnetophon was effective as a deception tool in the midst of the World War. It was absolutely impossible in many occasions for the Allies to determine Hitler's location because live quality broadcasts of his speech would be transmitted simultaneously from all corners of Germany. As two historians elaborated on the confusion:

> The allies suspected some sort of high-fidelity recording device, but they overlooked the fact that the Germans had an extremely advanced radio network. A complex web of high quality land lines . . . allowed remote broadcasts from any location to any other location. In addition, time delay broadcast had been standard procedure in Germany since the mid-1920s. To this day, old RRG engineers are amazed and baffled to hear that Americans thought the Magnetophons were being used to deliberately confuse the allies as to the location of high Nazi officials.[20]

The Magnetophon is the foundation for modern day magnetic tape recording equipment.

INTRODUCTION OF GERMAN RECORDING TECHNOLOGY IN THE UNITED STATES

A general concensus regarding the seemingly overnight spread of German-styled magnetic recorders in the United States during the postwar years has it that the Allies (including the United States) saw the German Magnetophons as "Spoils of war and therefore spirited them out of Germany with no legal rights."[21] Some writers have even gone as far as to claiming that the Germans kept the Magnetophon ideas strictly secret throughout the war period.

But on the contrary, the prewar research on Magnetophon in Germany was public. For example, Pfleumer's invention of tape was open because of his grant of a patent in 1928. Furthermore, there was the demonstration of the Magnetophon K1 at the Berlin Radio Fair in 1935,[22] and finally there was also continuous writings in radio magazines that were sold both in Germany and in neighboring Switzerland. The fact is that not only were most prewar activities on German Magnetophons publicized, the only improvements achieved during the war eluded the outside world.

Regarding the issue of inappropriate taking of patents, a vast majority of writers wrongly imply that the Allies (especially the Americans) exhibited a great deal of lawless behavior by invading the German magnetic recording industry without any proper legal authority. Prior to establishing the investigation committees to study the German technology following the end of the war, a major United States law was invoked and carried out in two phases. The law was the *Trading with the Enemy Act* of 1917, a bill originally passed at the outset of World War I. This law empowered the U.S. government to seize all enemy property. That included suspension of all patents held by any citizen of the enemy country or their assignors. Second, the law also authorized appropriate government bodies to organize a systematic seizure of all German industrial know-how.[23] On the basis of this law the Combined Intelligence Objectives Subcommittee (CIOS), Field Intelligence Agency Technical (FIAT), Technical Industrial Intelligence Committee (TIIC), and The Department of Commerce's Office of the Publication Board (OPS) were put to work to assess the advances made by war-time Germany. However, some writers could argue that this law really was just a justification for stealing German patents because it was a national law that countermanded international agreements to the advantage of particular economic interests of U.S. businesses and government.

Having used a national law to appropriate German technology, back in the United States, several confiscated items were exhibited by government and private concerns. Very popular among the equipment were the Magnetophons.[24] There was a clear interest in copying and manufacturing these machines. By mid-1945, over 7,000 American citizens and businesses had secured licenses for over 9,000 foreign patents vested with the Alien Property Custodian.[25] By June 1946, over $5,000 a week was collected by the Department of Commerce Office of Publication Board from American citizens and firms interested in buying details of German advanced technologies for further exploitation in the United States; over 1,300 of such detailed FIAT reports on German industrial establishments were released, and 20,000 vested patents were licensed.[26]

One allied soldier who was exposed to the hi-fi sound from the Magnetophon as early as 1944, but could not understand the source, was American Major John T. Mullin. Major Mullin was a member of an American Signal Corps unit stationed in England during the War. Mullin's background had been in electronics. He had a bachelor of science degree in electrical engineering from the University of Southern California.[27] He described his first encounter with the Magnetophon A.C. bias hi-fi recording as follows:

> Because of my background in electronics, I was assigned to the Signal Corps, troubleshooting a problem the Army was having with radio receivers that were picking up severe interference from the radar installations that blanketed Britain.
>
> I became so intrigued with what I was doing that I would work until two or three in the morning. I wanted music while I worked. The B.B.C. broadcast filled the bill until midnight, when they left the air. Then, fishing around the dial in search of further entertainment, I soon discovered that the German stations apparently were on the air twenty-four hours a day. They broadcast symphony concerts in the middle of the night—music that was very well played, and obviously by very large orchestras.
>
> I had some experience with broadcast music and knew what "canned"

music sounded like. The American network wouldn't permit the use of recordings in the early 1940s, because they claimed the quality was inferior. You
could always spot the surface noise and the relatively short playing time of
commercial 78 rpm discs. Even transcriptions had some needle scratch and a
limited frequency response. There was none of this in the music coming from
Germany. The frequency response was comparable to that of a live broadcast,
and a selection might continue for a quarter of an hour or more without
interruption.

In Germany at that stage, of course Hitler could have everything he wanted.
If he wanted a full symphony orchestra to play all night long, he could get it.
Still, it didn't seem very likely that even a madman would insist on live
concerts night after night. There had to be another answer, and I was curious
to know what it was.[28]

The music was appealing. Strauss and Lehar melodies played by a full
orchestra. Solo arias from Vienese operettas. What? At this hour? More full
orchestra—a male chorus singing songs of the Rhine and so on through the
night. How could they do it? The sound was so flawless that we were convinced we were hearing live performances. The audio deficiencies of record
scratch and other tell-tale distortions were completely absent.[29]

After the liberation of France by the Allied forces, Mullin's Technical Unit
Division of the U.S. Army Signal Corps was relocated in Paris. Here he was
assigned to investigate electronics developments in which the Germans
may have been active during the War.

On one of the many trips into Germany sometime later, the mystery
surrounding the full-live orchestra he thought he was listening to in the
early hours of the morning was solved. Mullin met a British officer who
shared one simple interest with him, good music. Asking Mullin if he had
ever heard of the German Magnetophon, the officer went on to assure
Mullin how much Mullin would like the equipment. Mullin and his com-
rades had already stockpiled about six Magnetophons in their laboratories
in Paris, where they had listened to sound produced by these machines and
even conducted several experiments with them. The DC-bias Magnetophons in Paris were as poor as 78 rpm shellac records, with poor dynamic range, and terrible background noise, so Mullin was neither impressed
nor convinced by his British counterpart's suggestion to audition the machines. Insisting, the British officer urged Mullin to visit Radio Frankfurt's
studios and listen to the performance of the machine. Thinking his friend
was not a genuine music enthusiast afterall, Mullin headed back to Paris,
but on reaching the crossroad to Paris and Frankfurt, he decided to visit the
studios as advised. While there, he ordered some music played on the
studio's Magnetophon. The resulting sound was unbelievably "pure" and
impressive. This was a sound of the same quality as that which he had heard

on German Radio while working late in England. Mullin described his experience:

> The mechanism appeared to be the same ones we had in Paris, but there was an obvious difference in the electronics.
>
> The technician placed a roll of tape on one of the machines and started it. Suddenly out of complete silence, an orchestra blossomed into being with fidelity such that I had never heard in my life. From deep resonant brass to the simmering of flute, it was all there. It was clean! It was free from any noticeable distortion. And as if that was not enough, the dynamic range was fantastic compared with anything I had ever previously experienced.[30]

Studying the schematic diagrams and instruction manuals of the "special" equipment, and later comparing it to those he had in his laboratories in Paris, Mullin discovered the missing link. The Magnetophons he had in his possession in Paris, were all equipped with D.C. biasing, whereas the one he encountered at Radio Frankfurt had an A.C. biasing.

FIG. 4.3.   Jack Mullin (left) and Murdo McKenzie. Mullin shows the Magnetophon to McKenzie, Bing Crosby's technical producer. The electronics was Mullin's design, entirely made in the United States while the tape transport was of German origin. (*Source:* Courtesy of Ampex Corporation, Redwood City, CA.)

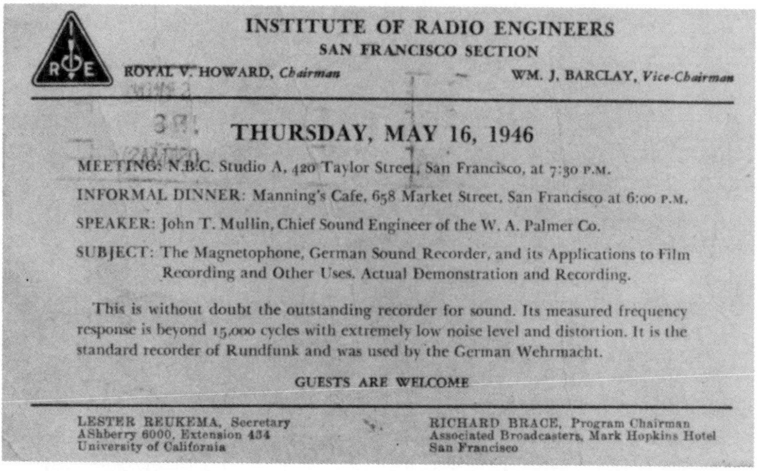

INSTITUTE OF RADIO ENGINEERS
SAN FRANCISCO SECTION
ROYAL V. HOWARD, *Chairman* WM. J. BARCLAY, *Vice-Chairman*

THURSDAY, MAY 16, 1946

MEETING: N.B.C. Studio A, 420 Taylor Street, San Francisco, at 7:30 P.M.

INFORMAL DINNER: Manning's Cafe, 658 Market Street, San Francisco at 6:00 P.M.

SPEAKER: John T. Mullin, Chief Sound Engineer of the W. A. Palmer Co.

SUBJECT: The Magnetophone, German Sound Recorder, and its Applications to Film Recording and Other Uses. Actual Demonstration and Recording.

This is without doubt the outstanding recorder for sound. Its measured frequency response is beyond 15,000 cycles with extremely low noise level and distortion. It is the standard recorder of Rundfunk and was used by the German Wehrmacht.

GUESTS ARE WELCOME

LESTER REUKEMA, Secretary
AShberry 6000, Extension 434
University of California

RICHARD BRACE, Program Chairman
Associated Broadcasters, Mark Hopkins Hotel
San Francisco

FIG. 4.4. Original announcement card for the Institute of Radio Engineers meeting in San Francisco on May 16, 1946. In this meeting Mullin introduced the magnetophon to radio engineers and enthusiasts in the United States for the first time. The response was overwhelmingly positive. (*Source:* Courtesy of Ampex Corporation, Redwood City, CA.)

After the exciting revelation of the differences between the D.C.- and-A.C.-biasing Magnetophon, Mullin proceeded with another colleague, Captain James Menard, to work on his D.C.-biasing Magnetophons, converting them to A.C. biasing by duplicating the electronics with the help of the schematic diagrams and instruction manuals he brought back from Frankfurt.

Mullin's final assignment in Europe after the war was to collect data and samples of German developments, and to forward them to the Signal Corps Laboratories and the Department of Commerce in the United States. After accomplishing his duties he was able to obtain two of the low quality DC-bias Magnetophons that he later sent piece by piece by mail to his home in San Francisco, California, as war souvenirs. Retiring from the U.S. Armed forces, Mullin modified his Magnetophons with custom-built A.C. bias electronics and joined an old friend, William A. Palmer, who owned a successful motion picture production company in San Francisco. The W.A. Palmer Company specialized in all facets of 16mm film work including color film duplication and sound recording. By 1946, the two converted Magnetophons were being used at W.A. Palmer's Studios to record off-screen voice and music for film.

On May 16, 1946, Mullin gave the first public demonstration of the Magnetophon in America at the local chapter of the Institute of Radio Engineers in San Francisco. Present in the audience were men who would later contribute immensely to the establishment of a magnetic tape industry in the United States, including engineers from Ampex and other Bay area companies. The demonstration was very successful. Mullin opened his presentation with slides, illustrating the technical description of the Magnetophon, then followed by playing back pre-recorded music, while intermittently, switching to live jazz music playing in an adjacent room using an A/B switch back and forth from live to tape.

An intrigued spectator described the scene as follows:

No one, but no one, in that audience of critical ears was able to detect a difference between live and tape. This brought forth a standing ovation from

FIG. 4.5. Demonstration of the magnetophon at the Institute of Radio Engineers meeting. At the Institute's meeting held in San Francisco May 16, 1946, Mullin gave the first demonstration of professional-quality recording in America with the magnetophon to the audience, most of whom had not been exposed to a "pure" recording sound such as that before. It was here that Harold W. Lindsay was first exposed to the "clean" sound of the magnetophon. He later confronted Mr. Poniatoff of Ampex, who later agreed to improve on the equipment and commence production in the United States of a new audio recording device. Mullin's partner, William Palmer, is shown with folded-horn speaker in a 4-foot-square enclosure, dubbed "the tub," which was made by Western Electric. (*Source*: Courtesy of Ampex Corporation, Redwood City, CA.)

FIG. 4.6. Jack Mullin gives a presentation slide show of high-fidelity audiotape. At the IRE meeting in San Francisco May 16, 1946, Mullin gave
presentation and slide show of the magnetophon. Seated in the front row
was Harold W. Lindsay and his wife, Margery. Lindsay would later be
responsible for pioneering the first commercially produced American audio recorder. About 200 radio engineers were being told about audio tape
technology for the first time. (*Source:* Courtesy of Ampex Corporation,
Redwood City, CA.)

the spellbound listeners. Equally amazing was the demonstration of the fascinating capabilities of tape editing, including a one-minute stretch of program containing twelve splices, none of which was detected by the listeners.

A deluge of questions followed the formal presentation, and Jack [Mullin]
fielded the questions in fine academic fashion. Adjournment brought a crash
and jam of the technically inclined to the lecture platform for a close look at
the fantastic Magnetophon.[31]

Harold Lindsay the future Chief Engineer of Ampex Corporation sought
out Mullin at the end of the meeting, saying "I've got a feeling this development is going to change the lives of millions of people. That's what I'd like
to do someday—work with magnetic recording."[32]

In his reply, Mullin assured Lindsay of his help. An engineer at Dalmo
Victor Company, a U.S. Navy contracting company involved in the manufacturing of radar equipment and located in San Carlos, California, Lindsay
knew Forrest Smith, who was the general manager for a young firm called

Ampex Electric Company. At the time, Ampex was a subcontractor to Dalmo Victor (supplying Dalmo with precision permanent magnetic motors and generators assembled in the Airborne radar) and had earlier ties to Dalmo. Both Lindsay and Smith were engaged in frequent discussions of their mutual interest in classical music and engineering design. Smith mentioned to Lindsay that Ampex intended to develop new products in view of the possibilities that, with the war ended, the navy might cancel most of Ampex's contracts. Furthermore, Smith told Lindsay that information concerning magnetic recording equipment would be welcomed by Ampex.

AMPEX'S DECISION TO MANUFACTURE
MAGNETIC TAPE RECORDERS

Ampex Corporation was a "brainchild" of Alexander Matthew Poniatoff, a Russian immigrant trained in electrical engineering who came to the United States in 1927. Once in the United States, Poniatoff worked for General Electric in New York, then Pacific Gas and Electric Company in San Francisco. Searching for a job in research and development, he was employed by T.I. Moseley, who owned Dalmo Victor Company. In 1942, as World War II continued, Dalmo won a contract to develop airborne radar scanners for the U.S. Navy. During 1943 and 1944, Dalmo Victor was having difficulties obtaining two important items: special motors and generators required in connection with the airborne radar scanners. Moseley then suggested that Poniatoff start a company that would manufacture these components.

On November 1, 1944, out of his personal resources, Poniatoff equipped an abandoned loft above Dalmo Victor plant and established Ampex Electrical and Manufacturing Company. A year later Ampex would boast of quality products.[33]

Poniatoff's quest for excellence was recognized and acclaimed as he remarked, "no effort was too great to develop." He believed in building products of highest performance and reliability. In designing these high critical motors and generators for the radar systems (see Fig. 4.7), Ampex used new Alnico 5 magnets developed to increase magnetic field to a high efficiency level. The General Electric Company (GE) held the patent for Alnico 5, but because the material was quite new and sophisticated, GE could not produce one single lot during the duration of the War.[34] Because of the quality of its products, Ampex was given a contract to replace all defective generators previously supplied by their competitors and became an exclusive supplier of all motors and generators required by the navy until the program terminated in August 1951.

The war was ended, so was the bulk of Navy contracts, and Ampex

FIG. 4.7.   Ampex Navy radar generator. While Mullin was redesigning the
magnetophon at W.A. Palmer, Ampex was still manufacturing (among
other things) generators for radar. Portrait shows one of the generators
developed by Ampex for Westinghouse. The product was used by the
Navy airbourne division. (*Source:* Courtesy of Ampex Corporation, Redwood City, CA.)

anxiously searched for new products to develop. Once Smith discussed
Lindsay's ideas of developing high fidelity amplifiers and speakers with
Poniatoff, Poniatoff immediately arranged for a meeting with Lindsay.

THE PRODUCTION OF THE FIRST COMMERCIAL
MAGNETIC TAPE RECORDERS IN THE UNITED
STATES

Early Research by Ampex

During the first meeting between Poniatoff and Lindsay, plans to develop a
postwar product for Ampex were discussed. Ampex was eagerly considering manufacturing studio turntables but decided to get an expert opinion.
Lindsay was hired as a part-time consultant to help in the new product
selection decision making. After several weeks of discussion, Lindsay finally

advised Poniatoff to consider upgrading the designs and manufacturing the German Magnetophon to meet radio broadcast qualities in the United States. The response from Poniatoff was very positive. Remembering his meeting with Mullin and the promise of assistance, Lindsay contacted Mullin. Preparing for the annual convention of the Society of Motion Picture Engineers (SMPE) in Los Angeles, Mullin suggested that Poniatoff meet him at the convention where he demonstrated the equipment.

Poniatoff was very impressed and excited by his introduction to professional magnetic recording, and Ampex moved to enter the new field. Lindsay was immediately hired as a full-time employee of Ampex and appointed to head the new tape recorder product development team. The development of a product for Ampex commenced once the staff was convinced of the possibilities of tape recording. Initial progress was slow, and this understandably was due to the fact that none of its engineers had any previous knowledge of magnetic recording.[35] Ampex's chances of success were also contingent upon producing the highest possible quality machine. Determined to be superior in all areas, Ampex desired to surpass the already superior performance demonstrated by the German Magnetophon.[36]

Several sources of information became available to the Ampex engineering team. First, they learned a lot by thoroughly researching both the mechanical and electronic aspects of Mullin's Magnetophon. Although a partner at W.A. Palmer Company, Mullin was very cooperative, allowing Ampex to examine the mechanical aspects of the machines but not permitting examination of the equipment's electronic circuits. The reason for the restriction was that Mullin had made a verbal agreement with Colonel Richard Ranger of Newark, New Jersey, who was also in the process of developing a similar machine. (Mullin's relationship with Ranger dated back to the years they spent in the U.S. Armed Forces in Europe during World War II.)

In addition to Mullin's help, Ampex engineers incorporated information from existing literature, spending evenings in research at Stanford University, which was a few miles away from Ampex. The problem here, however, was that in 1947, few written materials existed on magnetic recording in the United States. Nevertheless, their research was useful. Then a third source of information was the U.S. Government Intelligence Agency Reports on German industries (FIAT) written by American Technical representatives in Europe. By writing to the Department of Commerce's Office of Publications Board, Ampex secured microfilms of most of the reports. Of all these sources of information, the Intelligence Reports were the most useful. However, Lindsay and his small staff found that their best resource was their own engineering ability. He later said of the first Ampex tape recorder, "We had to re-invent the wheel." A major problem, and the most important aspect of concern in the development of magnetic tape recording equipment, was the design of a suitable magnetic playback head. The difficulty in designing the head would have been lessened if Ampex had been allowed to examine the head on Mullin's machine closely. Lindsay took responsibility of this facet of experiment, as with other mechanical designs.

Meanwhile, Mullin was active at his work at the W.A. Palmer Company. He and Palmer had given an impressive demonstration of the Magnetophon at MGM in Hollywood in October 1946, and were hoping to put the machines to a greater use. In New Jersey, Colonel Ranger was designing and developing a machine similar to the Magnetophon. Ranger relied on his and Mullin's machines as samples while working on his model.

THE FIRST USE OF MAGNETIC TAPE
RECORDING IN AMERICAN BROADCASTING

The practice of recording for later re-broadcast was practically rare in American broadcasting prior to 1946, apart from the standard practice of spot recording of important news events on disc (such as ticker-tape parades, the Hindenburg disaster, etc.). Only the Armed Forces, which were active in broadcasting during the war years, were known to have been making extensive use of the over 3,000 magnetic "wire" recorders manufactured by Armour Research Institute and Brush Development Company and others for broadcast transcription purposes.[37] Ignoring the regulation of the Department of War, the Mutual Broadcasting Service radio station (WOL) in Washington surreptitiously recorded on wire recorders the farewell press conference of Harold Ickes, Secretary of the Interior in February 1946, thereby paving the way for an important process. However, it was not until April 1946 that WMAQ, (an NBC affiliate in Chicago) aired the first completely wire-recorded news program, followed by a competitor, WBBM (a CBS Chicago affiliate), which also used wire recording for both spot-reporting and news events.[38]

The precedent set, most networks and local stations proceeded to record their news programs on wire recorders. Although a standard procedure in Europe, the ABC network began transcribing its evening programming for rebroadcast at a later, more convenient time on the west coast. The economic advantages accruing from this innovation led ABC to embark on a further $300,000 project involving recording its evening programs on discs at WENB studios in Chicago, with the cost spread among its various affiliates.[39]

As the youngest of the three radio networks, and trailing CBS and NBC, ABC acquired one of America's most popular entertainers, Bing Crosby (from NBC), for a weekly show in order to improve the popularity of their network.[40] Crosby, an ardent proponent of transcribed programs had left

FIG. 4.8. American-made audio wire recorder developed prior to World War II. American made wire recorder as perfected by Marvin Camras prior to World War II at the Armour Research Institute in Chicago. It was used for radio broadcasting by the U.S. Armed Forces. (*Source:* Courtesy of Ampex Corporation, Redwood City, CA.)

NBC because it would not pre-record his weekly "Kraft Music Hall Show." Beginning in the Fall of 1946, Crosby's "Philco Radio Time" show was premiered, with ABC giving Crosby "a free hand" to air pre-recorded programs edited on disc. Nevertheless, a clause in Crosby's contract with ABC stipulated that he return to live performance on air should his "Hooper" rating fall to an unacceptable level (60) (see Fig. 4.9).

By the end of the 1946 programming season, Crosby's show rating had dropped dramatically, and Crosby's associates blamed it on inconsistent style of editing from disc to disc, resulting in a drastic loss in sound quality. By the beginning of the 1947–1948 season, ABC was concerned enough to seek an alternative medium of recording (Crosby's Hooper rating had dipped to 62).

Meanwhile, early in 1947, Hugh King, a film producer and a W.A. Palmer

FIG. 4.9. Bing Crosby and Model 600. Bing Crosby in a promotional pose with the Model 600. This model was an ideal portable unit. (*Source:* Courtesy of Ampex Corporation, Redwood City, CA.)

Company client, had seen the Magnetophon being used for recording and editing at Palmer Studios. Aware of the problems with Crosby's radio program at ABC, King suggested that Mullin and his associates give a demonstration to the Crosby associates. Back in Hollywood, King contacted his friend Frank Healey, an agent, who in turn contacted Murdo McKenzie, the technical producer of the Crosby show. A demonstration was scheduled, and once again Mullin recorded and played back using the Magnetophon. He did some editing, and McKenzie was very impressed. But there was no

FIG. 4.10. (opposite page) (a) John Mullin's Magnetrack. Manufacturer: Allgemerne Elektizitats Gesellschaft, Berlin. Although originally manufactured by AEG of Germany, Mullin while reassembling it in the United States, made some major changes on this machine—changing its name from Magnetophon to Magnetrack. It was used for film track at W.A. Palmer and Company, where Mullin was a one-third partner. (*Source:* Courtesy of Ampex Corporation, Redwood City, CA.) (b) The Magnetrack system. Portrait of Jack Mullin's Magnetrack system used at W.A. Palmer company where he was a partner. This is an overhead view of the machine. Again this machine was half German, half American after being redesigned by Mullin. Mullin used these machines to record film tracks. (*Source:* Courtesy of Ampex Corporation, Redwood City, CA.)

a

b

commitment at the end of their first meeting. Instead, the Crosby associates elected to compare possible competitive machines.

Magnetic tape recorders of some quality were already beginning to appear in the American market. An example was the Brush Development Company of Cleveland's BK-401 "Sound Mirror," which was of considerable quality when judged against other machines available. This was a consumer machine introduced in 1946, making it the first American tape recorder. Ranger was also making a considerable progress in the development of his tape recorder and an accompanying tape using the German formula. Nevertheless, none of these machines were acceptable for professional broadcasting at the time.

Crosby was to record his first "Philco Show" for the 1947–1948 season in August 1947 at the ABC–NBC studios in Hollywood, and Mullin was invited to record the show on tape while Crosby technicians recorded theirs as usual on transcription disc. Ranger, who by now had completed his prototype machine that he called "Rangertone," was also invited. After the three parties ended the recording session, Ranger was asked to provide the first playback of the recordings. His was rejected outright due to excessive distortion and background noise. Mullin's Magnetophon performed excellently as usual, and Mullin received the commission to begin immediately recording and editing the Crosby show on tape for final transfer to disc for network broadcast.[41]

FIG. 4.11.   Merv Griffin. Musicians such as Merv Griffin benefited from the new audio recording innovation. This portrait shows a signed autograph of the Pander Records label on which Griffin recorded his first album with Lyle Bardo in 1946, using Jack Mullin's Magnetophon to master it. (*Source:* Courtesy of Ampex Corporation, Redwood City, CA.)

Ranger had invested a sizeable amount of money in the production of the Rangertone, yet he failed to achieve the professional standards needed. Later he would succeed in the application of magnetic tape recording to motion picture sound recording, but in consoling Ranger on the disastrous performance of his machine, Mullin advised him to sell, thereby cutting his losses. However, the task for Mullin was how to record a series of shows on two Magnetophons with almost no tape. Although he had returned from Germany with 50 tapes, by now most had been reused and edited several times. Because Ampex had made a considerable progress in developing their magnetic tape recorder (although they still needed some help in their electronic circuitry), Mullin turned to Ampex for help.

THE INTRODUCTION OF AMPEX MODEL 200 MAGNETIC TAPE RECORDER

After several months of intensive research, design, and development of their first model of magnetic tape recorder, Ampex believed it was time to test the head that they had just developed (see Fig. 4.12). Testing was done at W.A. Palmer Studios. First they listened subjectively to the best master tape material in the studio. Then they listened critically as it was played back with the German Magnetophon head, using their best monitoring equipment (see Fig. 4.13).

Finally, it was time to replace the German playback head with the prototype developed by Ampex. Great tension ensued as Lindsay explained:

> I have always remembered that next moment, just before pressing the button, as one of the most anxious times in my entire life—so much hung in the balance: a dismal failure or the beginning of an exciting future.
>
> The tape whipped up to speed; we were stunned, entranced, suspended in an eternity of mere seconds. Then cheers and hand shakes and clapping—the sounds of a wild celebration. Our ears had just told us what measurements later confirmed—we had outperformed the Magnetophon head. We were destined not to failure, but to fame. We followed the playback head with a successful record head and finally one for erase. These head successes and Alexander Poniatoff's unbending courage and confidence served to carry us through the very difficult months ahead, months when finances would dwindle to the near vanishing point, plus loss of credit, inability to get supplies where needed, weeks without paychecks and experimental and developmental reverses. Nevertheless, in the faces of all these obstacles we continued, stubbornly unwilling to give up.
>
> During these rough months Jack Mullin was helpful in many ways and on many occasions, allowing us to examine the mechanical portions of the Magnetophon, but never the electronics. The puzzling situation was later explained when we were told of his previous commitment and contract with

FIG. 4.12.   Harold Lindsay testing the Model 200. Lindsay, chief engineer at Ampex and developer of the Ampex audiotape recorder putting finishing touches to the Model 200. (*Source:* Courtesy of Ampex Corporation, Redwood City, CA.)

Col. Richard Ranger who was also helping to produce a domestic version of the German recorder. Jack had made certain improvements in the electronic circuitry which were to be exclusively used in the Rangertone equipment.

While unable because of these commitments to show us any of the electronic assembly beyond the front panel, Jack did, however, help us in many ways. His moral support, encouragement when going was rough, loan of a number of reels of German "L" type tape when he had precious little on hand, design suggestions, and last but certainly not least, his promotional efforts in Hollywood on behalf of our forthcoming product were vital to us.[42]

Recognition was accorded Ampex, which was by now concluding work on the Model 200, as Mullin telephoned long distance, to assure Ampex that Crosby/Philco was counting on Ampex's success in the manufacturing of a good quality machine. Not just a show of goodwill on Mullin's part, this was necessary in view of the fact that Mullin's two Magnetophons were insufficient for "Philco Shows" recordings. Representatives of Crosby/Philco visited Ampex and were satisfied with the progress made on the Model 200. They encouraged Ampex to notify them when the machine was completed.

Lindsay and his colleagues worked day and night from then on, frequently using Lindsay's home as their laboratory.[43] By the end of August 1947, Ampex reached the final stages of testing their prototype Model 200. A date was set for an early September demonstration for Crosby/Philco.

FIG. 4.13. Ampex Magnetic Audio Recorder Model 200. This was the first magnetic audiotape recording manufactured by an American company that met the FCC requirements for FM broadcasting. It added American engineering developments and "know-how" to the advancement made by Germans on their Magnetophon. The Model 200 was specially designed for radio network. Manufacturer: Ampex Corporation, Redwood City, CA. Recording duration: 35 minutes per reel; 30 inches per second for normal playing and over 300 inches per second average during rewind or fast forward. Frequency Response: 30 to 15,000 cycles within plus or minus 1 dB. (*Source:* Courtesy of Ampex Corporation, Redwood City, CA.)

FIG. 4.14.   Side view of the first Ampex audio head. This portrait shows
the first audio head designed by Harold W. Lindsay of Ampex Corporation. It was the first American audio playback head. (*Source:* Courtesy of
Ampex Corporation, Redwood City, CA.)

Unfortunately, a week prior to their appointment date, Ampex experienced a failure in the signal quality in the record mode of the machine.
Unsure whether they could rectify the problem in a week's time, they
contacted Mullin who in turn posed the question "Will it play back?".
When assured, that it would he encouraged them to keep the appointment.

The prototype of the Ampex Model 200 was then demonstrated for
Crosby and his associates in Crosby's listening room at Radio Center in
Hollywood. The spontaneity of action and interest expressed by the Crosby
engineers and other associates for the Ampex recorder was so great that the
demonstration continued for a full day. A few days later Ampex engineers
were awaiting the results, when representatives from Crosby Enterprises
visited them. They posed a question that would later eliminate Ampex's
anxieties: "We assume that you know you have taken Hollywood by storm,
now what are your plans for marketing it?"

FIG. 4.16.   (opposite page, bottom) Bing Crosby promoting the Ampex
Model 200. Crosby played a vital role in the final research and production
of Ampex's first audiotape recorder. He was therefore made an exclusive
national distributor. He appeared in a variety of advertisements to promote the equipment. (*Source:* Courtesy of Ampex Corporation, Redwood
City, CA.)

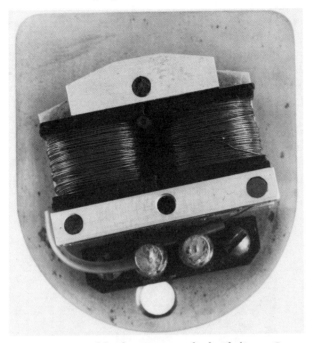

FIG. 4.15. Top view of the first Ampex audio head. (*Source:* Courtesy of Ampex Corporation, Redwood City, CA.)

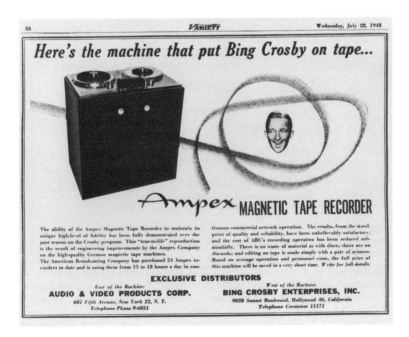

Ampex's product policy had favored the development of a high-quality professional type recorder targeted at the type of user interested in a rugged, reliable device capable of being used for day-in-day-out service rather than a product that would compete in the mass product market.

The historic Model 200 had an overall frequency response of 30 to 15,000 with a plus or minus 1 db, of 4% intermodulation using frequencies of 40 and 200 cycles, with signal to noise ratio being 60 db or better. The tape ran at a speed of 30 inches per second for normal playing, and over 300 inches per second average during rewind or fast forward, with an option of 600 inches per second upon request. A marking device was incorporated over the playback head for spotting tape in editing operations. The tape

HIGH-FIDELITY TAPE RECORDER DEVELOPED LOCALLY

Ampex Engineers Harold Lindsay and Myron Stolaroff thread a roll of plastic tape through the recorder, and prepare it to transcribe a musical program.

AMPEX ELECTRIC CORPORATION

Thomas Edison invented the phonograph in 1877—the world's best known recording device. Since then, scientists have experimented with disc, wire, and tape recording machines to achieve reproduction of music, speech, and other sounds as they are heard by the human ear.

Engineers at the AMPEX ELECTRIC CORPORATION in San Carlos have developed a machine which records music more perfectly than any other device. Theirs is a tape recorder which reproduces music and voice free of surface noise . . . and has a dynamic range which can recreate symphonic music in its original proportions.

You hear low and high notes of music, and delicate shadings and enunciation of voice tones which would be lost otherwise. You realize the high fidelity of these transcriptions as you enjoy a concert played over the recorder as if you were present in the concert hall. You hear the full range without distortion of such instruments as the double bass and the piccolo . . . and the singing or speaking voice in its natural timbre.

The Ampex machine records for 35 minutes on a 1 mile roll of plastic tape ¼" in width. Because the sounds are reproduced with the tape recorder by magnetic impulses, the tape can be used over and over; or the transcriptions erased. Editing a program on the tape recorder is simplified, since the tape can be cut, and better parts of a program substituted.

The market for the Ampex recorder is principally radio stations and networks. Bing Crosby and Burl Ives now use the recorder to transcribe their programs for broadcasting. Further research on a wider use of the machine continues.

Would You Like to Hear the Tape Recorder?

Alexander M. Poniatoff, founder and president of Ampex, invites you and your family to a demonstration next Monday evening, March 1 at 8 p. m., at the plant, 1155 Howard Avenue, San Carlos. *Free tickets to the demonstration are yours for the asking at this bank.*

Know Redwood City – San Carlos

The First National Bank of San Mateo County salutes the industries contributing to the progress and prosperity of this area . . . and takes pleasure in bringing them to your attention.

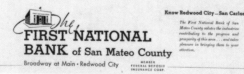

FIRST NATIONAL BANK of San Mateo County
Broadway at Main · Redwood City
MEMBER FEDERAL DEPOSIT INSURANCE CORP.

FIG. 4.17. First National Bank and Ampex. Initially, banks ignored Ampex's plea for funding. However, as Ampex proved that they were capable of producing quality products much needed in the industry, banks such as First National Bank of San Mateo County jumped into the scene. In this ad produced on February 25, 1948, First National tried to identify with Ampex. (Source: Courtesy of Ampex Corporation, Redwood City, CA.)

FIG. 4.18. Alex Poniatoff and some earlier investors. Portrait shows
Poniatoff, President of Ampex Corporation seated (center) with Forest
Smith (right) with some of the early Ampex investors. (*Source:* Courtesy of
Ampex Corporation, Redwood City, CA.)

recording time was 35 minutes per reel, enough to record the average
network program with a few minutes to spare.[44]

An Ampex promotional leaflet that carried a picture of Bing Crosby's
head-shot told the story:

Here's the Crosby Story:

The Bing Crosby show is considered one of the best produced programs
on the air. The half hour you hear broadcast is selected from 40 to 60 minutes
of recorded materials.

When Crosby first went on the ABC network 2 years ago, regular "platters"
were used, and in order to edit and re-arrange the material into the 30 minute
program, it was necessary to dub and redub from one platter to another. This
resulted in a serious loss of quality and unnecessary expense.

To solve this problem, ABC and Crosby experimented for 2 years with
every known recording medium and technique—finally selecting the Ampex
Magnetic Tape Recorder . . .

In the production of the program, Crosby's cast runs through the show.
The producer listens to the "playback" and immediately records improved
portions where necessary. The tape is then turned over to the writers and

FIG. 4.19. Ampex's ad with prices of equipment. This was one of the most important ads produced by Ampex depicting the prices of the Model 200 and 300 series. The equipment are also shown. The ad was released in 1949. It sums up the importance of these machines. (*Source:* Courtesy of Ampex Corporation, Redwood City, CA.)

producer for editing. The result is a perfect show—remarkably free from distortion and with a complete absence of "wow" or flutter. The speed is regulated so perfectly that even piano music is recorded without the slightest loss in quality. This is truly "true-to-life" reproduction.

Because Crosby was recorded on Ampex, other important shows such as Groucho Marx and Abbott & Costello have followed suite, and a number more are expected for the coming season.[45]

In April 1948, Mullin received the first two Ampex Model 200 tape recorders to leave the factory, as a present from Ampex to replace his two "tired" German Magnetophons.[46] Mullin later gave these first Ampex tape machines to ABC because of their bulkiness, and in turn received two specially constructed Model 200s, each half the original size—portable enough to travel with, as his job always called for traveling around and recording various performances of the Crosby shows on location.

By now Ampex was planning their first production run of Model 200, but unfortunately, the company was undercapitalized. They needed funds to purchase parts, and, unfortunately workers had not been paid for sometime. Banks would not give them a loan for such an uncertain investment. Unexpectedly, Ampex received an envelope with a Hollywood postmark on it. A check for $50,000 "with no strings attached or collateral requirements" enclosed carried Crosby's signature.[47]

Beside the problem of working capital, Ampex faced a scarcity of suitable

FIG. 4.20. Ampex audio recorders used at Capitol Records. One of Ampex's customers was not in radio, but record producing. Most of the recording studios turned to the professional quality audio recorders produced by Ampex. At Capitol Records' facilities, Ampex equipments were the centerpiece. (*Source:* Courtesy of Ampex Corporation, Redwood City, CA.)

FIG. 4.21. Ampex machines at Capitol Records. Behind these two men in the photographs are 1- Model 200 (far left), and 2- Model 300 series of Ampex recorders. They both have identical head assembly. (*Source:* Courtesy of Ampex Corporation, Redwood City, CA.)

magnetic recording tape. Two companies, Audio Devices of New York and 3M of Minnesota, had been working independently on the development of tapes. Both had heard of the new Ampex recorder and had at separate times contacted the California company. Their cooperation was useful for Ampex because both companies supplied many tape samples as they became available. Unfortunately, at the time of the Crosby/ABC demonstration by Ampex, neither of these companies had produced a good quality tape, and Ampex resorted to importing tapes from Germany.[48]

In the next 2 years, Ampex moved from a financially insecure situation to a marked degree of profitability. Basil Grillo, manager of Crosby Enterprises, and Charles McSharry, financial and production manager at Ampex, worked out an agreement in which Ampex supplied Crosby with 20 tape recorders at a price of $4,000 each, which Crosby in turn sold to ABC. In a short time Crosby ordered 30 more units. In addition, Bing Crosby Enterprises was made the sole distributor of Ampex products for the West Coast, while Audio & Video Corporation of New York represented Ampex on the East Coast.[49] Between 1947 and 1948, 112 Model 200 machines accounted for a sales income of $448,000. Ampex however had only spent $76,000 for the Model 200's development. By April 1948, ABC replaced its Daylight Saving Time-delayed programming transcribing equipment located at its Chicago WENR Studios with the new Ampex 200 and 2 million feet of red oxide tapes manufactured by 3M.[50]

After the Model 200 machines had been in service for seven months, Poniatoff received the following commendation from ABC:

> Commencing April 25, 1948, and continuing through September 25, 1948, [22 weeks], the American Broadcasting Company, in Chicago recorded on the Ampex tape recorders, approximately seventeen hours per day. For these 2618 hours of playback time, the air time loss was less than three minutes; a truly remarkable record. We believe that a large share of the successful operation was due to the use of the Ampex tape recorder manufactured by your

FIG. 4.22. Ampex recorders at ABC Studio in Hollywood. Picture shows Ampex recorders being used at ABC Studio in Hollywood. These are some of the few Model 300s made. (*Source:* Courtesy of Ampex Corporation, Redwood City, CA.)

company. We wish to thank you for your splendid cooperation in supplying us with this fine piece of equipment capable of withstanding the severe condition imposed during our delayed daylight savings time program.[51]

Very truly yours,

Frank Marx, V.P. in Charge of Engineering

American Broadcasting Corporation

Besides ABC, among the firms that purchased Ampex Model 200 machines were the broadcast companies of CBS, Mutual, and NBC and

FIG. 4.23.   Ampex Magnetic Audiotape Recorder Model 300. This equipment came as a result of a massive improvement on the Model 200. Ampex's goal in developing this machine was to reduce size, weight, and cost. By halving the tape speed, Ampex reduced the reel size and tape length and still maintained playing time of the Model 200. The Model 300 with its 10 $\frac{1}{2}$-inch reel, later modified eventually became the NAB standard. The portrait is that of the second prototype of Model 300 (1949) made of wood, but later changed to metal. This unit was designed for radio stations. (*Source:* Courtesy of Ampex Corporation, Redwood City, CA.)

FIG. 4.24.   Harold Lindsay (left) and Alex Poniatoff (right). Picture taken approximately 1977 shows Lindsay, Ampex's chief engineer and designer of Ampex's first audio recorder, and Poniatoff, founder of Ampex (with T.I. Moseley) with one of their products. Moseley did not believe that the tape recorder had a viable market in the United States, so he left the company. (*Source:* Courtesy of Ampex Corporation, Redwood City, CA.)

the recording studios of Capitol, RCA-Victor, Columbia, Decca, Gotham, and MGM.[52]

And so a small firm named Ampex manufactured the first professionally accepted magnetic tape recording machine in the United States. In the United Kingdom, the trend was similar to the events in the United States. The arrival of the "liberated" Magnetophons from Germany lent an impetus to the development of British's first postwar studio machine EMI BTR-1 in November 1947. The EMI BTR-1 installed at the EMI Abbey Road Studios, owed much to the Magnetophon, although several modifications were made which resulted in a credible performance. Radio-Gramophone Development Company was responsible for developing another early postwar machine in Britain.

FIG. 4.25. Magnetic Musak-Model 450. This equipment was the first magnetic musak player produced commercially. The Model 450 reproduced up to 8 hours of new program material from one reel of tape automatically and then automatically repeated. It used 16 × 3 ¾ inch reel bi-directional. Skating rinks, funeral homes, restaurants, banks, etcetra were users of this equipment. Special small and lightweight versions were developed for commercial aircrafts. Although commercial production began in April 1954, the Model 450 is still in use today. (*Source:* Courtesy of Ampex Corporation, Redwood City, CA.)

As with many other technological developments, Ampex did not rest on its laurels but continued research and improvement of its product. Although the first batch of the Model 200 series was still on the production line, Ampex introduced an improved machine, Ampex Model 300 in July 1948. This machine was an off-shoot of the considerable experience in the techniques of magnetic recording gained while working on Model 200. As the Model 200 was being introduced it became apparent that more sales would be realized if a moderately priced unit was produced. The Model 300, which had a lower tape speed but the same high quality performance, was introduced with a lower price tag. The Model 300 also provided improvements in head design, drive system and tape path; it was widely used in the industry and as of the end of the 1980s, hundreds of the machines are still in use around the world.

Initially, sales on the Model 300 were modest, because some broadcasters were still unaware of the possible advantages of a good magnetic tape recording system, but by June 1950, with prices around $1,500, success was imminent. Within a year, the Model 300 supplemented the list of Model 200 users with installations at the United Nations in New York, Radio Free Europe, Voice of America, ABC's Hollywood and Chicago Studios, Columbia Records in New York, the Naval Research Laboratory in Washington, Glenn Martin in Baltimore, and many other well-established clients. In 1950, the Ampex Model 300 was given the Certificate of Award for outstanding achievement in product development, design and engineering by *Electrical Engineering*, Cage Publishing Company's reputable publication.

The success that emanated from the Models 200 and 300 enabled Ampex to diversify into other areas of magnetic recording. Intensifying their new product research, Ampex was able to introduce such products as Magnetic Instrumentation Tape Recorder Models 302, 303, 322, and 500 in 1951,

FIG. 4.26. Arthur Fidler with the Model 600. Among the various celebraties used to promote Ampex Audio Tape Recorders was Arthur Fidler. In this photograph he is seen with the Model 600. (*Source:* Courtesy of Ampex Corporation, Redwood City, CA.)

FIG. 4.27. Judy Garland promoted the Model 600 Audio Tape Recorder for Ampex. (*Source:* Courtesy of Ampex Corporation, Redwood City, CA.)

Magnetic Duplication Model 3200 in 1952, the Motion Picture Sound System, and the Models 350 and 351 in 1953 and 1954. Ampex also introduced Digital Tape Drivers, CinemaScope Theater Sound Systems and branched into the consumer audio field, producing the first consumer stereo tape player, the Model 612 in 1955. Most significantly, research had already begun on the videotape recorder.

By the early 1950s, the economic success of the Ampex Models 200 and 300 coupled with the ideological realization of the need for such superior recording equipment by the broadcasting and recording industries, as well as other private organizations had greatly established and enhanced the audio magnetic recording industry in the United States. Such continued economic profitability and ideological factors overwhelmingly contributed to technological changes realized in the audio recording, and videotape recording industries to date.

Nonmagnetic Methods
of Recording Television

*I*t is surprising to note the amount of work done in the field of television recording in the early years, considering how undeveloped television, on one hand, and magnetic recording techniques, on the other, were in the 1920s.

A great number of television recording systems were proposed, but except for film, none worked efficiently enough to be diffused. Therefore, film was the only medium for television recording until the mid-1950s, despite its problems of poor picture quality.

This chapter examines the various nonmagnetic means of television recording employed and the difficulties encountered prior to an acceptable form of television recording equipment. Some of the systems that were initially regarded highly in the industry but failed are discussed.

EARLY METHODS
OF TELEVISION RECORDING

An early and important suggestion for the use of magnetic recording to preserve pictures was made by Boris Rtcheouloff in England on January 4, 1927.[1] A second convincing proposal was found in *Handbuch der Bildtelegraphie und des Fernsehens*, published in German in 1932. The author of this book was Fritz Schroeter, a professor at the Berlin Technische Hochschule and a former director of Telefunken.

In 1928, Luigi Marzocci, an Italian inventor filed a patent application for a variety of rotary heads intended for sound recording. Marzocci's process sufficiently foresaw concepts of video recording to allow the American company that acquired the rights to it considering litigation against Ampex Corporation many years later when videotape recorders were introduced.[2]

Since the early days of television, it was obvious that recording programs on film would play the same vital role in television as transcriptions and recordings in radio broadcasting.[3] Initial attention to solving most of television's problems was directed toward recording television programs on films in order to serve a variety of purposes. Among them were to delay broadcast of certain presentations to a more convenient time (in the United States, the 3-hour time differential between the East and West Coasts has been a major contributory factor to the need for an efficient television recording system), for "postmortem" (that is, enabling the television producer to have the advantage of seeing his finished work as transmitted), to extend network services to affiliate stations not linked by radio relay or coaxial cables, and for audition purposes. Furthermore, pre-recorded programs enabled television technicians to be occupied in some other operations at another location during the telecast, and it also allowed for a contingency material source in case of an emergency. And it could eliminate labor costs for night work.

Recording television programs by film was not without its problems. From the beginning, one problem was poor reproduction quality. Later, another problem concerned the recording of color values. Fortunately, color television was introduced almost simultaneously with the concept of magnetic tape recording of television signals, which alleviated this problem. Magnetic recording of television programs had enormous advantages over film, such as its capability of being reused many times, immediate playback, avoidance of picture development or chemical processing required by other methods, and ease of operation.[4]

These slowly came to outweigh the disadvantages (i.e., limited postproduction capabilities, reduced international exchange possibilities (at least initially), studio or remote unit organization). The balance between these pluses and minuses has meant that tape has taken over 30 years to match up to film's production flexibilities. The change over, however, appears to be inexorable within the television industry.

TELEVISION RECORDING:
A HISTORICAL PERSPECTIVE

As soon as Baird introduced his version of mechanically scanned television in England in 1926, he also started searching for convenient methods of recording his television programs. In his experiments, he developed a machine called the "phonoscope," which enabled him to research a process of recording television signals on phonograph records. Baird called the process "Phonovision."[5] His initial success on this project was possible because of the very low frequency signals carried on his television system— a 30-line picture at the rate of 12½ frames/sec. Due to this low frequency, it was possible to transmit the signal on telephone lines, or to impress it via a suitable transducer onto a wax or shellac 78 rpm record. Through an ordinary phonograph stylus head, the charged amplified signals converted the pictures into vibrations on the surface of the record.[6] Record reproduction was achieved by converting the vibration back into electrical impulses via a turntable synchronized with a scanning disc. Such recording and reproduction were always very poor in quality due to the crude nature of the mechanical system used.

On January 4, 1927, Boris Rtcheouloff filed a British patent application for a process of recording and reproducing television signals on magnetic materials. Rtcheouloff described his invention as:

> a method of recording and reproducing pictures, images and the like of the kind in which the picture, image or the like is scanned by an oscillatory vertical and horizontal movement and in which the luminosity of the various points of the picture is converted in electric currents by means of a photoelectric element, selenium cell or the like.[7]

Rtcheouloff's apparatus was capable of scanning and recording pictures by means of photoelectric currents. Furthermore, the recorded picture could be reproduced by reversing the recording procedure, that is by converting the impressions on the record electrically into a picture. The medium of recording assigned the apparatus was either a strip, disc, or iron cylinder or any other magnetic material referred to by Poulsen and Pedersen in connection with the Telegraphone. Pictures and accompanying sound were to be recorded synchronously, with the possibility of producing a master record for further magnetic reproductions.

The highlight of Rtcheoutoff's apparatus was the modification that provided for sound and picture recording on an endless piece of magnetic substance with reproduction and erasing capabilities.

ERPI EQUIPMENT

Thinking along the same line, two New Jersey inventors proposed a new method of television film recording at both the transmitting and receiving ends. In demonstrating their concept on September 14, 1927, Ralph Vinton Lyon Hartley and Herbert Eugene Ives, who worked for the AT&T Electrical Research Products, Inc. (ERPI) in New York claimed that their method had the advantage of providing an increase in the level of illumination needed in television transmission.[8] This adequacy in the amount of brightness then resulted in improved background details, hence, acceptable pictures especially when large or distant objects were involved. Their proposal involved conventionally taking a cinematographic film of the scene to be transmitted and later scanning the film for transmission. In addition, they recommended a step whereby film could be taken and developed at the receiver rather than at the transmitter, or at the receiver in addition to a similar step at the transmitter. This system later was similar to one independently developed in Germany—the "intermediate film" process. Equipment recommended for this method of television recording by Hartley and Ives included a cinematograph camera, film developing equipment, scanning apparatus, sound recording equipment, film, and sound projectors and equipment for "phonographically storing the sound and reproducing it in synchronism with the photographic film."

THE AMERICAN TELEVISION LABORATORIES, INC.
RECORDING APPARATUS

The American Television Laboratories, Inc., a Hollywood California firm in which Lee De Forest was a partner, filed a patent application on April 24, 1931, for a method of recording pictures transmitted electrically by exposing a coated film surface to a series of electrical charges controlled by the image to be transmitted, thereby resulting in an "etched image." The resulting picture could then be seen through a large-screen projector.[9] The equipment used was made up of a series of needle points attached to a revolving wheel that passed over a moving strip of pure metallic silver coated 35mm film. The needle points were connected to receiving apparatus that fed them with video signals. As these needle-points passed over the film, they created impulses and etching actions that varied simultaneously. A series of modulated lines were then formed on the film as a result, which was then projected on a standard motion picture projector.[10] This method was plagued by many technical problems and was therefore discarded.

THE INTERMEDIATE FILM
TRANSMITTER PROCESS

The German intermediate film process involved an initial photographing of the scene, panning the film through a dark tank where it was developed, fixed and washed, and rolling it on a drum while it was still wet, (or in some cases partially dried). It was then passed into television scanning apparatus where it was transmitted. After this initial use of the film, it was washed, dried, and ordinary positives were made out of it.

A.G. Fernseh demonstrated the intermediate film transmitter again at the Berlin Radio Exposition in 1933, introducing their "intermediate film receiver" for projection television. While in operation, television signals were received and recorded on motion picture film, processed immediately and screened by a standard motion picture machine onto a large screen. At the receiver, a Kerr cell stimulated the television signals causing them to modulate a strong beam of light. A scanning disk with 90 holes made hexagonally rotated at a speed of 3,000 rpm between the cell and the film, therefore making it possible to capture the resulting 180-line picture at 25 frames/second. The disk was focused directly on a sensitized film that was passing beneath a recording window, and when images of the aperture were made to fall on the film, they formed a variety of light and shades that built up a picture. After development, the film was fixed and screened through an intermittent type theater projector 10 ft × 13 ft in size.[11]

This was the first-known television film recording. This method was again demonstrated in the following year with the same instruments. A time lag of nearly 60 seconds occurred between the receiving and projecting of the pictures, and the picture quality was always poor due to blotches on the film. In 1934, Rolf Moller of Fernseh A.G. of Germany received a patent for television recording via the cathode-ray tube by continuous motion film.[12] Therefore, the first cathod-ray film was recorded in 1934 and demonstrated publicly in 1935. But this system was unsuccessful and was eliminated from the Radio Show in 1936.

THE VISIOGRAM

Continuous efforts directed toward television recording resulted in the introduction of a novel equipment called the "Visiogram" by Edison Bell Ltd. of England in 1934. A slightly different method from the previous recordings was used. Although motion picture film was used, the video signals were converted into modulated "sound" track of the image rather than being converted into light and shades as was common in other systems. According to the *London Times*, the first demonstration to the press yielded a disappointing result, as the picture quality was exceedingly poor.[13]

EARLY TELEVISION FILM RECORDING IN GREAT BRITAIN

Although progress on television technology was temporarily interrupted by World War II, it is nevertheless the case that the various wartime research and development projects contributed immensely to the development of television all over the world. By 1947, several methods of television recording were proposed both in Europe and in the United States, and all the methods had one thing in common—they all employed motion picture film as the photosensitive recording medium.

Recording conditions in motion picture and television were very different. In motion picture photography, a subject formed a complete image on each film frame and remained there until it was correctly exposed, after which a shutter was shut and a new unexposed frame took the place of the exposed frame, registered and then exposed. During exposure, every "picture element" of the emulsion received light of unproportional intensity to those received by the subject. The exposure time for all picture elements was equal, and it was about 50% of the total time of the cycle, or 1/48 th of a second at the standard rate of 24 frames per second.

Recording subject on television on the other hand was completely different. In this case, the image was visible as it was scanned line by line on television and would later be transferred onto the film. The exposure time for each picture element was comparatively short, while the picture elements were sequentially exposed as the television image scanning progressed. Almost all exposure took place as the electron beam exciting the fluorescent screen was actually focused upon the element of the screen concerned. The element continued to fluoresce (even though the beam had moved on to another position), its luminance weakening exponentially, while the afterglow supplied the rest of the exposure needed. The fluorescent screen was excited directly for only 0.3 microseconds while the time limit on the afterglow varied according to the strength of the fluorescent used. Broadcast television equipment therefore had limited intervals between successive pictures in order to economize on bandwidth.[14] As of 1949, all television recording systems utilized the cathode-ray tube as a modulating device but needed an alternate form of modulator because the cathode-ray tube resulted in poor picture quality. However, the demand for an adequate method of television recording was great particularly in England. The BBC was aware that many important news worthy events occurred during the day when a majority of viewers were at work, hence unable to see the direct transmission. Events such as the Royal Wedding in 1947, the Royal Silver Wedding drive, Olympic Games, Oxford and Cambridge boat races of 1948 and 1949, and F.A. cup finals of 1948 and 1949 were a few examples of such programs in need of time delay. Besides, the idea of assigning both film cameramen and television cameramen to cover the same news or major event was considered a waste of resources. Furthermore, the BBC producer and his team strongly encouraged the use of television recording for "postmortem" purposes. In addition, the British repeated much drama output a few days after the original live transmissions.

The British divided their telefilm system into two fundamental categories—those that used an intermittent movement and those in which the film movement was continuous. Among the intermittent-motion types was the 1947 BBC's effort of television recording using a 35mm camera. The problem with this method was that with the standard BBC television signal wave form of 405 lines, 50 frames per second (2 : 1 interlaced), a 25-frame television image had to be recorded at 24 frames per second. This hardly allowed enough time in between frames for pulldown. Therefore, a compromise was reached whereby only 50% of the television images were recorded, whereas the other 50% was used to pull down and register the film. The overall result of this method was that out of the British 405 lines, only 188½ active lines could be successfully recorded. The remaining lines were lost due to the fact that the shutter was closed every time each of these lines were to be scanned. Apart from the experimental use of this system to transmit the Centoph ceremony and Royal Wedding in 1947, this system was considered inadequate and therefore discontinued.

Later in 1947, another telefilm system was developed that used a standard 16mm film. This system was designed to record television pictures at an open shutter angle at 240°.[15] In 1 second, 50 television frames were displayed while 16⅔ film frames passed through the camera. Only two consecutive television frames were photographed on one film frame before the shutter closed, missing the third frame. The shutter opened again accommodating only the fourth and fifth frames, closing again during the sixth frame, and so on.[16] The result was a nonstandard telefilm recorder at 16⅔ frames/second.

Also proposed by the BBC was the Kemp–Duddington method on which a patent application was made in September 1950. This system required a double optical system and two-frame pulldown, making it possible to record two television scans at the bottom and two at the top apertures, and in the process duplicating the last second scan of the first picture and leaving out the second scan of the second picture, as the cycle was repeated.[17] The camera was phase locked to the television-frame pulses in order to maintain correct phasing. Tests showed a satisfactory movement sequence in this method compared to motion pictures.

Another proposal called for the use of cameras using two films, with two gates and film movements 180° out of phase. The first picture was recorded in gate 1 and the next in gate 2. They were both produced at 25 frames/second. The disadvantage in this system was mainly the complex editing system, higher cost of processing two films instead of one and the time factor involved.

Continuous-Motion Type TV Recording

In 1948, a continuous-motion type of television recording was introduced by BBC engineers by converting a Mechau telecine projector made by AEG of Germany into a 35mm camera. It was provided with a rotating mirror drum that coupled with a form of optical compensation, resulted in a perfect synchronization and as the successive tilts of the rotating mirrors repeated television images along as the film made its downward course, the images were stationary in relation to the film.[18] Successions of images were therefore formed as the film passed through the gate. Some of the advantages of this method included the elimination of using rate difference, pulldown, and the centerframe "picture splice" problem common in the United States. Besides, unlike previously described systems, no lines of television pictures were lost. A proposal to use this system in the United States was also considered by blacking out a segment of the mirrors, thereby avoiding the possibility of recording more than two fields on a single frame.[19] This was the first competent system used by the BBC, although the transport system failed to provide a correspondingly high performance. This machine was redesigned with the intention of providing a new film traction mechanism, and it was installed at the BBC's Lime Grove television studios in 1953.[20]

Apart from the continuous-motion and intermittent-motion systems of television recording, an old and efficient method existed that incidentally was the basis for the "intermediate" film receiver developed by A.G. Fernseh in the early 1930s. Images were recorded continuously from a cathode-ray tube by using decay and built-up phosphorus. This was accomplished by running and guiding the film vertically while the complete content of each frame of the television image spread on the length of the film. The camera had no shutter. Therefore differences in frame frequency and shutter frequency problems were eliminated. In the early 1943s, this method of recording was used as a basis for a new system known as "ultrafax" facsimile recording equipment.[21]

EARLY TELEVISION FILM RECORDING
IN THE UNITED STATES

A major consideration in designing early television recording equipment in America centered on the fact that the television picture rate transmission was 30 frames per second as opposed to the standard motion picture recording rate of 24 frames per second.

Attempts to record television programs on film from the face of the cathode-ray tube using both still cameras and motion picture cameras commenced in the United States around 1937. Conventional silent 16mm spring-wound cameras operating at 16 frames/second were employed. Due to the inadequacy of luminance on the monitor, very fast film emulsions were used. The cameras were non-synchronous with the television system;

hence, the films were marred by stroboscopic patterns of blanking (shutter bar), overexposure, and underexposure.

The Synchronous Camera

Later a synchronous camera was developed to operate at 15 frames per second, and recording every other television frame. The fault with this camera was that it produced a nonstandard film that was difficult to use for regular viewing or for rebroadcast purposes.

The need was to record the 30 frames/second television picture on a 24 frames/second film so as to correspond with the speed of a 16mm sound film. Efforts to develop this type of equipment was pioneered by Allen B. DuMont Laboratories, Inc., (New Jersey), a company that was in the business of photographing television programs; they in turn assigned the development task to Eastman Kodak Company.[22] Eastman Kodak later announced the technology of a new 16mm motion picture camera for recording television programs in January 1948.

A separate development in television recording began during World War II. Progress in commercial television scientific research had been slowed down because of the war. Nevertheless, the U.S. military conducted a series of experiments with television using it in a variety of ways. Significant among the military television hardware was the "Project Block"[23] and "Ring" system developed for airborne transmission during World War II, for the purpose of permanently recording various transmissions.[24] Motion picture film cameras installed on the ground and in various aircrafts were able to record occurrences from aircrafts and guided missiles. The U.S. Air Force developed a standard camera with a speed range of 8 frames/second to 4 frames/second for airborne television recording purposes. Due to changing standards of transmissions, the many photographic processing steps involved, and low light intensities of the recording monitors, the recorded picture qualities were very poor. A 15 frame-per-second, 170° open shutter cine special camera was then recommended for further recordings.[25]

Significant experiments continued into the postwar period in the military as the U.S. Navy experimented on color television recording. With a special 25mm focal length lens developed by Polaroid Corporation and mounted on the Cine Special 16mm film camera, successful pictures of the Plan Position Indicator (PPI) type of radar scope images were obtained.[26] But because this was not quite a successful lens, Polaroid was asked to build an improved 25mm f/o.7 lens for the same assignment. During a public demonstration of the Navy "Block" and "Ring" airborne television apparatus on March 21, 1946, the Navy successfully made its first postwar black-and-white television recording at the Naval Air Station at Anacostia, DC.

On August 18, 1949, the Navy employed their Berndt–Maurer film camera with a 25mm fl 1.4 Cine Ektar lens to make the first color film recording. Exposures were made at 15 frames/second synchronous, and at approximately 8 and 4 frames using the hand crank. Both exposures at 8 and 4 frames were adequate; hence, this system was considered promising. But the first completely successful experiment color recordings were made from CBS color television receiver (modified by Naval technicians) and demonstrated before the FCC in September 1949 in Washington DC. Sound was added to it, to make the first sound and color picture film recording on February 6, 7, and 8, 1950.

RCA's Dot Sequential Color Recording

RCA made its first "dot sequential" color recording in its laboratories in Silver Spring Maryland on March 10, 1950. RCA achieved this by recording at a 15 frames/second with a 180° open shutter, and exposure time of one-thirtieth of a second. Film and filters used included: Daylight Kodachrome with Harrison C; Daylight Kodachrome with no filter; Commercial Kodachrome with Wratten No. 83 and Ansco Tungsten with Ansco No. 11 conversion filter. All the exposures were good, but strangely enough, the general opinion was that the film record was superior in quality to the original television image. This phenomenon may have been partially explained by the fact that the recording camera lens was located on the axis of, and normal to, the color television image, whereas the observers were forced to view the image from an "off center" position. The "line sequential" system of Color Television, Inc., of San Francisco concluded the three experimental systems and recorded from an RCA Receiver on March 16, 1950.[27]

Kinescope Recording

National Broadcasting Company (NBC), American Broadcasting Company (ABC), and Columbia Broadcasting Service (CBS) were all eager to solve the 3-hour east–west time differential through a reliable television recording system. This would enable them to broadcast their important news items almost simultaneously both on the East Coast, and at corresponding time periods on the West Coast; as opposed to the uncertainties and difficulties in program scheduling resulting from live television. In 1955, "kinescope recording" was the established system and looked upon as the major recording instrument for the three networks. "Hot-kines" or "quick-kines," as the systems were known, made it possible to record and playback a black-and-white television program in less than 3 hours. Most programs were recorded on the west coast with two machines simultaneously, one 35mm and the other 16mm. These recordings were made directly from the face of the cathode-ray tube, or "kinescope," concurrently with the live transmission of the program. On the 35mm film, the accompanying sound was recorded either on magnetic audio tape or on magnetic film because of the absence of a recording track. (The 16mm did have an optical track.) As a rule, the programs were recorded in segments of 20 minutes each. These were later rushed to be developed, washed, dried, and projected as negatives. The 35mm was used as "air copy," whereas the 16mm was the reserve.

The popularity of the "hot kine" depended on the fast speed involved in processing and having the 35mm film ready for broadcast. Color transmission and recording were finally introduced in December 1953 when the NTSC color system was approved in the United States. In 1954, NBC developed a special color-kine system that used a Triniscope (three different 10-inch kinescopes) held together optically by mirrors and recorded on 35mm color negative film. The performance of this system was unimpressive, therefore NBC resorted to other means of recording.[28] The utmost concern was the need to show any given program on the East as well as West Coast at their respective corresponding time slots and thus create for advertisers one national audience. Therefore, there was a massive attempt to create an efficient and effective television recording system reflecting the belief that a breakthrough in this area would directly result in great economic rewards. This being the case, network television as well as other private organizations were eager to fund series of technical developments in television recording.

Eastman Kodak's Contribution to TV Recordings

Eastman Kodak's contribution to monochrome television recording was centered on a new special film, "Eastman television recording safety film." This film was available in 16mm as well as 35mm. It was widely preferred due to "its greater definition and speed, improved gray scale and its flexibility which made it possible to be used with either the conventional P-11 phosphor, or the ultraviolet P-16 phosphor."[29]

For color, Kodak, working with NBC, introduced a lenticular stock in 1955, reviving a line of development that the company had abandoned in the 1930s when Tripac Kodachrome was introduced. Recording and processing color television images on monochrome film emulsion was made feasible by means of small vertical lenticles or lenses, which were embossed on the base of a specially prepared film surface. These served as prisms to isolate the color into color difference stripes. By using an additive projection system (that is via tri-color filters), a composite color picture could be created on the screen from conventional monochrome film and thus would be quicker to develop. Still bent on bridging the 3-hour time-zone delay gap with color television recording, NBC announced plans to install television recording equipment using this Kodak system. This partnership and financial linkage between RCA, NBC, and Eastman Kodak was in line with RCA's objective of broadcast technological supremacy. (It should be noted that CBS was committed to Ampex's videotape recording system.) On September 26, 1956, NBC inaugurated its Burbank California plant, whose equipment was built by RCA. This system continued daily until February 19, 1958, when NBC gave up film and followed CBS into color videotape recording. Several experiments on kinescope were nevertheless continued in order to perfect a system that would take advantage of its flexibility and interchangeability, which were outstanding.[30] In many instances, videotape recording was impossible, due to inconveniences of transporting it to various locations; in such cases, color kinescopes were made. Continued interest in hot-kine was therefore maintained by such an advantage.

By 1958, the only reported new development in kinescope recording was a device known as an "ultrasonic light modulator," designed and built by the Fairchild Controls Corporation for airborne, photographic recording of radar information.[31]

Another interesting method of recording color television images was used at the Walter Reed Army Medical Center in Washington DC. A triniscope monitor using red, green, and blue phosphor kinescopes provided a superimposed color image, and a camera containing a 16mm subtractive color film was used to photograph it. Color prints were then made and distributed to medical facilities as training films.[32] The triniscope monitor was made available commercially by the Telechrome Company.

At NBC in New York, a 16mm Ansco-chrome was used on an experimental basis to photograph color images from a 21-inch shadow-mask kinescope. The resulting picture quality was used for reference purposes. The soundtrack was obtained by single system direct positive recording, but it gave less acceptable results. However, the sound quality was improved remarkably by the use of a blue-sensitive photocell in the projector.[33] Kinescope recording lingered on into the 1960s when in 1962 NBC announced its specially designed 7-inch (178mm) color kinescope with dichroic mirrors. Attempts were made, resulting in successful recording of tricolor 21-inch kinescopes. Developed concurrently was another experimental system called the "telecentric lens system" that employed three 5-inch color projection kinescopes.[34] The resulting three images were added together by means of front surface reflectors only. A demonstration of this system was given that resulted in a recording made on 16mm film (Ektachrome Commercial) and printed into internegative and then into positive color prints, a 16mm print made from an original 35mm camera negative, and a 35mm print made from the same camera negative as the 16mm print.

The BRYG System

In April 1958, a nonstandard color television recording system, known as the BRYG system, was introduced. This method proposed separating the color information on the basis of luminance, red and blue.[35] BRYG was designed to use either 35mm or 16mm film travel or optics, with luminance information stored on a large film area, while red and blue information was stored on two smaller areas, one quarter of the area of the luminance. The color green was to be produced by electronic matrixing involving the subtraction of red and blue from the luminance signals. The BRYG was supposed to be used in direct color photography for color TV transmission and kinescope recording of live color television programs.[36]

These were some of the various television recording systems that were introduced at one time or another before the advent of the videotape recorder. Most of these systems did not work. Even the kinescope that was adopted as the standard in the industry was problematic. Kinescope never progressed beyond poor quality pictures and used an enormous amount of film stock. It was, however, the only system that was used after the introduction of videotape recorder.

Although these systems had their faults, it is important to mention that their introductions were indications that there existed a unique problem in television recording; one that needed immediate attention. Their shortcomings exerted a huge economic pressure on the stations as they spent enormously on film stock and manpower. And the consistently poor quality picture that resulted was detrimental especially to west coast viewers. The urge to contain these problems therefore led to a massive technological change that heralded in the videotape recording technology.

The Advent of the
Videotape Recorder

✳ **A**s commercial television expanded in the early 1950s, the problem posed by the ineffective ways of recording television on film became insurmountable. The quest for fresh ideas was therefore imminent. The major proposal was to capitalize on the already successful audio magnetic tape recording medium, improving its technical quality in order to make it viable to recording both sound and photographs. Four organizations, Bing Crosby Enterprises, RCA, BBC, and Ampex Corporation, were central in this early research. The breakthrough in modern television recording therefore occurred in the early 1950s through these efforts when audio magnetic recording principles were transformed to make possible the recording of video signals. This chapter examines this early research tradition.

MAGNETIC RECORDING:
FROM AUDIO TO VIDEO

On November 14, 1950, Bing Crosby Enterprises filed a patent application for a "video recording method." Three years later on December 1, 1953, RCA publicly gave a demonstration of recording television pictures on magnetic tape in black and white and in color.[1] But in April 1956, Ampex Corporation provided the most sensational demonstration of a magnetic recording equipment thus far.[2]

The videotape machine was capable of recording both sound and picture on tape. It is difficult however, to delve into the principle of video application without some knowledge of conventional magnetic recording theory. So far, this study has given an in-depth history of magnetic recording from its inception, but to comprehend fully videotape recording, an analysis of the techniques of audio recording on magnetic tape is discussed with emphasis on the characteristics relevant to videotape. This is necessary because some of the problems of video recording are similar to those present in audio, whereas the limits of both techniques are also identical.

Principles of Magnetic Recording—Audio

The principles of magnetic recording have been known since Valdemar Poulsen first patented the Telegraphone in 1898. Magnetic recording and reproducing equipments have gone through a variety of changes since then. But, although outstanding improvements have been effected on the mechanical as well as electronical units of the magnetic recorder over the years, the general principle of magnetic recording remains the same. In describing the principle of his Telegraphone, Poulsen wrote:

> The present invention represents a very essential advance in the branch of sciences as it provides for receiving and temporarily storing messages and the like by magnetically exciting paramagnetic bodies. The solution of this problem is based on the discovery that a paramagnetic body, such as a steel wire or ribbon, which is moved past an electromagnet connected with an electric or magnetic transmitter, such as a telephone, is magnetically excited along its length in exact correspondence with the signals, messages or speech delivered to the transmitter, and further, that when the magnetically excited wire is again moved past the electromagnet it will reproduce the said signals messages, or speech in a telephone-receiver connected with the said electromagnet.[3]

Magnetic tape recording is used widely in the acquisition; storage; and reproduction of sound, vibration, acceleration, temperature, other phenomena and numeral data that have been converted to electrical signals. With modern electronic equipment, almost every type of information is reduced with minimum distortion and over a wide range of electrical frequencies. During the recording process, a transducer is used to convert sound or other phenomena to electrical current.

A magnetic recorder is made up of various important components including magnetic tape that consists of a plastic base coated with minute iron oxide particles suspended in a synthetic resin binder. The metallic oxide, which is the actual magnetization medium that results in excellent performance is distributed uniformly on the face of the tape. The magnetic heads are the most important component in a magnetic recording system. The responsibility of converting electrical current to magnetizing force when recording and then reconverting the magnetism to an electrical current during reproducing is accomplished by the heads. Most magnetic recorders of professional caliber utilize three heads for erasing, recording, and reproducing, respectively. The tape transport, which consists of three important divisions of tape supply systems, tape drive system, and a tape take-up system accounts for the tape movement properly across the head at constant speed.

The magnetic tape is drawn past the three heads in succession. These heads consist of a core shaped like an incomplete ring, inserted in a coil of wire. "The discontinuity in the ring forms the nonmagnetic head gap in series with the magnetic path of the core."[4] The magnetic circuit is therefore complete when the magnetic tape bridges the gap. The actual recording process occurs when the iron oxide particles are permanently magnetized proportionately to the magnetic flux as soon as those particles move out of the gap. Variation in the signals cause the head magnet to vary the field it produces and to align the magnetic fields of the iron oxide particles on the tape. When the process is reversed, and the recorded signal amplified through a loud speaker, the original sound is reproduced. Traces of previous recording are removed when the tape is brought up to the maximum saturation point as it passes through the erasing head. In longitudinal recording, the tape is drawn across a fixed magnetic head, and the standard speed may range from $1\frac{7}{8}$, $3\frac{3}{4}$, $7\frac{1}{2}$, 15, 30, 60, 75, 120, or 150 inches per second. The higher speeds are used only in instrumentation and computer recorders.

Principles of Magnetic Recording—Video

The principle of videotape recording was established from the foundation laid by magnetic sound recording techniques, and there are a great number of similarities, although there are also some major differences between the two techniques. Many of the conventional principles that worked perfectly in audio recording surprisingly would later create an enormous problem in the recording of video signals. The central difficulty was the enormously greater bandwidth of the video as opposed to the audio signal.

A magnetic recorder for audio applications, operating at a 7.5 inch per second tape speed, will record at 15 kc signal at a rate of 2 kc for each inch of tape. Thus the recorded wavelength of that signal on the tape will be 0.5 mil (or 0.0005 inch). Achieving this same recorded wavelength for a four-megacycle signal would require a tape speed of 2,000 inches per second—which works out to be 10,000 feet per minute or over 113 miles per hour.

Of course this assumes the use of a standard audio head, which is rather impractical assumption. However, the use of the most precise heads—

assembled under laboratory conditions and incapable of being produced in quantity—still would require a tape speed of 200 inches per second. It is interesting to note that 60,000 feet of tape on a reel 38 inches in diameter would be necessary to provide a one hour program at this absolute minimum speed. Our tape transport would have to be built like a diesel truck.

Thus the problems of high frequency response and adequate playing time were seemingly not compatible. Many early experiments (not conducted at Ampex) had as their goals multi-channel time multiplex or frequency—multiplex devices in which the frequency response requirement would be approximately divided by the number of channels provided. These experiments, however, have never resulted in practical equipment.[5]

It was this problem of accommodating video frequencies that thwarted early research efforts, thereby making it impossible to record both sound and sight on video equipment.

Longitudinal Recording

Longitudinal recording that was a standard in audio recording was clearly too practical for videotape recording. From 1950, it was thought that an extension of this stationary head and fast speed principle would solve the bandwidth problem, and by 1954, RCA demonstrated a longitudinal track video recorder operating at 360 inches per second. However, the recorder not only failed to provide full bandwidth capabilities, but the quantity of tape and the size of the spool used were intolerable. Besides, it was very difficult to control the tape speed accurately.[6]

Despite the quality engineering technique built into the early RCA video recording machine, it was impossible to produce an acceptable machine because of the "fixed head" technique used in the system. The RCA model demonstrated in 1953 used a cellulose acetate base coated with a red iron oxide. For color television recording, a tape $\frac{1}{2}$-inch wide was used, whereas $\frac{1}{4}$-inch wide tape was used for monochrome television. The tape transport mechanism was designed to prevent any jitter in the picture, and the tape speed was approximately 30 revolutions per second.[7]

While recording and reproducing, the composite color signal was decoded into red, blue, and green video signals and a synchronized signal. Three separate channels were devoted to the red, blue, and green video signals recorded with bandwidth of 1.5 megacycles, whereas the fourth channel was assigned a combined high frequency video channel containing the combined high frequency responses of the red, blue, and green video signals from 1.5 to 3.5 megacycles. The horizontal synchronizing signal was recorded on the fifth channel. All signals in these channels were then recorded on tape by a quintuplex head.[8] The sound was recorded on two amplitude-modulated carriers at about 80 and 150 kilocycles. The sound could also be recorded on frequency-modulated carrier at 90 kilocycles. The whole set of television signals was therefore recorded through six channels on seven magnetic tracks on the tape. Recording and reproducing video signals have since been improved by modern techniques, which are discussed later in this chapter.

Combining Magnetic (Audio) Recording Techniques With Videotape Recording Techniques

Audiotape recorders record sound either from microphones, radio receivers, or by duplication from another recording. Similarly, videotape recorders record television pictures from a television camera, from a television receiver, or by duplication from another recording. Additionally, sound tracks on the videotape permit audio recording from microphone or television set on the same tape with the television picture, but the audio quality is in most cases inferior to audio recording of similar standards because of the proximity of stray fields (magnetic particle orientation being on the wrong axis), poor contact on tape edges, and reduction in track width.[9]

Nevertheless, the basic method in audiotape recording and videotape recording is the same. Sounds and visual images are converted to electrical signals by a microphone or camera. The electrical current varies in direct relationship to the sound or picture and produces a comparable varying flux in an electromagnet (the recording head). Magnetic tape, coated with iron oxide, is moved past heads that create fields around the tape and so align the particles in specific patterns that correspond to the original sound or picture. When the process is reversed and the electrical signal detected from the tape is amplified through a speaker or television tube, the original sound or picture is reproduced.[10] As with audio recorders, videotapes may be played back immediately without processing by connecting the video tape recorder to a television set. Recorded tapes may be erased on the recorder in part or entirely, and reused hundreds of times without loss of quality.

Of the various closed circuit television devices used in homes, commercial and industrial establishments, only those using magnetic recording techniques are capable of *recording* and *playing back* pictures and sound. Those not using magnetic recording are good for *playback* only. These playback-only devices are only capable of playing pre-recorded programs.

Audiotape recorders provide high fidelity stereo music at frequency responses up to 20,000 cycles per second (20,000 Hertz). But much higher frequencies are required to record television pictures. Studio videotape recorders made specifically for the broadcast industry record at more than

5,000,000 cycles per second (5 megaHertz).[11] Due to these differences in frequency levels, there had been a great number of problems surrounding the recording of audio on videotape. Recording the audio signals is now accomplished by conventional magnetic recording techniques discussed earlier under audio recording.

Frequency response is directly related to the speed at which a tape moves past recording and playback heads. In audio recorders, tape moves past the heads at $7\frac{1}{2}$ inches per second, which is the accepted standard speed for high quality performance. Slower speeds of $3\frac{3}{4}$ and $1\frac{7}{8}$ ips are used, but each provides relatively lower quality. In making the transition upwards from audio recording frequencies to video recording frequencies, engineers have successfully used two basic techniques (transverse [quadruplex], and helical-scan) to increase the relative tape to head speed.[12] A third method (longitudinal) has been tried unsuccessfully.

Transverse Recording

In 1956, after experiencing many problems in various techniques of video recording, Ampex developed the rotary recording head and a technique called "transverse recording."[13] In a transverse recording technique, a magnetic videotape 2 inches wide is moved past recording heads at 15 or $7\frac{1}{2}$ inches per second. Rotating rapidly across the tape at a 90° angle to the path of the tape are four recording/playback heads mounted on a disk. The relative tape-to-head speed is increased to 1,500 inches per second resulting in frequencies of over 5 megaHertz. At this bandwidth color or monochrome quality television pictures of broadcast standards are produced. Transverse (otherwise known as quadruplex) recorders are complex and expensive, but solve the mechanical problems associated with longitudinal systems.[14] They have largely been replaced in the 1980s with other video recording formats.

THE CREATION OF CROSBY ENTERPRISES' ELECTRONIC DIVISION

By 1950, the television industry was on the verge of converting to recording television signals on magnetic materials as established back in 1927 by B. Rtcheouloff.[15]

While pondering over the huge success realized from the manufacture of audio magnetic tape recorders by Ampex, for which he was a direct contributor, John T. Mullin, approached a highly reputable engineer, Wayne R. Johnson, with the idea of recording television on tape. Both men were optimistic, and convincing Frank Healey, Crosby's technical manager, they approached Bing Crosby who arranged for a small shop to be opened for the venture under the auspices of Bing Crosby Enterprises. This was the beginning of Crosby Enterprises Electronic's Division, whose laboratory was opened in June 1951.[16] Their determination was further boosted as they were awarded a $1 million contract by the U.S. government for the development of videotape recorders that were to be used for military purposes. Mullin had filed a patent application for "video recording methods" on November 14, 1950, but a year later, after the demonstration of their videotape recorder, the machine was still at a very premature stage of development as his comment later suggested.

> Our first demonstration was pretty crude. We had "recorded," if it could be called that, some TV pictures of airplanes landing and taking off. Whenever we gave a demonstration, Frank would stand by the monitor and say, "Now watch this plane come in for a landing," or "There goes a guy on take off." It is doubtful the viewer would have known what he was seeing without his running commentary.[17]

The growing frustration did not deter Mullin and his associates. On November 11, 1951, Bing Crosby Enterprises gave its first demonstration of a videotape recorder in black and white to the members of its staff, and on the next day they gave the first public demonstration. This videotape recorder was operated on a multitrack system. The system used 12 (recording) heads (10 for recording video signals, the eleventh for horizontal and vertical synchronizing of signals, while the twelfth was used exclusively for recording audio).[18] Initial prototypes of this recorder used brown oxide tape one-inch wide with a tape speed of 100 inches per second. The unit accommodated reels of tape capable of playing continuously for 16 minutes.[19] The machine was technically unsuccessful, therefore Crosby Enterprises, in cooperation with General Electric, tried another approach by dividing the video signals into 10 channels for recording on a half-inch tape. Even with this method, there were many difficulties in recording complete video signals.[20]

In 1956, after several trials and less hope for success, Bing Crosby Enterprises gave up every attempt to develop an industry-accepted videotape recorder, especially after witnessing a demonstration of the Ampex prototype VTR whose picture quality was by far superior to what Crosby's engineers had developed to date. After the introduction of the Ampex videotape recorder, Bing Crosby Enterprises was acquired on August 31, 1956, by the 3M Company and incorporated into their Mincom Division, which would later specialize in the instrumentation field. Crosby Enterprise built 4 very expensive high frequency data recorders for the U.S. Army

FIG. 6.1.   Bing Crosby shows his VTR to female visitor. One of the first researches on VTR was done by the Crosby group in the early 1950s. This group produced a VTR that although left much to be desired, provided directions into further research for viable VTR. Most parts of the machine were extracted from Ampex's audio machines. To Crosby's right is the video-processing amps consisting of 11 video and 1 audio track. (*Source:* courtesy of Ampex Corporation, Redwood City, CA.)

Signal Corps. These machines were based on the longitudinal VTR. The only surviving machine in this category is at UCLA.

By the time Bing Crosby Enterprises finally merged with 3M, the concept of videotape recording had been demonstrated several times to the public, who in turn expected an improved videotape system in the near future.

RCA AND BBC INVOLVEMENT IN RESEARCH AND MANUFACTURE OF THE VIDEOTAPE RECORDER

Besides Crosby Enterprises and Ampex, RCA deserves credit as a company that helped pioneer videotape recording. On September 27, 1951, Brigadier General David Sarnoff, chairman of the Board of RCA, delivered a speech in which he asked for three presents from RCA engineers for his 50th anniversary in radio (which would be in 1956). The first present he requested was an electronic air conditioner; second, a lightweight picture recorder capable of recording video signals off television, and third, a true amplifier of light.[21] Sarnoff put greater emphasis on the second device. He stressed that such a television recording device would enable television pictures to be reproduced in the home, theaters, or anywhere at anytime. This call by Sarnoff for his "presents" provided an impetus to his company and Ampex at the time, and, in response, from the magnetic recording industry as a whole to strive toward the development of videotape recording.

RCA Demonstrates Its First Black-and-White and Color Magnetic Video Recorder

The original compact experimental videotape recorder developed by RCA was the responsibility of a seven-man team of RCA engineers consisting of Harry F. Olsen and William D. Houghton, who headed the development program, and Maurice Artzt, J.T. Fischer, A.R. Morgan, J.G. Woodward, and Joseph Zenel.[22] Presiding over the occasion was Sarnoff, who enumerated the potentials of the tape recording technique for television, the national defense, motion pictures in theaters, home movies, and for industrial and educational purposes. Apart from its status as a communications giant and, having established itself firmly in radio and television (especially in equipment manufacturing), RCA was also the parent company of NBC. This corporate relationship therefore played a great role in RCA's quest for supremacy in videotape technology in the early 1950s. For obvious economic reasons, RCA was bent on making NBC the top-ranking television system in the nation through new technologies.

When the RCA longitudinal videotape recorder was ready for its first public trial, the highlight of the demonstration was a carefully selected program that was beamed via radio microwave, originating in the NBC Studios in New York City, to RCA's David Sarnoff Research Center at Princeton, New Jersey—a distance of about 45 miles. The program presented consisted of:

1. An introductory message by television and film actress Margaret Hayes, taped several days before the demonstration and reproduced on monochrome television signals.
2. The reproduction of a pre-taped Christmas sketch by Margaret Hayes in color.
3. The reproduction of a pre-taped monochrome television signal containing a Victorian sketch by Margaret Hayes in color.
4. A live program of a Victorian sketch by Margaret Hayes beamed via microwave radio relay to the two receivers used at the demonstra-

tion followed halfway through the sketch by one receiver switching to a taped version of the program with the other receiver remaining live, enabling the viewers to make comparison between the live and taped presentations.

5. A playback of the whole presentation.[23]

Color telecasting was still on an experimental basis in December 1951, so the results of this presentation alone were already of substantial news interest. One common consensus was that color television would make the average person more conscious of and appreciative of the colors of his or her environment. Commenting on color television, a *New York Times* editor wrote:

> A new color age will soon be upon us. With the advent of tinted television the country is going to be conscious of color to a degree scarcely imaginable at the moment . . . in fashions, decorations, art appreciation, entertainment, advertising methods and public tastes.
>
> Psychologically, watching color TV in the familiar surroundings of one's own home produces an almost uncanny reaction. Actually turning a knob and seeing the screen light up in different hues amounts in some ways to an almost completely new experience in the meaning of color. What was taken as a matter of course . . . the colors with which one lives . . . suddenly and rather strangely takes a new importance, pertinence and interest.
>
> How often, for instance, does the man of the household worry whether yellow is lemon or chartreuse? Or when did he sheepishly ask for advice as to whether the cyan was distinguishable between blue blue and green green? With color TV he may do both as a matter of course.[24]

For color conscious individuals who were particular about what constituted a good and acceptable color, color television then offered a facility uncompared to other color media—the ability of the television set owner, through the "chroma" control, to adjust instantly the hues and tints to suit his or her own temperament. But these were of course more apparent than real choices given the limits of realistic modes of representation.

Speaking at the demonstration of the RCA videotape recorder at Princeton, Sarnoff described the similarities between sound and visual recording, describing the latest video recording as a major step into an era of 'electronic photography' in which motion pictures in color or black-and-white would be produced quickly and economically without any photographic development or processing." Publicizing the advantages of the videotape recorder, Sarnoff explained:

> Magnetic tape requires no chemical processing. The pictures can be viewed the instant they are taken, which adds new flexibility in making motion pictures. An unlimited number of copies of magnetic tape recordings can be

made quickly. Recorded tapes can be preserved indefinitely for historic references or, if desired, can be electronically 'wiped off' and reused again and again.

With further development of videotape techniques, numerous possibilities will open up. Small portable television cameras are already in wide use in industry, in stores, in banks, in schools and colleges. Low-cost television cameras that work like satellites off home television receivers are ultimately possible. Eventually, low-cost videotape equipment of simpler and more compact design than the studio-type equipment shown today can be made available as attachment for these cameras.[25]

Sarnoff further stressed that the new line of the "all-electronic" portable television camera, videotape recorder, and standard television receiver would revolutionize both amateur and professional motion pictures and furthermore, would speed newsreel preparation as well as making the reporters' job easier. This equipment could also be used at home to make home movies or to record television programs.

Sarnoff also gave the impression that the videotape recording process was only the beginning of a revolution in the electronic field:

Electronic motion pictures . . . in black-and-white and color . . . for television, for the theatre and for the home will stem from this remarkable development. Today we are only on the threshold. But the electronic door has been opened wide and gives us a fascinating vista of the future.

The media present at the RCA demonstration were spontaneous in their review of the new videotape recording equipment as the Newark Evening News reported that the demonstration was staged for open-jawed members of the press by Radio Corporation of America at its laboratories in Princeton and the preview of things to come . . . perhaps in 2 years . . . was commercially unveiled. It concluded that this new method of recording sight, similar in basic aspects to tape recording of sound, might eventually end the use of movie films, kinescope, and similar film-based systems of delayed telecasts prevalent at the time. The press delegation, usually a hard-boiled bunch of cynics, actually burst into spontaneous applause after witnessing a series of black-and-white and color transmissions.[26]

The New York Times wrote that after the demonstration, the viewers generally agreed that the results were remarkably effective and that the system possessed great potential advantages for use in television and, more remotely, for the motion picture screen.[27]

Stressing some basic features and the principles on which the videotape recorder operated, the New York Times further stated that the implications of this innovation entered far beyond the home. The consensus was that in the distant future motion picture theatres will dispense with film and throw picture plays on the screen with a special television projector. For the immediate future, RCA promised no more than an inexpensive method of dispensing with kinescope (picture tube) film recording now widely used in television studios.[28]

Finally, the radio editor of New York Times observed:

> What perhaps will interest the lay viewer at home the most is that visual recordings promise relief from the inferior quality of kinescope films, especially where color is concerned. . . . According to reports of observers at RCA demonstration, the tape recordings of pictures already are superior in quality to Kinescope if somewhat below the level of 'live' telecasts. But the long range promise is that ultimately tape recording and 'live' broadcasts will be so nearly the same in quality that a viewer would be hard put to tell the difference.[29]

Obviously what is at work here is not just the economic advantages of magnetic video recording but also an ideologically determined standard of quality reproduction . . . the duplication of the 'live' broadcast.

E.W. Enstron, Vice President in charge of RCA Laboratories Division summarized the status of RCA research and engineering problems as related to videotape recording in December 1953 by confirming that although some technical problems had to be surmounted before videotape equipment could be made available commercially, RCA considered that the most problematic had been conquered and that further development was certain to solve the remainder. The demonstration of the RCA videotape recording system was regarded as a huge success. Several hundred members of the press, industry, and a variety of interest groups were present at the demonstrations. Generally, the black-and-white and color pictures were considered to be nearly as good as pictures received by live transmission.

Basic Technical Problems and Solutions
in the RCA Longitudinal Videotape Recorder

It used to be a rule of thumb in the magnetic recording field that both very high and very low frequencies cannot be put on the same tape if one expects a good signal-to-noise ratio from both. The reason is that audio signals are in the range of 15 to 20 cycles per second, which represent the bass sound level; whereas video signals range up to 4 million cycles per second. In the RCA videotape machine, the audio receiving and reproducing heads were essentially the same used in the video channels. Furthermore, the principle involved in the recording of color video signals was quite different from that used in the recording of monochrome video signals. The composite color video was linked with a color demodulator that produced the three color video signals (red, green, and blue) and the separate synchronizing components on separate outputs. The resulting four signals were then linked to their respective recording heads through four recording amplifier units. The audio was handled through a corresponding fifth amplifier unit. Thus, the color signals were recorded on five separate channels of ½-inch wide magnetic tape. One track was assigned to each primary color video component (red, green, and blue), one for the accompanying synchronizing information, and one for audio signals. On the other hand, the recording of monochrome video signals required only two tracks on a ¼-inch tape. One track was assigned to carry the complete video signal and the other for audio signal. The tape speed of the RCA videotape recorder demonstrated on December 1, 1953, was 30 feet per second, but RCA was determined to reduce the tape speed to a much lower level in order to enhance maneuvability and to reduce the amount of tape used. The sizes of the magnetic tape reels were 17 inches in diameter but could only record 4 minutes of television program. Even at this time, RCA was developing a reel 19 inches in diameter capable of recording and playing for 15 minutes.

RCA's initial equipment design was unable to resolve satisfactorily these difficulties. Although RCA continued in its quest to perfect videotape recording equipment, the breakthrough occurred 3 years after the first RCA demonstration. This time, however it was by another company, Ampex Corporation—until then unknown in the TV industry. The RCA equipment had many innovations that became subsequent video recording (VR) standards; among them were tape tension servos, eddy current brakes, luminance/chrominance separation, and sync reinsertation, most of which are familiar components in today's VTRs.

However, it is now possible to record high quality video signals on one channel, even at a low speed of 6 meters per second, but in the early 1950s, available technology was so premature that the system was far from being successful.[30]

FIRST PUBLIC DEMONSTRATION OF AMPEX VIDEOTAPE RECORDER

In 1951, while still enjoying the fortune brought about by its success in the audio magnetic tape recording industry, Ampex Corporation decided to apply the basic principles of magnetic tape recording used in audio and data recording to the recording of television signals. Ampex Corporation's president, Alexander M. Poniatoff, and his two senior engineers, Myron Stolaroff and Walter Selsted, agreed to allocate a meagre sum of $14,500 to the investigation of the possibility of developing a tape recorder capable of recording television programs.[31] If any company could capitalize on the magnetic tape technology in the United States during the period, it was Ampex Corporation. Their experience in audio and data magnetic recording technology and the resulting economic profit were convincing enough to encourage them to embark on the development of the technology for video recording. Media publicity concerning video recording at Crosby Enterprises and RCA was extensive. Videotape technology was therefore regarded as one of the most important technologies of the decade, even though it was far from perfect. Networks, as well as government interest, in this technology and the continuous publicity accorded the new video phenomenon by the news media in view of the poor quality of television recording (which especially affected the west coast), were the major economic reasons behind Ampex's persistence in the attempt to develop an acceptable videotape recording system.

The first idea was to investigate the rotary head approach that was capable of achieving high relative head-to-tape speeds necessary for recording television signals. This method was invented by Dr. Marvin Camras of Armour Research Foundation, Illinois, of which Ampex was a licensee.[32] At the same time, an electrical engineer with 10 years experience in radio broadcasting, who was tired of the radio business, contacted Ampex Corporation for a possible employment opportunity. Eventually, he was hired to take charge of the new television magnetic tape recording project. His name was Charles P. Ginsburg.

Ginsburg was excited about this project. Before its start, the project's itinerary was to build a machine with three heads mounted on the flat surface of a drum scanning the surface of a 2-inch wide tape in an arcuate fashion. The head-to-tape speed of about 2,500 inches per second and a tape speed of 30 inches per second would ensure a dependable recording bandwidth of $2\frac{1}{2}$ megacycles.[33] Ampex was not quite ready for the project although it had budgeted some money for it. For instance, Ginsburg spent his first week on the job working on the floor until eventually his laboratory was ready—a tiny converted ladies room. In fact, the magnetic tape recording of a television signal was given such a low priority at Ampex that in May 1952 the project was suspended for 3 months in favor of the production of a sophisticated type of instrumentation recorder. Despite the optimism exhibited by most of the personnel involved in the video recording development at Ampex, management was somehow pessimistic due to the persistent poor quality demonstrated each time Crosby or RCA showed their respective equipment.

During the video hiatus, Ginsburg met Ray Dolby, (later of audio noise reduction fame) an exceptionally brilliant 19-year-old high school graduate who had just enrolled as an engineering freshman at Stanford University. Dolby dropped out of college to join the Ampex team in August 1952.

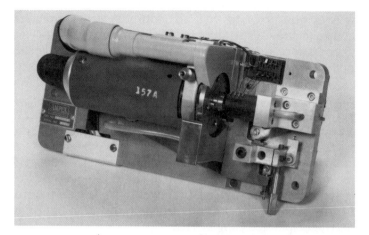

FIG. 6.2.   Ampex Video Head. This is an Ampex Video Head assembly on the VR-1000. It is the transverse head showing the head wheel. The plastic hose that runs into the female guide controls the air pressure. Cubicle metal object at the bottom and in front of the female guide is the control track head. One of the four video heads drum can be seen in front of the top of the female guide. (*Source:* Courtesy of Ampex Corporation, Redwood City, CA.)

Although Dolby lacked the necessary academic training in engineering, his ingenuity and understanding of technical matters made his contributions in the Ampex television recording project invaluable. It was Dolby who created the basic block diagram of VTR circuitry that is still used in the most recorders today.

The project team gave their first internal demonstration of blurry pictures in October 1952. This was promising enough to reaffirm management support for the project. By march 19, 1953, the team had redesigned and built a second system that was operational, correcting most of the faults of the earlier machine. Instead of the previous three heads, the new machine had four heads and a two-way switcher that could select during playback either of the sets of diametrically opposed heads. The rotating head described a radius of an arc of $1\frac{1}{4}$ inches, which resulted in a range of 105 degrees for each head as it scanned the 2-inch wide tape. The video processing system utilized amplitude modulation (AM). The capstan motor ran off the 60 cycle line frequency, whereas the drum motor was powered from the fifth harmonic of line frequency. An optical sensor translated the impulses from the 300 cycle rotating video head, recording the signal longitudinally on one edge of the tape. During playback, the 300 cycle tape signal was converted and used to drive the head drum motor. Evidently, many old components were still included in this system. Ginsburg later commented on their difficulties:

Although we were rather pleased by some aspects of the reproduced picture, the pleasure was attenuated close to the vanishing point by the number of unexpected problems confronting us. The pitfalls of the discontinuous method of recording were becoming painfully obvious. The odious label "Venetian blinds" came into being to describe certain very unpleasant flaws at the points representing the cross-over from one head to the next in the reproduced picture. The unsuitability of the method of control and the necessity for extreme accuracy in the positioning of the tape relative to the rotating heads became quite apparent and a good many hours devoted to analyzing the complexity of potential errors in the accurate sweep geometry indicated that major revisions would be in order before the rotating head VTR could be successful.[34]

As promising as the early efforts were, the project was again suspended in June 1953. In the midst of the frustration, Dolby, who had dropped out of Stanford, was drafted into the U.S. Army and despite fruitless pleas by his colleagues he left sadly on March 18, 1953. Before departing, Dolby would stay up late with Ginsburg. Ginsburg, an ardent mathematician, pre-

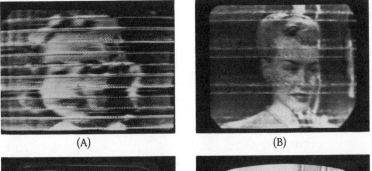

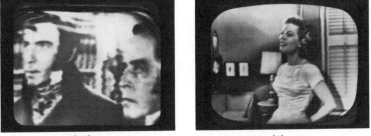

FIG. 6.3. Banding adjustment. Progression of photographs showing the effect of quadruplex banding that is out of alignment. During development, Ampex engineers kept adjusting the head during playback until the best quality picture was obtained. Picture A is very bad. Picture B is better. Picture BB is better. Picture C is best. (*Source:* Courtesy of Ampex Corporation, Redwood City, CA.)

calculated every intricate component, which Dolby thought through, as both were eager to build a machine. Dolby's involvement in the project climaxed on a Sunday morning just before he left as he pondered over a recent but sketchy idea of rotary head switching, the means by which most of the ideas that today's videotape systems operate. He wrote of his idea:

> I got up and quickly, sketched the scheme on paper, dressed and made a beeline for Charlie's (Ginsburg) house in Los Altos. It was a warm sunny Sunday morning and we walked on Charlie's front steps. I explained every-thing, and we both went over the system point by point. We could not find a flaw, and it seemed to be all advantages. It is difficult to appreciate what a tremendous lift an idea like this gives, but it is really something. Things like this were what made work exciting. All of a sudden, what seemed a foggy, dim, even dismal, future suddenly becomes bright and optimistic. I think I got more excited over the rotary switching idea than I have about any other. Work on the new system was begun the very next day. I did not realize it at the time, but in my present estimation, this idea was the last really significant contribution which I was to make to the VTR as it is today. The rest of my work was just moderately competent engineering.[35]

While he was in the Armed Forces, Dolby exchanged notes with Ginsburg. During the project's period of official suspension (June 1953 through August 1954), considerable progress was made on the VTR project despite the few man hours and the little financial allotment assigned it, both by authorized and unauthorized means. An 80 man-hour allocation was requested by Ginsburg to modify and demonstrate the equipment that was now christened the Mark 1 machine. The project was reactivated in Sep-tember 1954, nearly 9 months after RCA's December 1953 demonstration of its video recorder. By October, the team had been boosted to include a total of five members—Ginsburg, Charles Anderson (who was later known for his proposal of the FM video signal processing system), Shelby Hender-son, and later engineers Fred Pfost and Alex Maxey (see Fig. 6.4). The engineering group was ready, and a final assault was made. The group had found that transverse scanning using four heads worked better than arcuate scanning. Although everyone worked as a group and shared information, an informal division of labor was established. Maxey did a lot of off-hours research during February 1955 and discovered some strange phenomena connected with the characteristics of pictures reproduced from tape. He worked on a way of controlling the amount of information read out during playback by each of the four heads of the transverse scan by varying the tape tension in any of three ways: at the reel, by moving a vacuum-based female guide toward or away from the edge of the spinning drum, or by varying the vacuum which was pulled from the non-contact side of the tape. These were major breakthroughs. Pfost developed a new head system using new

FIG. 6.4.   Original Ampex VTR development team. This was the original
Ampex VTR development team. From left to right—Fred Pfost, Shelby
Henderson, Ray Dolby, Alex Maxey, Charles Ginsburg (team leader), and
Charles E. Anderson. Pfost was responsible for developing the video
heads. Henderson was the model maker. He designed the machine. Dolby designed all basic block diagrams. Maxey was the resident inventor of
the group. He did early experiment on elasticity of tape and development
of female guide which was highly important to the success of proper
tracking. Anderson developed the FM signal recording. (*Source:* Courtesy
of Ampex Corporation, Redwood City, CA.)

magnetic alloys for which he substituted the previously used AM with a
new FM system. Dolby (having concluded his tour of duty and returning to
Ampex on a part-time basis while registered at Stanford University as a full-
time student), designed and built a multivibrator modulator that resulted in
excellent picture quality. Anderson designed the mark IV console that was
to become the basis for Ampex VTRs for the next half decade.

At an internal demonstration at the end of 1955, it was suggested that the
package for this very expensive machine must be made as attractive as
possible. Combining these breakthroughs and convinced of the high standard they had achieved, the team agreed to demonstrate the machine to a
group of 30 Ampex executives. Excitement and rumors brought in more
guests than expected. April 14, 1956, was set as the date for a full-scale

public demonstration. Six weeks before that public showing, Ampex invited several network representatives, including Bill Lodge of CBS, Frank Marx of ABC, and representatives of both Canadian Broadcasting Corporation (CBC) and the BBC to visit the video recording laboratories. They were sworn to absolute secrecy and even ushered in and out separately. Ampex was sure that its machine was far ahead of others in the industry. As a result of that preview, Ampex agreed to unveil the machine one day earlier than planned to CBS affiliates. At the Chicago convention of the National Association of Radio and Television Broadcasters (now NAB), the machine was demonstrated to the 200 owners and station managers of the CBS affiliates, it received a long-standing ovation. Ampex personnel were mobbed with questions about prices, delivery, and so on. The following day, the machine (later named the "VRX-1000") was demonstrated to the rest of the convention at the same time as the original prototype (known as "Mark III") was being shown at Ampex in Redwood City. The press and viewers were elated by the demonstration. Welcoming a new era in west coast television, a San Francisco correspondent wrote:

> For seven suffering years, West Coast viewers have taken most "live" network programs with a grain of Schmaltz. Though New Yorkers always have seen them in unflickering perfection, we, on the wrong west end of the continental time zones, have had to squint at fuzzy, delayed kinescope. We still do.
>
> But not for long. While the rest of us moaned, the Ampex Corporation of Redwood City put its electronic experts to successful work. After four years of intensive experiments they have perfected a video magnetic tape recording system that will revolutionize the sights and sound delayed network telecasting. Their machines can record a television program and play it back (instantly, if necessary) with all the clarity of a "live" program or a motion picture film.
>
> After previewing the first public demonstration two weeks ago, I reported the system as "flawless." So now, has the entire television industry. CBS and NBC have acquired machines for use this fall. More than seventy have been ordered by independent stations, including channel 4, here. Thanks to a revolt in Redwood City, all of us will soon enjoy clear viewing all the time.[36]

Prior to the demonstration, Ampex estimated that it would sell 30 machines worldwide by 1960 at about $30,000 each if the result was favorable.[37] As it turned out, orders received at the NAB meeting alone amounted to $1 million, and within 4 weeks after the demonstration, Ampex had orders totalling $4.5 million.[38] By 1962, Ampex had delivered 1,000 videotape recorders, including several accessories, at an average price of more than $50,000.[39]

The tape used during experimentation and at the NAB in Chicago was supplied by 3M of Minnesota. With the encouragement of Philip Gundy,

FIG. 6.5. Ampex VR-1000. The VR-1000 was the production model of the VRX-1000. Within a period of one year this television tape recording system moved from research and experimentation status to an ideal stage. The Model VR-1000 was the first practical commercially accepted VTR ever produced. It was produced in 1956. Manufacturer: Ampex Corporation, Redwood City, California. Size: Console 55¼ inches long, 42 inches high, 35 inches deep. Recording time: up to 64 minutes on 12½ inch reel. Playback timing synchronous with system timing reference. Rewind Time: Approximately 180 seconds for full reel. Weight: Approximately 1,350 pounds. Video Head Life: 100 hours minimum with normal maintenance. (*Source:* Courtesy of Ampex Corporation, Redwood City, CA.)

general manager of the Audio Department of Ampex; W.W. Wetzel; Robert von Behren; and their associates, 3M developed a 2-inch wide video tape sample for Ampex.[40]

Among the videotape recorder orders taken by Ampex at the NAB convention were those from ABC, CBS, NBC (for use in network delay broadcast), and the U.S. government. George Gould ordered one for use in television program production and formed Telestudios, Incorporated, the first independent videotape production facility. Two models of the VRX-1000 were delivered to CBS Television City and two to NBC–Hollywood in November 1956. CBS became the first network to use videotape for a coast-to-coast delayed broadcast of a news program, "Douglas Edwards and The News" on November 30, 1956.

In March 1957, Ampex was awarded an Emmy from the Academy of Television Arts and Sciences at its Ninth Annual Emmy Awards presentation in recognition of the videotape recorder as the most significant technical achievement in the television industry in 1956. Ginsburg accepted the award on behalf of Ampex Corporation. For his personal involvement in the development of the videotape recorder, Ginsburg was also awarded the David Sarnoff Gold Medal of the Society of Motion Picture and Television Engineers in 1957, the Vladimir K. Zworykin Television Prize of the Institute of Radio Engineers in 1958, and the Valdemar Poulsen Gold Medal (awarded the Danish Academy of Technical Sciences) in 1960.

COMPETITION FOR AMPEX VIDEOTAPE RECORDING

The VRX-1000

In the next three decades since the introduction of the VRX-1000, all subsequent broadcast videotape recorders have followed the standard set by the Ampex machine. Other companies were able to compete in this industrial market only by employing Ampex's scanning head and transverse system.

The instant success brought about by the first public demonstration of the VRX-1000 at the NARTB Convention catapulted Ampex into the limelight. With many orders taken at Chicago and some technical problems still outstanding on the machine, Ampex engineers returned to hard work in their laboratories, trying to improve the whole system. The Mark IV cabinet used in the demonstration at Chicago would not fit through a standard doorway and so it was reduced in size. Dolby designed an outstanding amplifier system for the machine, and all the experimental heads were improved.[41] Building the machines to meet the burgeoning orders was now a top priority, even amidst further assignments relating to the achievement of interchangeability (the first machines being unable to playback tape originated on another VRX-1000), editing, and color. Thus, the first 16 machines were handbuilt and considered experimental models. Users were advised to save the head and any tape made on it for repeated replay purposes.

When full production began, the VRX-1000 became the production model VR-1000, and in just 1 year, tape recorded television moved from research and experimentation status to accepted technology. The VTR was subjected to every conceivable test and analysis by television's leading engineers and found competent both in performance quality and in complete adaptability as a functional integrated part of modern broadcasting operations. Supervised by Kurt Machein, an Ampex project engineer, the first of

FIG. 6.6. Ampex VR-1000 with racks. This is a complete portrait of the
VR-1000 with electronic racks. It was later expanded to three racks when
color was introduced. Racks (2) each 25 inches wide × 20 inches deep ×
84 inches high. 98 inches × 130 inches required for door clearance and
full access. (*Source*: Courtesy of Ampex Corporation, Redwood City, CA.)

the VR-1000s was delivered to KING-TV in Seattle, Oregon, in November,
1957.

By 1959, VR-1000s had interchange capability, able to play tapes made on
any other videotape recorder. Initially, editing considerations also constituted a problem to video recorder purchasers because no pictures were
visible on the tape and none were visible on the screen unless a tape was in
stable motion. Therefore, to solve this problem Ampex included an exclusive editing exercise in the training given to various industry engineers
who represented a cross-section of their clients. Editing entailed splicing
precisely so that the waveform of the recorded control track was smooth
and continuous, so that a transition from one recorded tape to the next
occurred at the end of a field or frame. The process was laborious and
difficult. In addition to the minimal tolerances involved in lining up the
fields, sound ran a little behind picture, making smooth edits difficult to
achieve. But because the machine's prime purpose was to record multi-
camera studio (out), these problems meant little.

The Ampex Model VR-1000 was a monochrome videotape recorder and

although RCA had demonstrated color television in 1953, many video recorder purchasers were also aware of the advantages of the medium. The
consensus among them was that the excellent operational savings realized
from the use of the monochrome videotape recorder, would help pay for
the eventual explosive conversions of their stations to color.[42] Thus, stations invested in the monochrome VCRs, while awaiting an acceptable
color recorder.

RCA AND AMPEX
CROSS-LICENSING AGREEMENT

It was clear to Ampex that the market for the monochrome videotape
recorder would be short-lived. Therefore, the company experimented seriously with color. At the same time RCA, despite its wide spread publicity
on its 1953 longitudinal videotape recorder had failed to produce a practical
machine accepted by the industry. Nevertheless, RCA had the best color
technology know-how in the television industry. After carefully studying
the electronic components of the Ampex VR-1000 purchased by NBC in
late 1956 (which initially spent more time in RCA laboratories than in NBC
News Studios), RCA engineers concluded that it would be economically
wasteful and time consuming to try to redesign the Ampex components
without infringing its patents. However, RCA successfully upgraded the
VR-1000 to their color technology. On the other hand, Ampex was aware of
the difficulties in researching this technology and, turned to RCA. Ampex
had the VTR technology, whereas RCA had the color technology. On October 14, 1957, RCA, signed a cross-licensing agreement, trading its color
technology for Ampex's transverse technology.[43] (This technology exchange was agreed upon by both companies to last for a period of 3
months.) But it was extended after the expiration of the initial agreement to
cover another 3-month period. Shortly afterward, both companies were
producing similar machines in both monochrome and color, and competing strongly against each other.

On October 25, 1957, RCA demonstrated its prototype color videotape
recorder to the press from Camden, New Jersey. The machine was a low
band quadruplex recorder designated the VTRX. It was capable of recording in color as well as in monochrome, although it was said to be designed
specifically for color. These prototype VTRX's were used solely by NBC for
delayed broadcast of color programs between the East and West coasts.
Regarded as laboratory prototypes, these units were subjected to intensive
development especially in the video signal-handling circuitry, servo mechanism, electro-mechanical, and precision mechanical assemblies. Rapid design and improvements on the VTRX resulted in the first production

model, named the TRT-1A. The most outstanding improvements over the VTRX visible in the TRT-1A were in the stability of servo mechanism and superiority of the video headwheel panel. The TRT-1A was first used commercially in 1959. Feedback from the performance of the TRT-1A resulted in further development and redesigning of a new machine, designated the TRT-1B, which was introduced in 1960. Noticeable improvements on the TRT-1B included an "increased operational flexibility, better monitoring facilities, which included a signal processing amplifier that provided clean sync and blanking in the output signal." This was the first transistorized unit.[44]

By December 1957, Ampex had introduced their "10–10 color kit," a conversion accessory unit used for recording and reproducing color television. This kit was attached to each VR-1000 machine. In developing the VR-1000 color accessory, Ampex engineers made its attachment to the monochrome machine as simple as possible to aid in interchangeability and to keep costs of conversion low. Adaptation to color in the console involved the addition of a single rack of electronics involving some few minor resistor changes.

By April 1958, Ampex had fulfilled a promise to its clients by making the VR-1000 a complete system with the following important features: a color component, employing an electronic accessory to the basic recorder; complete interchangeability of tapes from one machine to another; and a functional editing procedure.[45]

A 1958 advertisement for the VR-1000 displayed the economic and ideological claims of the technology:

> The Ampex VR-1000 is the ultimate in television recording and playback. Both picture and sound match the realism of the original performance. Telecasts played back from the Ampex VR-1000 appear identical to live TV.
>
> The Ampex VR-1000 is a complete television recording and playback facility. Playbacks are immediate or they may be delayed indefinitely. Tapes are interchangeable and *reusable*. Editing is *proved* and practical. Thus the Ampex VR-1000 brings new flexibility into all station operations . . . in scheduling programs, commercials and special events . . . and in scheduling performers, camera crews and studio time.
>
> The Ampex VR-1000 *Videotape* Recorder has been in daily use by the networks since November 30, 1957, and by farsighted independent stations since November 30, 1957. Accelerated production of the VR-1000 assures delivery of all back orders before Daylight Savings Time in April, 1958, with prompt delivery on subsequent orders.
>
> The Ampex VR-1000 repays its cost in a hurry, starts paying for itself immediately in your black and white operations, adapting to color whenever you're ready for it. The Ampex VR-1000 adapts to color by adding a single rack of electronics, with necessary inter-connections. Then, every subtle gradation in

FIG. 6.7.   Alexander Poniatoff with the VR-1000. Picture shows Ampex's
founder, Alexander Poniatoff with the VR-1000. The racks are behind Mr.
Poniatoff. (*Source:* Courtesy of Ampex Corporation, Redwood City, CA.)

color is recorded and playbacks are brilliantly "live." Using this Ampex accessory, your station's changeover to color not only costs less but is greatly
simplified. Color conversion assemblies are available beginning mid-summer
1958.

Ampex would like to tell you more about *Videotape* recording and playback—how stations increase their efficiency and potentials, how sponsors
benefit from fluffless, pre-recorded live quality commercials. The complete
story is covered in a fully illustrated booklet."[46]

Interestingly, in the 1950s, Ampex owned the name "Videotape" as a
trademark.

Progress at Ampex Corporation

Ampex extended the use of its videotape recorder into the educational
broadcasting field with an order from the National Educational Television
and Radio Center in Ann Arbor, Michigan, a recipient of a multi-million
dollar grant from the Ford Foundation. Initially, 43 educational television
stations were equipped with Ampex videotape recorders through the Na-

tional Educational Television and Radio Center of New York. This network of affiliated educational stations was able to interchange and broadcast tapes produced, duplicated, and syndicated from the duplicating center in Ann Arbor, Michigan, or from any of the affiliated stations. This order led to the installations of Ampex videotape recorders in educational television stations throughout the United States. Selling the idea of using videotape equipment for educational purposes, Ampex stressed the necessities of such applications in areas such as pre-recording television lessons; recording a lesson while in session for later use by other institutions or individuals; creating a library of recorded tapes for use in class presentations; using it for scholastic training and self-improvement of TV teachers; and videotaping materials that could be useful with parent groups, visiting educators, professional educational meetings, boards of education, PTA meetings, and evening adult education courses.[47]

Videotape recorders were considered to be practical in virtually every television field. A videotape recorder was available to record President Eisenhower's inauguration, as a *Time Magazine* correspondent reported:

President Eisenhower took his inaugural oath last week twice within half an hour—or so it looked to millions of viewers on CBS and NBC. The trick was done not by mirrors but their electronic equipment: the new videotape recorder, a 900-lb machine that captures images as well as sound on magnetic tape and can play them back instantly—or whenever the user wants them—with fidelity approaching the original picture.[48]

The public was also exposed to videotape recording through network sports broadcasts. For the television industry, the large sport recording involving the use of videotape was the occasion of the Eighth Winter Olympic Games, held at Squaw Valley, California, in 1960. Already, history was made on July 25, 1959, when 75 million Americans as well as several hundred million Russians and others watched Nixon's tour and debate with Khrushchev in Moscow through the facility of an Ampex color videotape recorder. This was the first promotion of "live" playback from magnetic tape. Ampex consolidated its rising financial status with a listing on the New York and Pacific Stock Exchanges.

Meanwhile, in 1952, the BBC commenced work on a videotape recorder that was known as Vision Electronic Recording Apparatus (VERA) using the same longitudinal format seen earlier on the machines built by Bing Crosby Enterprises and RCA. The VERA was unveiled by the BBC in April 1958. It was a large machine which employed $\frac{1}{2}$-inch magnetic tape running at a speed of 200 inches per second on a $20\frac{1}{2}$-inch reel that had a 15-minute operating time. Vera had three recording heads employing a three-track system, with two of the tracks used to store video signals (one track for direct video and the other for low frequency video signals using FM modulating), and a third track for carrying the sound that was FM-modulated onto a carrier. For editing purposes, a 30-KHz signal burst switch was activated on to the sound track to make the sound audible. Although they had spent 5 years developing the VERA, only two prototypes were in use.[49] The BBC concluded the VERA project immediately after the Ampex demonstration in April 1956. Following the footsteps of early longitudinal videotape recording systems, VERA did not reach a production stage and for the same reasons.

By May 1958, the Ampex VR-1000 had been introduced in Europe. The first two VR-1000 videotape recorders to be used in Europe were delivered to Associated-Rediffusion in London. The machines were adjusted to the British 405 line standard by Rank-Cintel Limited. The price tag was 20,000 pounds.

The BBC continued to use the Ampex VR-1000 for all its video recording until the implementation in 1962 of a change from 405 lines to 625 lines. The BBC was seeking a videotape recorder that was capable of providing more detail at the new broadcasting standard. Once more, they contacted Ampex with the request for a high quality black-and-white video recorder capable of meeting high picture fidelity.

Work on the VR-1000D, a prototype being developed for the BBC was immediately applied to a new machine, one of the most important developments in Ampex history, the high-band VR-2000. The new transistorized "color" videotape recorder came in time for the color boom that began in late 1964. Unveiled at the NAB show in 1965, the high band VR-2000 was the only videotape recorder on the market capable of the level of color fidelity demanded by broadcasting stations. The BBC whose initial requests for high band color started it all, was the first to order these machines due to their satisfaction with the VR-1000D. In fact, the first six VR-2000s were shipped to the BBC even before the unveiling at the NAB show.

With the expansion of color in the industry, Ampex had developed a new version of its Intersync control system, a picture synchronizer that improved horizontal phase stability for VTRs. Coupled with the introduction of the Philips Plumbicon tube that guaranteed an excellent color fidelity in the cameras, Ampex was equipped with the complete accessories to make a better color recorder. Therefore, at the 1964 NAB convention, history repeated itself, for the VR-2000 was not only considered a unique engineering achievement, but a necessity for all the networks in the United States. It was claimed that the high-band VR-2000 was the only videotape recorder on the market capable for the kind of color fidelity needed to make good quality color broadcasting feasible. Ampex was honored on June 4, 1967 with its second Emmy Award by the Academy of Television

Arts and Sciences, acknowledging the VR-2000 contributions to television recording technology.

However, a relationship that began in 1957 with an agreement to the exchange ideas developed into competition between RCA and Ampex. This time Ampex had not only transistorized and "colorized" its equipment, but it entered Europe, previously an exclusive RCA territory, in full force. But now the low-band RCA TR-22 VTR, the first transistorized VTR was surpassed by the VR-2000 in both function and design. Ampex would later have a terrible backlog in production, due to the excessive demand for the VR-2000 from the United States and Canada as well as these newer markets. Once again, Ampex's marketing forecast was inadequate to market demands.

Just before the unveiling of Ampex's first videotape recorder, the VR-1000 at the NAB convention at Chicago in 1956, Ampex market studies showed that if the machines could be made to work in both monochrome and color, that total sales between 1956 and 1960 would be 26 units at $30,000 each. As it turned out, Ampex was shipping 30 units per month at $75,000 by spring 1958.[50] This time the argument made by Ampex management in connection with the VR-2000 was that because television stations had just acquired the highly priced VR-1000 machines whose capabilities had not been fully realized yet, it was difficult to see how even a superior product such as the proposed VR-2000 would rapidly replace the recent VR-1000 purchases. Furthermore, management believed that better color recording, which was an important feature of the new machine, would not be a sufficient incentive to dump the VR-1000 because color broadcasting had not fully penetrated the industry. Ampex was wrong again.

The 1961 RCA TR-22 (see Fig. 6.8) remained the VR-2000's main competition for several years. It was the most ergonomic machine yet—a result of a human engineering studies organized by RCA that coupled the recorder to its human operation because of its ease of operation.[51] The TR-22 was a gratifying commercial success. Apart from the vacuum tubes in the picture and waveform monitors, this machine was completely solid state. It was exceedingly different from its predecessor, the TRT-1B.[52] Two versions of the TR-22 were introduced by RCA: "A domestic model for 525-line, 60-field TV signals with 60-cycle AC power." Next was a three-standard switchable recorder designed to accommodate 525-line, 60 field; 625-line, 50-field (UK/Germany, etc.); and either 405-line (UK), 50-field or 819-line (France), 50-field signals. From this analysis, it is clear that RCA was not only preparing an "onslaught" in the U.S. market, but was also bracing for a mass competition in foreign markets, especially in Europe.

In 1969 RCA introduced the TC-100, a videotape cartridge for playback of commercials and other small videotape segments, for automated station

FIG. 6.8.   The RCA TR-22. Manufacturer: RCA. The Model TR-22 was the
first "all transistor VTR." It was introduced in 1961. Some important characteristics were its smaller size; single-packed machines (no external racks
or accessories); lighter weight; reduced power consumption, and ease of
operation. With the production of this model, RCA established itself as a
major competitor in the market. (*Source*: RCA Consumer Electronics Division, Indianapolis, IN.)

breaks. The TC-100 contained a short videotape segment placed in separate
cartridges. Instructions for the desired sequence of playing were then
punched into the built-in memory. Using a pulse code to signify "start of
message" and "end of message," it provided 10 seconds to the 3 minutes of
playing time. The machine was capable of taking up to 22 cartridges in its
magazine.

In 1974, RCA introduced a device called "a cue-operated programmer"
otherwise known as The RCA TAC-1. This was a sequential switcher with a
built-in memory, which could be programmed to maneuver up to 15
source sequences in any desired order. These different source sequences
could be cartridge VTRs, reel-type VTRs cartridge, reel-type film projectors,

or slide projectors. The TAC-1 could be programmed to run a complete station break no matter upon what station equipment the discrete message were stored.

But all this failed to deter Ampex. By mid-1969, 1,000 Ampex VR-2000 high band recorders had been sold. The VR-2000, and a second high-band model named VR-1200 introduced in 1966, continued to dominate the monochrome and color videotape recording market all over the world. Ampex's 1,000th high-band color videotape recorder was sold to the CBS Television Network in New York in June 1969.[53]

By 1970, Ampex had expanded to include seven major fields, the first five being the most dynamic growth fields in the world—communications, leisure/entertainment, computer peripherals, information storage and re-

FIG. 6.9.   Sony's Video Recorder BVH1000. This was Sony's answer to portability. Capitalizing on helical technology, Sony developed a reputation that had since extended into the home video industry. (*Source:* Sony Corporation of America, Park Ridge, NJ.)

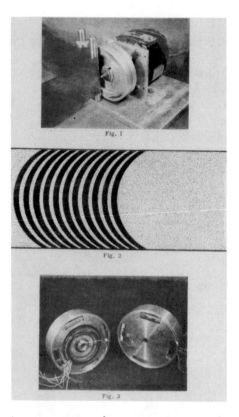

FIG. 6.10. Arcuate scan recording system. Figures 1 through 3 show Ampex's attempt to scan the tape in an arcuate scan rather than transverse or quadruplex to the path of the tape. The resulting problem was that the arcs would never be exactly spaced (Figure 2) therefore a huge time based error occurred while playing back. Transverse won over this system. (*Source:* Courtesy of Ampex Corporation, Redwood City, CA.)

trievals, educational technology, instrumentation, and geophysical research. Credit must be given as well to the 3M Company for pioneering and supplying most of the tapes that made Ampex's products as successful as they were. Ampex continued to benefit from its command of video recording stemming from their achievement of the first practical method of videotape recording introduced in 1956.

By 1956, it was established that videotape technology could cut costs, deliver quality pictures, and yield impressive revenues for the television industry.

Chapter 7

The Home Video Revolution

*I*n the late 1970s and early 1980s home video was often described in a drawing of a television set from which a dozen lines pointing to all directions emanated. A line linked to a home videocassette recorder; one connected to a videodisc machine; another hooked up cable; yet another went to the videogame machine or to a home computer, or other data-retrieval system; and finally the last tied in the audio stereo system. This was a picture of the home video/entertainment center. But this dream has not exactly materialized as planned. Videodisc players that were once thought to be a strong competitor to videocassette recorders have not yet succeeded; the videogame machine seems to have completed its life cycle, resulting in a downward trend in its sales; the home computer market has begun to level off, whereas all data-retrieval systems are underused. Cable too has slowed, although it now reaches into 51% of all American homes. Only the home VCR, now with 58.1% penetration, has continued to show strong growth in the home; and with the advent of a built-in hi-fi system in modern VCRs, linkages of VCRs to stereo systems have become a trend. Of all these home devices, the videocassette recorder is currently enjoying the greatest popularity—a growth curve parallel to that of color receivers two decades earlier.

In discussing the home video environment it is important to trace its history back to the development of the helical-scan system. This was the clue to reducing the VTR's size, which facilitated the development of the home video recording system. The importance of Sony's U-matic technology as the main foundation on which a successful consumer video system was developed is established. In addition, the economic impact of consumer video, public acceptance, and VCR usage are also analyzed in this chapter.

HELICAL-SCAN FORMAT VIDEOTAPE RECORDERS

In September 1959, a new approach to video recording was introduced by Toshiba of Japan. The Toshiba VTR-1 prototype videotape recorder was demonstrated to the public at the Matsuda Research Laboratory, Kawasaki, Japan (see Fig. 7.1).[1] Toshiba had started work on this system in 1953, completing its first experimental prototype in 1958. The major difference

FIG. 7.1. Prototype of Helical-Scan machines. Alex Maxey of Ampex was interested in alternative scanning and confided in the advantages of the helical system. He therefore developed prototypes as shown in this picture from 1956 to 1959. Helical had several advantages over the quad system. It was problematic in the beginning, but soon became a universal standard. (*Source:* Courtesy of Ampex Corporation, Redwood City, CA.)

between it and the RCA and Ampex recorders was in the relationship of tape to head. The VTR-1 was equipped with only one video head with tape running around a cylinder housing the video head in a helical loop. The signal was transversely recorded across the width of the 2-inch wide tape and initially operated at a speed of 15 inches per second. An FM modulation system was employed to record the signal on tape. In January 1961, Ampex introduced its first commercial helical-scan unit. Sony followed suit in November 1961 with its SV-201. By December 1961, a prototype VTR-1 was delivered to NHK (the Japanese state television network) for testing and evaluation. Toshiba also designed another helical-scan model that employed two heads with the tape half wrapped around the video head.[2]

The helical-scan format was not a completely new technique to Ampex engineers because they had been experimenting with it since 1956, and in 1957, Maxey introduced a prototype.[3] The main advantage of the recording technique had been well known since its inception to include low operation costs, simplicity, and the possibility of slow motion and stillframing. These were the same advantages that would later make helical-scan the standard in the home video industry. However, it was also evident that the helical-scan constituted a severe handicap in some areas. As a rule of thumb in video recording systems, high quality corresponds directly to high video writing speed, which ranges from 1,500 inches per second for quadruplex down to a few hundred for some low-cost-inch consumer formats.[4]

To achieve a high band, 800 to 1,000 inches per second (ips) writing speed was required, or a scan length of up to 17 inches. This was an extremely difficult task to accomplish on a mechanical transport. A popular method used to contain this problem had been the application of a heterodyne color recovery system (introduced by Ampex) to reduce the writing speed and to ensure the quality of signal mechanical format.

The answer finally was an electronic programmable video head (PVH) and a micropositioning servo system that automatically traced the video track as recorded on tape. Research commenced on this system at Ampex in the late 1950s, while Toshiba was also perfecting an identical solution. The PVH could simultaneously scan two tracks and accurately trace a track that actually crossed over to an adjacent track position by means of a sinusoidal dithering scheme used to sense track boundaries.[5]

Some outstanding features of this micropositioning, and ones that broadcast engineers hated to forgo, where its capabilities to produce broadcastable slow-motion and a stillframed video, eliminating the noise-bar characteristic of earlier helical VTRs.

The rationale behind Ampex's decision to pursue both transverse (quad) and helical-scan videotape recording programs at the same time in the 1950s was clear. The transverse recorders were complex and expensive, although very tolerant as far as mechanical problems were concerned;

helical-scan recorders, on the other hand, were simpler, were capable of certain special effects (e.g., stillframing/slow motion), and were much less expensive. Unfortunately, the problems inherent in helical-scan recorders seemed so insurmountable that the project was suspended. Ampex revived the helical-scan project again in 1961 when it attempted to develop the VR-8000, a professional broadcast-quality monochrome helical recorder. The recorder had several unique features including easily removable heads. Several production prototypes were built, but the technical problems characteristic of early helical format finally destroyed it, too, and no model was mass-produced. Ampex did reconsider and perfected a helical-scan system but only after other companies had introduced their systems.

However, industry attention was turned to the development of lower performance units that were targeted at semi- or nonprofessional markets. Following Toshiba's example in 1959, a variety of successful helical VTRs were manufactured by several companies, including a two-head helical-scan videotape recorder introduced in January 1961 by the Victor Company of Japan. This machine was marketed in the United States under the trade name Telechrome JVC Model 770.[6]

Helical VTRs were available in $\frac{1}{4}$-, $\frac{1}{2}$-, $\frac{3}{4}$-, 1-, and 2-inch wide tape by 1976. Ampex alone manufactured over 26,000 1 and 2-inch helical-scan industrial-quality VTRs, and the last of the three types in this category was the VPR-7900A. By 1964, Japanese manufacturers had made videotape recorders available in their home entertainment market. In 1965, Sony introduced its SV-201 helical-scan model, following its predecessor, the Sony PV-100 videocorder introduced in July 1964. By 1966, Sony's presence in the U.S. market marked the first appearance of an inexpensive videotape recorder.

As the 1960s progressed, videotape recorder manufacturers were moving toward a new market, the domestic market. Rapid changes in equipment design were obvious as portable, battery powered machines were being unveiled one after the other.

In 1963, Ampex formed a new consumer and educational product division located in a 75,000 square foot building outside Chicago. The division combined all Ampex consumer products in one market organization for the first time. In that same year, Ampex produced several futuristic home entertainment systems. The most elaborate was the Signature V, it was a complete home entertainment center consisting of a compact videotape recorder (a VR-1500, the first successful Ampex helical-scan VTR), black-and-white camera, television receivers, and a home music center. At 9 feet long, it allowed the owner to "tape" one program for later viewing while watching another. Featured in the 1963 Neiman-Marcus Christmas Catalog, this unit sold for $30,000.[7]

On September 21, 1964, an agreement was made whereby Ampex entered into a joint venture manufacturing agreement with Toshiba (Tokyo-

Shibaura Electric Company) to enter the Japanese market. The joint venture company known as Toamco (Toshiba–Ampex K.K.), would manufacture and market videotape recorders, computer memories, and instrumentation equipment in Japan.[8] This was an advantage of Ampex's new consumer division because Toshiba was already known for its compact home videotape recorders.

Ampex announced new plans in the summer of 1965 to develop another home videotape recorder that would be capable of recording television programs off the air for viewing at a more convenient time. By coupling it to a CCTV camera, "instant films" could be taken and played back at anytime on a standard television. This unit was designated the 6200 HVR and its basic price was at $1,095 and above.

The Mobile "Videotrainer," which combined Ampex's VR-7000 with television camera and receiver, was introduced in November 1965. It was specially designed for educational uses and bridged the gap between broadcast quality portable videotape recorders and home videotape recorders. The price for the package was down to $6,000. Only one other development was necessary before home VTRs would become a standard consumer durable.

By 1976, Ampex and Sony had very similar but incompatible professional helical VTR formats. During the Society of Motion Picture and Television Engineers Winter Television Conference held in January 1977 in San Francisco, a document known as the "White Paper" was submitted. It suggested 1-inch helical-scan video format. This led to the formation of two working groups in the committee for Videotape Recording Technology. One group was responsible for the development of a segmented, and the other for nonsegmented 1-inch video formats. These formats had since been approved for standardization. A major advantage was the interchangeability with other machines built to the same formats by different manufacturers.[9]

However, despite the large publicity accorded these two formats in the industry, little was mentioned of a third format.[10] This was also a 1-inch format manufactured for several years by Ampex, and later in the 1970s, by "Video Memories" which acquired the rights to build and sell the format.

The three formats were labeled Type "A," "B," and "C." The Ampex Type "A" format, the Ampex Video Memories format, was equipped with two audio tracks and a video track. There was a gap during the vertical interval, and the vertical sync was not recorded. The Bosch Type "B" format, the segmented 1-inch format, had five video recorded segments, using two heads, and had three audio channels. The Type "C" format was a compromise 1-inch format whose beginning was with the "White Paper." It contained three audio tracks and a video track, and an optional sync track to provide a guarantee against loss of video signals.

These 1-inch machines were to provide two main objectives for broadcasters:

1. To provide a replacement for first generation electronic news gathering (ENG) equipment. The new machines would provide optimum technical quality over existing machines.
2. To be useful in editing. Their stop action and slow- and fast-motion viewing abilities allowed a system of video editing using film techniques.

SONY INTRODUCES A NEW EQUIPMENT FOR HOME RECORDINGS

In 1975 Sony introduced lower cost $\frac{1}{2}$-inch tape in cassette form. In April 1969, Sony had announced its first color cassette videotape recorder. The cassette used 1-inch tape running on two tracks at $3\frac{1}{2}$ ips. It measured $6 \times 10 \times 3\frac{3}{4}$ inches and the two reels were mounted coaxially. The tape panned from one reel to another around a hub slightly larger than the head drum. When the cassette was slipped into the machine, the hub stopped over the drum, locking the cassette in place, and rotating the hub so that a window in it allowed the tape to make contact with the drum. The recording of the color was a modification of the NTSC. Later in November of the same year, Sony announced a new home color recorder whose cassettes measured $8 \times 5 \times 1\frac{1}{2}$ inches and were capable of recording as well as playing back for 90 minutes. It had a 250-line color resolution and a processed NTSC recorded signal. In addition to the video tracks, there were two audio tracks for either stereo recording or dual languages.

As the 1970s approached, the industry was thus rapidly moving toward the consumer market. But a number of companies that were considering the home entertainment market came to the same conclusion as did Sony during the early 1970s—open reel 1- or $\frac{3}{4}$-inch tape was too expensive and complicated.

With the advent of Sony's revised $\frac{3}{4}$-inch U-matic format in 1972, the videotape industry had a new standard, this time for cassettes. This was the world's first successful intermanufacturer standard for encapsulated helical videotape system. The Sony U-matic used a two-head helical-scan format with two audio channels allowing for stereo record/playback. The cassettes ran for up to 60 minutes and the machine could record and playback a full color signal. The U-matic's reliability made it a widely accepted product. Sony's strategic department was convinced that their new U-matic would soon be a passing fad as soon as another manufacturer duplicated its electronics. Therefore, Sony decided that it was best to give the technology to the industry rather than having it "stolen." Providing it legally to the industry through licensing would not only enable Sony to retain claim on the U-matic, but would also allow them to receive some type of concessions or payment beneficial to Sony. A major contributing factor to the worldwide use of the U-matic was the signing of the first inter-manufacturer agreements initially with Matsushita (Panasonic) and Victor Company of Japan (JVC). U-matic products are now available in consumer, industrial (i.e., broadcasting), and commercial formats. As of the end of 1983, industry studies indicated that over 31 different ¾-inch U-matic models were available.

In the 1960s when companies such as RCA, Ampex, and Toshiba announced their interest in the VCR market, skeptics—especially in the professional videotape production world—assumed that cassettes could not possess the quality for broadcast applications. Of course the skeptics were proved wrong before the 1960s were over. VCRs soon became a fact of life worldwide in broadcasting, cable, video facilities, and even home television use. Thus, the helican-scan system and the small videocassette paved the way for marketing the home videocassette recorder.

INTRODUCTION AND DIFFUSION
OF VIDEOCASSETTE RECORDERS

Early Home Video Recorders

In the early 1960s, most videotape recorder manufacturers were searching for markets for the videotape recorder other than in broadcasting, and it was evident that the likely sector to be targeted was the consumer although many in the industry questioned the possible extent of this.

The first video recorders (all noncassette and even some nonmagnetic) made available for home use were made by a number of firms. These models were built in an open-reel format until Avco, then Ampex and Toshiba introduced cartridges in 1970.

An early open-reel machine that used small enough tape to make it a possibility for home use was the Telcan longitudinal scan machine available by June 1963. The Telcan unit was one of the first to employ ¼-inch tape, and at a reduced cost of 59 guineas it could be used to record television programs and also record from an industrial television camera for instant home movies.[11] In April 1964, Winston Research Corporation, a Division of Fairchild Camera and Instrument Corporation of Los Angeles, introduced a low-cost four-track television tape recorder that recorded on ¼-inch tape. The picture quality of this machine has been described as comparable to normal home viewing.

Yet, Sony claimed major credit for expanding video recording beyond the professional sphere and into the home. In 1964, Sony described its dream product and argued that it "will change the whole concept of prime time television . . . because any time will be prime time." Unveiling a helical-scan monochrome open-reel machine, they dubbed it the first home consumer videotape recorder. By summer 1965, Ampex Corporation responded, announcing its home videotape recorder that recorded television programs off the air for viewing at a more convenient time and allowed for immediate playback. This machine was the 6200-HVR and cost $1,095.

However, the advantages in ease and simplicity of operation made videocassettes and cassette recorders more desirable. In October 1967, CBS introduced a video recorder called Electronic Video Recording (EVR).[12] This system was video playback only for pre-recorded or television taped programs on conventional television receivers (monochrome or color). Analog signals were recorded in a 7-inch cartridge on 8mm lenticular film. The first public demonstration of the EVR prototype occurred in December 1968, and CBS was very optimistic about the results. Eventually, on March 24, 1970, CBS gave a public demonstration of a color EVR.[13] But the system could not survive against the burgeoning world of magnetic-tape cassettes.

By the late 1960s and early 1970s, virtually every company in the videotape manufacturing business was involved in introducing new video products for home consumption. Besides Sony, Ampex, and CBS, these included, Toshiba, Matsushita (Panasonic), North American N.V. Philips, Telefunken, RCA, Avco, American Photocopy Equipment, Arvin, Technical Operations, Inc., and Japan Electron Laboratory Company. The specifics of some of these machines are important for understanding the subsequent need for standardization and interchangeability of formats to encourage and retain consumer access to the programmed material.

In November 1969, Panasonic unveiled a prototype two-reel magazine-loading color videotape recorder based on the "cassette" principle. This system measured 13.9 × 14 × 5.1 inches, and used $\frac{1}{2}$-inch tape with a speed of 7.5 inches per second capsuled in a cassette 10.6 × 6.4 × 0.9 inches in size. With an improved double heterodyne automatic phase control system that made the playback signals jitterfree, the machine was claimed to be the "cassette" system ready to compete with open-reel recorders in such fields as education, business, research, and even some professional broadcast applications.[14]

Also in November 1969, Sony introduced a new color video player. This unit was different from the one introduced only 6 months earlier. The latest equipment ran at 3.15 inches per second and had a cassette measuring 8 × 5 × 1$\frac{1}{4}$ inch with a $\frac{3}{4}$-inch tape. It recorded with NTSC color standard, yielding a 250-line color resolution and stereophonic sound of very good quality. It was capable of playing up to 100 minutes.[15] Sony's player was also portable and cost under $400. However, in order to record off the air, another device costing $150 was needed. A vidicon monochrome camera was also available for recording home movies at a cost of $100. Each blank cassette sold for about $20. Marketed in Japan from 1969, it was not available for U.S. consumers until December 1971.

In June 1970, N.V. Philips announced the videocassette recorder, which was able to record and playback in both color and black and white. Measuring $22 \times 13 \times 16\frac{1}{2}$ inches, the machine used a cassette measuring $5.8 \times 5.0 \times 1.4$ inches with concentric hubs, capable of playing for 60 minutes, with a tape speed of 5.6 inches per second. Its other features included recording audio signals independently on the tracks, sound dubbing and "stop motion." Philips proposed producing a variety of black-and-white and color components with tuners in the future.[16]

One month later, Avco Corporation of New York publicized its Avco CTV Cartrivision. This was a solid state unit consisting of a receiver–recorder–playback system built into a self-contained compact unit. Pre-recorded cassettes as well as off-air recorded television programs could be played back instantly. Home movies were to be made by a specially constructed camera that was to be available at a later date.

In September 1970, Ampex introduced a cartridge system called "Instavision," a product of Toamco, the joint venture concern between Ampex and Toshiba in Japan. The system was hearlded as the "smallest cartridge-loading video recorder and/or player ever made." The Instavision recorder/player used standard $\frac{1}{2}$-inch videotape enclosed in a small circular plastic cartridge measuring 4.6 inches in diameter and .7 inches thick. The deck weighted about 15 points with batteries and measured $11 \times 13 \times 4\frac{1}{4}$ inches. Included in the package were a choice of recorder/players and players operating on batteries or AC power with auxiliary power pack. Effects such as slow and stop motion as well as simple assembly editing could be performed on the system. Audio recording was done through two independent audio tracks that included a stereo playback. Beside the recorder/player, other components included a camera, power pack, tape cartridge, and accessories. The camera was a Vidicon type weighing 5 pounds, with an electronic view finder, hand-held trigger operated and equipped with a standard 4-to-1 zoom lens. The tape cartridge could be played on any other $\frac{1}{2}$-inch standard 1 reel videotape machine. Video resolution was 300 lines for monochrome. Color resolution corresponded with standard color television receivers. Signal to noise ratio was 42 db.[17] Ampex later changed the name from "Instavision" to "Instavideo" before dropping the project in 1972.

Within less than 1 year, five major firms moved into open competition

TABLE 7.1
Home Video Systems and Their Prices as Available in the Early 1970

	Recording Medium	Date on Market	Unit to Price**	Ability to Record	Freeze Frame Capability
CBS/EVR Industrial Model	Film	Late '70	$795	No	Yes
Consumer Model		Mid '72	$350		
Ampex Instavision	Magnetic Tape	Mid '72	$900	Yes	Yes
RCA SelectaVision	Hologram/Tape	Late '72	$400	No	Yes
Sony Video	Magnetic Tape	Late '71	$400	Yes	No
AVCO: TV Cartrivision*	Magnetic Tape	Mid '71	$895	Yes	No
Nordmende Colorvision	Film	Mid '71	$850	No	Yes

*Television included with units
**Prices as at date on the market

for the home video market (see Table 7.1). In 1971, describing the sudden rush into the home video field, Chase Morsey Jr., RCA's executive vice president who headed its SelectaVision project, said:

> Everybody is sitting there worrying which system will make it big, and completely missing the point. The point is that by 1980 it will be a billion dollar annual business. Our market research suggests that figure is probably conservative. I think this stuff is going to be bigger than television. In fact, video cassettes would give television sales a tremendous shot in the arm: each family will have good reason to want several color sets. Some people don't realize that this isn't just another gadget. If you want to calculate the market for video playback, just add up the collective market for movies, books, records, audio cassettes, adult courses, encyclopedias, business magazines and fairy tales. All of this and more could go on video cassettes to be played either in motion or a frame at a time.
>
> I believe that video cassettes will be the 'razor blades' of the home entertainment business.[18]

Sorting Out the Possible Systems

The introduction of home video recording or the cartridge system as it was known was grandly heralded. Of course this prediction was delayed, coming only in the mid-1980s. The publicity and high hopes accorded the cartridge and its usefulness in homes created a new set of ideological concerns, similar to those created earlier by VTRs. The variety of choices allowed by home video systems, which included recording, playing back, making home movies, and functioning in slow, freeze-stop motion, and editing modes were the main reasons why home video's arrival aroused so much interest and stirred such excitement among consumers as well as in the entertainment and communication industries. It was predicted that in time, home video would radically alter the status quo in television, motion pictures, theater, music, journalism, book publishing and several other fields. Analysts went as far as predicting that the growing video cartridge industry would become a mainstay of the U.S. economy. For instance, Morsey of RCA believed that the home video industry would reach the $1 billion revenue mark by 1980, and even more optimistic analysts put it at about $3 billion. Actually, Morsey's prediction was close to the actual sales revenue.

Despite the Electronics Industries Association of Japan's (EIA-J) effort to standardize various video recorders and equipment, the majority of the equipment manufactured were still incompatible with each other. Only in the late 1970s did Sony's BETA and VHS format finally begin to control the market, becoming *defacto* standards for the field. In fact, the fate of a late entry, Philips Video 2000, is instructive as to the strength of these two dominant formats.[19]

The Betamax System

Sony, introduced its Beta format VCR in 1975 to counter Philip's original VCR format (now obsolete).[20] Before the introduction of Betamax, Sony was well known for its U-matic format, and open-reel industrial VTRs for professional use.[21] The basic principles of the U-matic were translated into the development of an innovated VCR called Betamax.

The reason for the wide adoption of tape was partly due to Sony's efforts and concern over interchangeability of various home video recorders being manufactured at the time. Although Sony, Avco, and Ampex adopted tape for their various systems, the equipment was incompatible. Sony, in a bid to create the market's compatibility, rallied seven companies, convincing them to agree on a policy of interchangeability. Thus, Matsushita Electrical Industrial Co. (Panasonic), Victor Company of Japan, Industria A. Zanussi S.P.A. of Italy, Grundig Werke GMBH, AEG-Telefunken of Germany, N.V. Philips Gloeilmapenfabrieken (Norelco) of Netherlands, and North American Philips Corporation proceeded to manufacture home video recorders that were compatible. Sony's Beta tape format became the standard as had U-matic before it.

The Betamax used a $\frac{1}{2}$-inch magnetic tape. Initially presented as a 1-hour recording equipment, Beta has been improved. Now three different playing lengths exist: Beta I with a 1 hour recording capability; Beta II, 2 hours; and Beta III, which increased recording time 50% by stretching a 3-hour recording on an L-750 tape to $4\frac{1}{2}$ hours and up to 5 hours on the newly developed L-830.[22] All use the same size cassette, however, and all Beta format machines can play Beta tapes.

A major difference between Beta and VHS is that they record electronic signals with different methods.

With only a fraction of the VCR market, Beta has a bleak future. In January 1988, Sony, the inventor and major manufacturer of Beta announced their plan to sell VHS models. Statistics as of January 1988 indicate that of the 170 million home video recorders that have been manufactured worldwide since 1975, only 20 million, or 12% are Beta systems. Sony's intention is to offer its VHS model for sale in Europe by mid-1988. Initially, Sony will buy VHS manufactured by Hitachi Limited, but they will be marketed under the Sony label. Sony intends to produce the hardware eventually.

Sony's decision will likely result in further reduction in programming selection for Beta consumers. The availability of a much larger selection of VHS pre-recorded movies has been a major contributing factor to the boom in that market. Over the years, Sony has fought to maintain the Beta market as well as staging a come back by introducing a variety of new products including the 8mm video recorder system, and a similar camcorder. These equipment use tapes smaller than those used by Beta and VHS. Beta's poor performance in the marketplace has been a major concern to Sony in recent years. In effect, this resulted in Sony's involvement in offering VHS tapes in the United States in 1983 and in Japan in 1985 in view of the increasing market for music video pre-recorded tapes. Sony has also been involved in producing parts for VHS recorders. These moves were instrumental to Sony's recent decision to offer VHS recorders.

Despite the low share of the Beta format worldwide, it continues to maintain record shares in countries such as Mexico where it commands 90% of the market and Indonesia where it has a 70% share.

VHS (The Video Home System)

A year after the 1975 introduction of the Beta format, Matsushita and its Victor Company of Japan (JVC) subsidiary unveiled their VHS (video home system) technology in direct competition and incompatible with Beta. At the outset, Beta was technologically superior to VHS, employing the slogan: "Beta is Better." But VHS manufacturers had not entered the battle with an intent to let Beta control the market. RCA, which was first to market a VHS machine in 1977, supported its campaign with a solid marketing strategy in the United States, reciprocating and updating every innovation effected on the Beta, so much so that Beta's technological superiority notwithstanding, VHS became the leader in the competitive war that immediately followed.

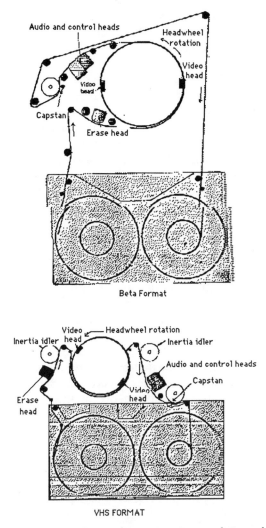

FIG. 7.2.   Beta and VHS formats (Source: CMPTE Journal, December 1985.)

Superceding Beta I, VHS had its initial edge when VHS users were able to enjoy 2 hours of recording as opposed to Beta I's 1 hour. The engineering trick that resulted in the extra hour bonus for VHS formatted equipment was the ability of the VHS engineers to slow the tape speed, thereby increasing recording time.[23] Beside the tape length, other advantageous factors of VHS included portability and cost, contributing to a decreasing market performance by Beta. Thus, although neither Beta nor VHS format per se determined the winner, engineering advances on the VCRs played a primary role in the outcome. Once in place, however, VHS' impetus is now also a factor in its maintenance as the industry standard.

Although the home video market continues to surge and VCR sales of both formats are increasing, VHS has continued to outsell Beta by a comfortable margin of 4 : 1. The latest VCR usage study indicates that VHS has 78.5% of the market, whereas Beta takes 21.5%. Due to the continuous poor (sales) performance of Beta in the market and its waning in popularity among consumers, Zenith, which was Sony's first Beta licensee, discontinued its Beta line of products, switching over to VHS. Sanyo followed suit in 1982, now manufacturing VHS systems instead of Beta. Nevertheless, Beta and VHS are still the predominant formats in the market and dedicated through market competition to producing better electronic equipment.

Eventual success notwithstanding, VHS was not initially free from technical problems. Just as Betamax adopted a previous system—the U-format-loading system, VHS used JVC's M-Loading System. This system involved a complex tape-threading and path system that sometimes resulted in over-stretching tapes during fast winding. This, in turn, resulted in a blank screen whenever the tape was in a fast-wind mode as the tape separated from the heads. However, JVC quickly corrected this problem, eliminating any likelihood of tape damage and restoring the screen pictures even during fast wind.[24]

Besides the fast-wind/no picture drawback, the early VHS had another problem. The head drum was 2.6 inches in diameter with a 7.3-inch revolution per second, resulting in a slower speed than Beta. This slower speed, although an advantage in increasing recording time, resulted theoretically

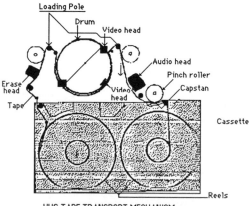

VHS TAPE TRANSPORT MECHANISM

FIG. 7.3.   VHS tape transport mechanism (Source: SMPTE Journal, December 1985.)

FIG. 7.4.   JVC's Model HR-3300, the first VHS manufactured.

in an inferior picture quality. But actually, it was the audio quality that seemed to falter. Again, improvements corrected this shortcoming.

Originally VHS was introduced with JVC's 2-hour VCR (see Fig. 7.4). Shortly thereafter, other equipment was able to record with a dual-speed 2- and 4-hour mode, followed by a 6-hour mode introduced in 1979. With a variety of product lines in the marketplace, some machines were able to accommodate a dual 2-hour/6-hour recording capability, whereas others such as the Panasonic VHS offered all three speeds: 2-, 4-, and 6-hour modes.[25]

Another VHS competitive advantage was the introduction of programming capacities. In fall 1978, RCA surprised Sony by introducing the first deluxe programmable VCR, the VCT 400, which was capable of being preset to record up to four programs on different channels as much as a week in advance, or, as consumers soon discovered, four different shows a night. Toshiba V-5420, which would be the first rival in this area, did not appear in the market until a year later. It was not until 1980 that Sony's four-event/14-day programmable (below the RCA capabilities) was available, by which time VHS had advanced to seven or eight events/14-day programs. Ironically, and despite the considerable video engineering innovations of Sony and other "Beta faithfuls," there is little they can invent, even at the present, that cannot eventually be duplicated by VHS.

Video 2000

Jointly invented by N.V. Philips, the Dutch electronic conglomerate, and Grundig, Video 2000 was introduced to compete with the Japanese-made VCRs especially in the European market. Based on its audio cassette (which was accepted as the industry standard) principle, N.V. Philips designed the

Video 2000 with two channels so that after concluding a 4-hour recording in one direction, the videocassette is flipped over for another 4 hours of recording in the opposite direction. Video 2000, like Betamax and VHS, uses a $\frac{1}{2}$-inch wide tape. It also employs a Dynamic Track Following System whereby a flexible video head is capable of sensing and tracing the exact path of each video track. With this system, there is no need for a tracking control. This system also allows better use of the tape that results in a longer recording time on the two-track system, as well as smooth freeze-frame and slow-motion pictures.

Being a late comer in the VCR market, Video 2000 faced an "identity crisis" although it was judged technologically superior. Furthermore, unlike the other formats that had long lists of licensees, N.V. Philips and Grundig had only a few licensees who were willing to produce and distribute Video 2000. These included ITT, Pye, and Bang & Olufsen.

For several years, there has been serious competition between Philip's Video 2000 and Japan's Matsushita Electric Industrial Company and its Victor Company of Japan European affiliate. This competition has been simply described by many in the industry as "war." Later, this battle expanded to include Betamax. By October 1983, it was obvious that the still new and little-heard-of Video 2000 was taking a back seat as its principal inventors signed a joint venture agreement with JVC, Britain's Thorn-EMI, and France's Thomson–Brandt to invest in a ½-inch machine in order to exploit the opportunities created by Japanese export restraints in Europe. In December 1983, N.V. Philips announced its decision to "supplement its own Video 2000 system with VCRs under Matsushita VHS patents." This decision signaled the end of the format wars (because Beta and VHS coexist) and thus opened up the European market for more innovative VCR marketing. Suspending the Video 2000 line was, therefore, seen as a painful concession of defeat for N.V. Philips, whose 1983 loss on the VCR amounted to $55 million. This loss was in turn blamed on unfair Japanese competition, as Philips tried unsuccessfully to limit Japanese VCR exports to Europe. Although Philips succeeded in convincing the European Commission and Japan's Ministry of International Trade & Industry early in 1983 to guarantee a market for 1.2 million of its Video 2000 machines for 1983, the company had still fallen short of realizing its sales goal.

Most European retailers were disappointed and believed that N.V. Philips was totally eliminating the Video 2000 from its inventory although it claimed that it was merely adding VHS to its product line. A video department head for a large French retailer stated:

> Philips, whenever it changes its policy, says it is simply adding an additional model to its existing product line. But two weeks or a month later, they tell you they are all out of the old models.[26]

On the other hand, Philips continued to lament that it introduced Video 2000 too late when Beta and VHS were already established in the European market in 1980.

Blank Tape

Achievements in video technology are not made possible exclusively by high-tech machines. Credit for the present advancement in video technology is shared equally by improvements made in videotape. Blank videotape manufacturers are equally serious, applying every sophisticated technical know-how in the production of tapes as hardware manufacturers.

A tape's quality is dependent on its ability to deliver a superior sound as well as "color-perfect" pictures. The most prevalent problem area in most videotape concerns is missing picture information—spots of black and

FIG. 7.5. BASF audio tape. BASF has been in the magnetic tape production business for almost six decades. Their contribution and reputation in the production of blank audiotape is outstanding. (*Source:* Courtesy of BASF Corporation, Bedford, MA.)

white. These "dropouts" as they are called, are caused by debris on the tape surface, spots lacking oxide coating, or parts of the coating with fewer than normal magnetic particles. Tapes with higher grades contain less dropouts.

Another problem area concerns color variation. This occurs in two phases: color intensity change referred to in numerical application as chrome AM (Amplitude Modulation), S/N (Signal to Noise), and changes in color shade or hue, referred to as chroma PM (Phase Modulation) S/N. These changes are not the same color (intensity) or tint (shade or hue) referred to in television manuals when you need to adjust your television set.

The sound effect or graininess is a result of changes in the contrast's random noise. It is calculated in terms of video or luminance S/N. Color noise is always evidence in large picture areas of similar color such as cartoons. Improvement in chroma noise has been encouraging due in part to high quality VCRs and from advancement in blank tape technology.

As a rule of thumb in understanding simple dB variations, doubling (+) or halving (−) the value of a power measurement results in a 3 dB change, while quartering results in a 6 dB (3dB + 3dB) change. Recent VCRs, such as the S-VHS and Beta, have contributed immensely to changes in all three types of S/N. Other improvements have been a result of technical superi-

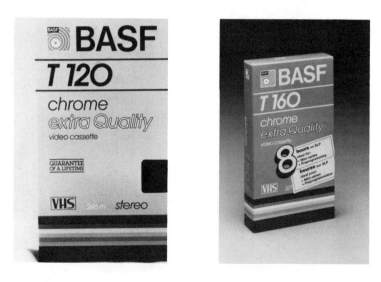

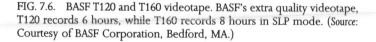

FIG. 7.6.   BASF T120 and T160 videotape. BASF's extra quality videotape, T120 records 6 hours, while T160 records 8 hours in SLP mode. (*Source:* Courtesy of BASF Corporation, Bedford, MA.)

TABLE 7.2
Factor Sales* of Blank Videocassettes
(Thousands of Units and Dollars; United States, 1982–1986)

Year	Retail Distribution		Industrial and Bulk Distribution		Total Units	Sales Dollars
	Units	Dollars	Units	Dollars		
1982	24,672	$279,674	8,857	$77,766	33,529	$357,420
1983	60,368	$485,926	14,635	$94,516	75,003	$580,442
1984	133,185	$770,555	33,284	$161,376	166,469	$931,931
1985	233,021	$1,054,825	60,638	$229,704	293,659	$1,284,529
1986	296,253	$1,234,689	71,138	$245,526	367,391	$1,480,215

*Includes factor sales to distributors and factory-direct sales to dealers
Excludes sales to duplicators
Source: EIA Marketing Services

ority in tapes. It is now possible to squeeze a greater amount of magnetic particles into a smaller and tighter space on the tape. Such fineness is commonly expressed in terms of surface area, weight, or square meter per gram. Other contributions to today's better quality tapes is a result of smoothness of base films, specialized coatings or layers of runability, additives, surface polishing (calendering) and accurate, debris-free slitting of bulk tape.

Blank tape manufacturers have been keeping up with VCR equipment manufacturers, providing every latest product with complementary tapes of similar quality. The S-VHS for instance uses a specialized high quality tape.

It is estimated that 300 million blank videocassettes were sold to dealers in 1987 at a total cost of $1.12 billion. In 1988, it is projected that 325 million blank videocassettes will be sold at $1.16 billion. Growth in blank tape sales has been declining, as consumer demand continues to fall. The main reason for this decrease is that there is a rise in the percentage of second-time VCR buyers among total VCR sales. It can be said that the blank tape market is suffering from the effect of the maturing VCR market. Because major buyers are no longer new owners, but second-time owners who are owners of "crowded tape libraries," they have little or no need for further recording activity. The increasing number of camcorders sold in the last few years was to remedy the blank tape market, however, they are being bought by consumers who already own VCR decks.

First-time VCR owners account for the largest percent of blank tapes. Purchase of blank tape among this group drops after their 9–12 tape in the first year of VCR ownership. In 1987, the blank tape industry's problem was compounded by fierce competition, severe price erosion, lack of brand

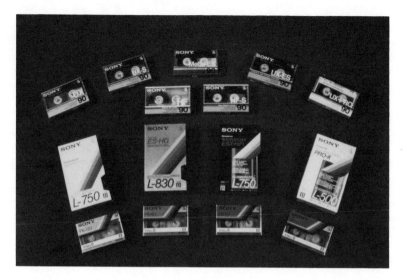

FIG. 7.7. Sony audio and videotape. (*Source:* Sony Corporation of America, Park Ridge, NJ.)

loyalty, lackluster demand, and oversupply. The industry saw the price of a T-120 dropping 19% from $4 to $3.25.

Adding to this dilema was the increasing number of brands and distributional channels that has surfaced in the past few years (see Table 7.3).

TABLE 7.3
Major Blank Tapes

1. BASF
2. Fuji
3. Kodak
4. JVC
5. Konica
6. Maxwell
7. Memorex
8. Panasonic
9. Polaroid
10. Quasar
11. RCA
12. Scotch
13. Sony
14. SKC
15. TDK
16. Zenith
17. Goldstar
18. Magnavox
19. Qua

Ironically, second-time VCR buyers could also become a blessing to the blank tape industry. Because they are regarded as educated consumers in the market, they are most likely to purchase advanced equipment, hence become prospects for high-grade tapes. Due to the increasing S-VHS and S-VHS-C market, high-grade tape sales, which grew by 20% in 1987, are expected to experience more growth in succeeding years.

VCR Market Growth

VCRs can now be obtained for less than $200; $1,000 less than the price in 1978. The VCR market has continued on an upward trend. By 1979, 4 years after Sony's introduction of Beta, approximately 1 million American households contained VCRs. By May 1985, VCR penetration was at 21% of U.S. television homes, far exceeding the 7% level that in the past has signaled the beginning of mass acceptance of other consumer electronic products. About 17 million VCRs were sold in 1984 to users in the United States, whereas retail sales were estimated by the Electronic Industries Association to be in excess of $6 billion. This rapid growth has been spurred by a steady decline in VCR prices that in turn has been the result of the strong competition present in the industry. As competition raged, the number of features increased—speed search with picture, wireless remote control, maximum record time of 6 to 8 hours, cable-ready, adjustable timers to record multiple programs over 7 or more days, built in hi-fi (stereo), and four recording heads, and so on.

As the VCR penetration increased so did the number of hardware manufacturers. In 1984, four additional companies joined the list of VCR manufacturers, bringing the total to 34. The top 10 manufacturers then and their respective current market share are listed in Table 8.1.

Although RCA has continued to dominate the VCR market right from its inception, both RCA and Panasonic showed substantial decreases in sales in 1984 over the previous year. The market shares lost by these two manufacturers were gained by several small brands such as Fisher, JVC, and Magnavox. The blank tape market is equally as spread out as the VCR market. The top-ranking blank tape manufacturers include those listed in Table 8.2.

TABLE 8.1
Top 10 VCR Manufacturers
and Current Market Share

RCA/Selectavision	20
Panasonic	16
Sony	9
Sanyo	6
Quasar	6
Fisher	6
Magnavox	6
JVC	5
Sears	5
AE	5

Continued rapid growth should be expected in the home video industry as sales continue to increase. Manufacturers will be able to lower prices due to economics of scale, on the one hand, and competition, on the other. Technological improvements on VCRs are now at a point of diminishing returns; improvements in video quality would probably be undetectable by most viewers, and very few consumers need a 30-day event adjustable time.[1] Price, therefore, will be the prime focus of competition.

Apart from price and the variety of features available, other factors that contribute to the increasing VCR penetration include:

- Taping programs off the air from network television including cable.
- Growth in available software and software outlets, allowing access to programs not presently available off air or on cable.
- Availability of over 15,000 titles on pre-recorded cassettes.

TABLE 8.2
Top-Ranking Blank Tape Manufacturers

TDK	21
Scotch	18
Memorex	13
Sony	12
Maxell	10
Polaroid	8
Fuji	8
BASF	6
Ampex	6
Kodak	6

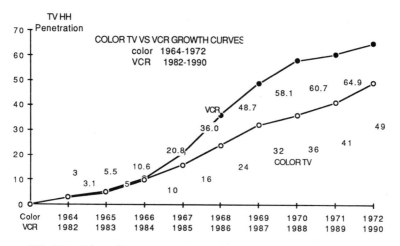

FIG. 8.1. Color television versus VCR growth curve. (*Source:* Television Digest [color television] VCR—author's projection.)

- Growing consumer awareness.
- Production of VCR better "human engineering" units that are easier to operate, thereby overcoming one source of consumer resistance.
- The prestige of VCR ownership.[2]

As color television improved and more programs were available, consumers embraced color as the new standard. The similarities between the growth curves of color television lend support for a similar projection for the VCR.

Although several analysts expect the growth of the VCR to level off sooner than did color television, it is likely that VCR will continue its increasing growth rate until it surpasses color television's 15-year growth level by 1990.

Following a normal product life cycle, beginning with the introduction, then growth, and maturity level of sales, VCR appears now to be in its growth phase. This is a period of rapid market acceptance.

VCR USAGE

The VCR user uses the equipment for four major purposes:

1. Recording for time-shifting.

2. Playingback of pre-recorded, rented, purchased, or borrowed tapes.
3. Recording for "library" retention.
4. Making and playing home movies.

Typically, most consumers use the VCR for either of the first two purposes. After time-shifting, the second reason given by VCR owners for purchasing their VCR is their ability to rent pre-recorded cassettes. The third reason was for "building videocassette libraries." This factor was predominant among heavy users (a category described by A.C. Nielsen as comprised mainly of women who record mostly daytime soap operas and movies), purchasers of blank tapes, and viewers in pay television homes.[3] A much smaller segment, 12% of VCR owners who own portable video cameras, use their equipment for home movie purposes. This application could expand with the introduction of the 8mm and VHS camcorders in the consumer market.[4]

Renting pre-recorded tapes constitutes a major part of the VCR activity. Recent VCR studies indicated that 83% of VCR owners have rented a pre-recorded cassette at one time or another. For the past 4 years, the videocassette rental market has been expanding to accommodate the increasing number of viewers. As discussed in chapter 11, Hollywood saw profits available, and leased rights, thereby increasing the variety of feature films available. The most rented program types were drama/mystery/suspense— with 31% of VCR households renting these, followed by comedy with 24%.

Unlike rental, only 27% of VCR households have ever purchased pre-recorded cassettes. Moreover, purchases have been decreasing, as only 3% of VCR households purchased one or more cassettes during an average month in 1984, as opposed to 5% in 1983. High prices, ability to borrow or rent tapes, and the fact that viewers watch video tapes only once or twice were given as the main reasons for not buying pre-recorded cassettes. However, when purchased, movies remained the most popular program type, whereas sales of exercise, instructional, and musical programs have increased.

High Fidelity VCR System

A recent major addition to the VCR has been its capability to produce stereophonic (hi-fi) sounds. The use of videocassette recorders for high fidelity audio recording and playback has been an important industry trend toward the integration of electronic home entertainment systems. The reality of this trend became evident when Sony Corporation of Tokyo equipped its Beta System with extra accessories, turning it into Beta Hi-fi. This was immediately followed by NEC Corporation, and lately all other VCR manufacturers have inaugurated similar versions of high-fidelity audio into their various systems.

Improved sound quality for VCRs have been desired by most users. As discussed earlier, "as the tape velocity becomes smaller according to the high density recording, the conventional fixed sound head gives poor quality sound and frequency response." Sound quality is greatly improved by recording the sound signals with rotary heads. Using this concept, VHS VCRs borrowed from the 8mm VCR system, the methods of utilizing FM sound multiplex that was developed and standardized in March 1983. However, because there is no vacant frequency band for sound signals, an initial problem involving compatibility was inevitable. This was later overcome with the introduction of the hi-fi VHS standard based on a multilayer recording method that was developed to record two different signals at different depths of a magnetic tape. Hi-fi VCR was therefore developed to realize two main goals:

1. Achieving high quality sound, better than hi-fi audio cassette deck.
2. Having complete compatibility with conventional VCRs.

In order to obtain high quality sound, a method coupling FM with a noise-reduction circuit utilizing unique compression and expansion were used to obtain the required high dynamic range of over 80 dB. Furthermore, the hi-fi VHS system uses rotary heads, therefore it is not affected by fluctuation of the tape speed. This resulted in Wow flutter characteristics that were superior when compared with an audio deck.

In order to ensure compatibility, the luminance signal was frequency modulated and the chrominance signal was down-converted by 629 KHz. There was therefore no vacant band for sound signals without cutting the luminance or chrominance band. Therefore, the new FM sound multiplex recording system utilized extra sound heads in addition to video heads. The video heads record the video the same way the conventional VCRs do, and the sound heads record the frequency modulated sound signals. The multilayer recording method enables interference between sound and video signals to be achieved. The sound head precedes the video head and records the sound signal deep in the magnetic layer. The video head erases the surface of the sound signal already recorded and records the video signal instead and thus the multilayer recording is achieved.[5]

From a marketing standpoint, the integration of video with audio is logical. With color television penetration over the 85% mark in Europe and North America (even higher in Japan), a phenomenon that continues to increase demand for VCRs, the desire to integrate television, VCR, and stereo components is imminent.

Therefore, the inclusion of hi-fi audio capability in VCRs is an important and strategic factor both for consumers whose new equipment supplies audio quality that is upgraded to audio system quality, and to the manufacturers whose appeal to the product is increased because of this new feature. Despite its importance, the inclusion of audio high fidelity does not add significant costs to the VCR production. In both Beta and VHS, the system is based on frequency modulation of the high frequency carrier, which television and VCR already use for their audio signals. FM signals are relatively immune to interfacing noises, so costly noise-protection circuitry does not have to be built in.

The videocassette recorder is not the first consumer electronic product to capture the consumer market with such a great intensity. The phonograph, radio, television (black and white), color television, and cable TV made different impressions in the home at different times in the history of consumer electronics. It is the cosmetics, functions, timeliness, and innovativeness of the VCR technology that makes it such a unique phenomenon in the home. Videocassette recorders have turned out to be the fastest growing home electronic systems in the U.S. history.

VCR MARKET PENETRATION

Sometime in 1987, the 50 millioneth VCR was shipped to a retail store. The buyer probably would not realize what significant part he or she has played in the history of this industry. But that single machine has gone down in history as the midpoint to winning the favor of all American television homes. For a high-tech gadget first introduced just 12 years ago, that is no small feat. Simply stated, with about 13.5 million units sold in 1987, 50% of all homes in the United States had a VCR in 1987. The surge in VCR penetration continues. As of February 1988, there are VCRs in 58% of all U.S. households containing TVs. Considering that there are 88.6 million households with television in the United States (98% of total U.S. homes), the total number of VCR households has increased to 51.5 million (58% of TV household). In 1980, the VCR was only 5 years old, and its penetration was just 1.1%. VCR growth has been remarkable (see Table 8.3).

When further broken down by demographics, county size A had the highest penetration at 59.1%. There were VCRs in 60.8% of television households in the pacific region (see Table 8.4).

For statistical purposes, A.C. Nielsen divides the country into counties. "A" Counties is defined as all counties belonging to the 25 largest metropolitan areas. Corresponding to the Standard Metropolitan Statistical Area

TABLE 8.3
VCR Households and Percent Penetration

	TV Households (000)	VCR Households (000)	% of TV Households
1975	68,500	—	—
1976	69,600	—	—
1977	71,200	—	—
1978	72,900	200	0.3
1979	74,500	400	0.5
1980	76,300	840	1.1
1981	79,900	1,440	1.8
1982	81,500	2,530	3.1
1983	83,300	4,580	5.5
1984	83,800	8,880	10.6
1985	84,900	17,600	20.8
1986	85,900	30,920	36.0
1987	87,400	42,560	48.7
1988	88,600	51,480	58.0

Source: VCR—A.C. Nielsen (NSI) February each year TVB
estimates prior to 1984
TV Households—A.C. Nielsen (NTI) January each
year

(SMSA), these counties include the largest cities and consolidated areas in the United States. "B" counties are smaller than "A." They have populations over 150,000 or are located in metropolitan areas of over 150,000 according to the latest census. "C" counties are under "A," and "B." They are all counties not included in "A" or "B," and are over 35,000 population, or in a metropolitan area having over 35,000 according to the latest census (see Tables 8.5 and 8.6).

The highest VCR penetration in the United States is in Anchorage, followed by Fairbanks, Alaska, which has 78% and 76.2% respectively. On the other hand, Laredo has the lowest penetration at 39.1% (see Table 8.7).

TABLE 8.4
VCR Penetration by Demographics

By County Size	Nov. 1986	Nov. 1987
A	50.1%	59.1%
B	41.9	52.1
C	38.7	49.2
D	31.9	42.0

TABLE 8.5
VCR Penetration by Territory

Territory	Nov. 1986	Nov. 1987
Northeast	47.7%	51.1%
East Central	37.4	49.4
West Central	40.9	50.8
South	39.6	49.1
Pacific	52.2	60.8

Contrary to forecasts by some pessimists in the industry, VCRs will continue to record a strong growth through 1996 (see Table 8.8). The key to this growth will depend on continued production of state-of-the-art and innovative VCRs, and availability of high quality programmings.

VCR EQUIPMENT SALES

Since 1987 there has been mass publicity about the new generation of video equipment. Unquestionably, these are the type of hardware that will lead the VCR industry into the 21st century. Much has been written in this text about such high technology equipment as the HDTV, S-VHC Camcorders, Ed Beta, and 8mm Hi-Band. For the average video enthusiast and innovator, this list of video equipment means a renewed confidence in the industry. The impact of these high tech products however, will not be immediate in the market.

VCR Sales

Since January 1988, production and sales of most video hardware including the VCR deck has dropped by 20% when compared against 1987 (see Table

TABLE 8.6
VCR Penetration by Market Size

	Nov. 1986	Nov. 1987
1–10	52.1%	60.7%
11–20	43.2	52.5
21–50	40.9	51.4
51–100	38.2	48.5
100+	36.6	47.4

Source: A.C. Nielsen (NSI)

TABLE 8.7		TABLE 8.7	
November 1987 VCR Penetration by Market		(Continued)	
Abilene-Sweetwater	40.2	Clarksburg-Weston	37.7
Ada-Ardmore	43.0	Cleveland, Akron	52.9
Albany, GA	50.1	Colorado Springs-Pueblo	53.2
Albany-Schenectady-Troy	51.4	Columbia, SC	47.2
Albuquerque-Santa Fe	47.4	Columbia-Jefferson City	43.6
Alexandria, LA	47.7	Columbus, GA	38.7
Alexandria, MN	34.9	Columbus, OH	48.7
Alpena	32.7	Columbus-Tupelo-West Point	37.9
Amarillo	50.4	Corpus Christi	46.7
Anchorage	76.8	Dallas-FT Worth	59.9
Atlanta	56.5	Davenport-R. Island-Moline	47.4
Augusta	45.0	Dayton	46.6
Austin	51.7	Denver	55.4
Bakersfield	52.5	Des Moines-Ames	42.7
Baltimore	59.9	Detroit	52.6
Bangor	50.2	Dothan	44.0
Baton Rouge	48.3	Duluth-Superior	41.9
Beaumont-Port Arthur	49.0	El Paso	47.1
Beckley-Bluefield-Oak Hill	39.9	Elmira	46.5
Bend, OR	53.1	Erie	38.2
Billings	47.9	Eugene	54.0
Biloxi-Gulfport	46.9	Eureka	54.9
Binghamton	47.3	Evansville	46.1
Birmingham, Anniston	44.9	Fairbanks	70.0
Boise	45.4	Fargo-Valley City	35.1
Boston	57.0	Flint-Saginaw-Bay City	54.3
Bowling Green	38.5	Florence, SC	38.9
Buffalo	46.0	Fresno-Visalia	57.3
Burington-Plattsburgh	48.6	FT. Myers-Naples	46.5
Butte	43.6	FT. Smith	43.8
Casper-Riverton	51.1	FT. Wayne	54.3
Cedar Rapids-Waterloo & DUBQ	44.9	Gainesville	47.3
Champaign & Springfld-Decatur	48.4	Glendive	38.3
Charleston, SC	53.1	Grand Junction-Montrose	52.1
Charleston-Huntington	45.6	Grand Rapids-Kalmzoo-B.CRK	49.1
Charlotte	47.6	Great Falls	45.8
Chattanooga	53.8	Green Bay-Appleton	50.7
Cheyenne-Scottsbluff	51.1	Greensboro-H. Point-W. Salem	44.7
Chicago	61.6	Greenville-N. Bern-Washngtn	44.5
Chico-Redding	56.4	Greenwood-Greenville	37.5
Cincinnati	48.4	Harlingen-Weslaco-Brnsville	37.5

TABLE 8.7
(*Continued*)

TABLE 8.7
(*Continued*)

Harrisburg-Lncstr-Leb-York	51.3	Minot-Bismarck-Dickinson	41.4
Harrisonburg	42.4	Missoula	38.0
Hartford & New Haven	57.1	Mobile-Pensacola	56.2
Hattiesburg-Laurel	50.2	Monroe-El Dorado	42.7
Helena	51.7	Monterey-Salinas	62.9
Honolulu	58.7	Montgomery	47.4
Houston	56.7	Nashville	43.1
Huntsville-Decatur	52.4	New Orleans	51.6
Idaho Falls-Pacatello	51.6	New York	62.3
Jackson, MS	43.3	Norfolk-Portsmth-Nwpt NWS	51.2
Jackson, TN	42.8	North Platte	42.9
Jacksonville	49.9	Odessa-Midland	52.3
Johnstown-Altoona	41.7	Oklahoma City	49.9
Jonesboro	34.3	Orlando-Daytona Bch-Melbrn	48.6
Hoplin-Pittsburg	44.5	Ottumwa-Kirksville	34.1
Kansas City	49.9	Paducah-C. Girardeau-Harrbg	40.8
Knoxville	44.3	Palm Springs	55.4
La Croose-Eau Claire	47.0	Panama City	56.8
LaFayette, LA	53.2	Parkersburg	51.0
Lake Charles	46.6	Peoria-Bloomington	50.2
Lansing	53.4	Philadelphia	57.9
Laredo	33.6	Phoenix	56.9
Las Vegas	65.8	Pittsburg	46.1
Lexington	47.4	Portland, OR	55.6
Lima	41.3	Portland-Auburn	51.9
Lincoln & Hstings-Krny Plus	37.2	Presque Isle	50.3
Little Rock-Pine Bluff	42.7	Providence-New Bedford	53.1
Los Angeles	64.3	Quincy-Hannibal-Keokuk	37.0
Louisville	50.1	Releigh-Durban	47.9
Lubbock	48.9	Rapid City	43.3
Macon	50.3	Reno	64.1
Madison	45.3	Richmond-Petrsbg. Charltsvl	47.9
Mankato	32.6	Roanoke-Lynchburg	43.6
Marquette	41.6	Rochester	50.9
Mason City-Austin-Rochestr	43.9	Rockford	57.6
Medford-Klamath Falls	51.5	Sacramento-Stockton	63.8
Memphis	43.6	Salisbury	62.9
Meridian	33.8	Salt Lake City	60.3
Miami-Ft. Lauderdale	49.3	San Angelo	48.3
Milwaukee	52.7	San Antonio	51.6
Minneapolis-St Paul	54.3	San Diego	63.9

TABLE 8.7
(*Continued*)

San Francisco-Oakland	63.8
Santa Barbara-Sanmar-Sanluob	58.1
Savannah	50.3
Seattle-Tacoma	57.5
Shreveport	45.1
Sioux City	36.3
Sioux Falls (Mitchell)	32.7
South Bend-Elkhart	50.8
Spokane	50.4
Springfield, MO	54.1
St. Joseph	45.2
St. Louis	51.9
Syracuse	49.7
Tallahassee-Thomasville	46.0
Tampa-St. Pete, Sarasota	45.1
Terre Haute	44.3
Toledo	56.4
Topeka	50.0
Traverse City-Cadillac	45.0
Tri-Cities, TN-VA	46.3
Tucson (Nogales)	53.0
Tulsa	47.5
Twin Falls	44.1
Tyler	45.2
Utica	40.2
Victoria	54.9
Waco-Temple	51.8
Washington, DC	59.5
Watertown	48.2
Wausau-Rhinelander	44.3
West Palm Beach-FT. Pierce	49.4
Whelling-Steaubenville	46.9
Wichita Falls & Lawton	44.3
Wichita-Hutchinson Plus	44.1
Wilkes Barre-Scranton	40.3
Wilmington	42.6
Yakima	52.4
Youngstown	45.3
Yuma-El Centro	46.6
Zanesville	51.4

Source: A.C. Nielsen (NSI)

TABLE 8.8
VCR Households Projections to 1996

	TV Households (000)	VCR Households (000)	% of TV Households
1989	89,500	54,300	60.7
1990	90,500	58,770	64.9
1991	91,500	61,620	67.3
1992	92,500	63,620	68.8
1993	93,500	65,470	70.0
1994	94,500	67,800	71.7
1995	95,500	70,570	73.9
1996	96,500	73,710	76.45

Source: Paul Kegan Associates

8.9). This trend is supposed to continue, but rather very mild as long as the yen remains stronger than the dollars, thereby increasing the average cost of a VCR in the United States. Also, as a result of a decline in Japanese export, VCR production fell 9.5% to 30.65 million in 1987.

The Electronics Industries Association estimates that 11.9 million VCRs valued at $3.57 billion were shipped in 1987. Production for 1988 puts it at 11.9 million units and $3.51 billion.

VCR OWNERSHIP

In 1987, growth in VCR ownership dropped by 47%. An estimated 8.1 million consumers purchased their first VCRs in 1987, just over half of 15.3

TABLE 8.9
Comparison of Sales—VCR Against Other Home Electronic Systems

Product	March 1988	March 1987	% Change	March 1986
Total Home VCR	997,373	1,025,596	− 2.8	1,030,373*
Decks	880,713	948,453	− 7.1	973,262*
Camcorders	116,550*	77,143	+51.2	57,111
Total TV	1,927,143	1,979,747	− 2.7	1,874,431
Total Color	1,741,749	1,733,182	+ 0.5	1,629,540
Direct-View	1,718,993*	1,710,779	+ 0.5	1,604,668
Projection	22,156	22,403	− 1.1	24,872*
Monochrome	208,150	268,968	−22.5	244,891
TV excl. Project	1,927,143	1,979,747	− 2.7	1,849,559

*Record for any March
Source: Video Week, April 18, 1988

million first-time buyers in 1986. This was in turn a sharp reversal from 1988 when new VCR ownership rose 72% from 8.9 million.

More consumers are purchasing replacement or second VCRs. Particularly, most consumers who already own VCR decks are buying a significant number of camcorders.

VCR SOFTWARE

Pre-Recorded Cassettes

The Electronic Industries Association estimates that sales of pre-recorded cassettes was 110 million units amounting to $2.77 billion in 1987. It is also predicted that a growth of 18.2%, or 130 million units, estimated at $2.99 billion will be experienced in 1988.

Availability of program source is a vital organ in the VCR market. Of all program sources, 15 recorded shares of 1% and above in 1987 (see Table 8.10). In preceding years CBS/FOX has led the industry as top pre-recorded cassette supplier, however, in 1987, Paramount toppled CBS/FOX. Current wholesale shipments excluding budget and adult labels is at $2.3 billion, a 15% growth over the previous year.

TABLE 8.10
1987 Market Shares (dollars in million)

	1987		1986	
	% Share	$ Share	% Share	$ Sales
1. Paramount	12.8	294	11.0	220
2. CBS/Fox	10.0	230	13.7	275
3. Warner	9.1	212	8.5	170
4. Disney	8.9	205	8.2	164
5. RCA/Columbia	7.8	179	9.2	184
6. HBO	6.6	152	6.4	128
7. Vestron	6.4	147	8.0	160
8. Heron	5.5	127	3.4	68
9. MCA	5.3	122	7.1	142
10. Lorimar	4.7	108	3.4	68
11. MGM/UA	4.3	99	7.5	150
12. Nelson	3.7	85	3.4	68
13. New World	3.0	69	2.4	48
14. Ive	1.4	32	1.8	36
15. Prism	1.0	23	1.2	24
Cinema Group	1.0	23	—	—
All others	8.5	196	4.8	96

Source: Video Week, January 4, 1988

TABLE 8.11
Price Levels on Prerecorded Cassette Sales

	1987	1986
$80–$90	32.0%	N/A
$60–$80	27.4	58.3%
$40–$60	1.7	4.2
$30–$40	1.7	4.5
$20–$30	14.1	16.2
$10–$20	18.1	12.6
Under $10	5.0	4.2

Source: Video Week, January 11, 1988

Most of the growth is credited rackjobbers, direct sales, and mail-order channels. This, however, does not bode well with small labels with limited overhead. Major titles generated more than $400 million in wholesale revenue, about 17% of entire market in 1987, while rental cassettes produced $242.2 million.

Price Polarization

The sale price of an average pre-recorded video has always been alarming to consumers (see Table 8.11). Most box office hits released on videocassettes would cost about $86. This in turn makes it almost impossible for an average consumer to purchase it. The industry on the other hand prefers this high price, and seems to be profiting through high price rather than sales volume. Thirty-two percent of revenues from pre-recorded cassette sales are from those sold at the $89.96 price level. Paramount occasionally promotes its labels by offering them at special discount prices of about $20 to $30.

Rentals

A typical videocassette rental outlet now offers about 2,500 titles—a marked increased over 1985 level of 2,000. Although these stores are a vital part of the VCR industry, most are poorly organized. As with any rapidly growing industry, most rental outlets have gone out of business as fast as they were started. Arrangements of titles are grossly ignored by some stores, whereas others thrive on poor quality and illegally duplicated tapes. Range of selection varies from store to store, and store owners tend to focus more on new releases rather than on well-stocked libraries. This accounts for the sluggish pace of availability of pre-recorded titles among half of the households with VCRs. Often, rental stores offer low budget films that cater to

TABLE 8.12
Estimated Distribution of Prerecorded Tape
Sales/Rentals by Genre: 1986–1987

"Adult"	10
Children	10
Action-adventure	18
Comedy	17
Drama	13
Horror	11
Sci-Fi	7
Classics	3
Foreign	1
Music video	2
Sports/fitness	3
Other	5

Source: Media Matters, August 1987

specialized audiences such as science fiction, Kung fu, adult films, and the like. Feature and children films account for a significant portion of the market. Adult films have grown to be an important segment of the market whose target is mainly the middle class category (see Table 8.12).

Price increases on theatrical films will continue (see Table 8.13 for the top sellthrough and rental titles, 1987). Therefore, more VCR owners will turn to rentals rather than purchasing their programs. A $99 price tag on a title will be prevalent, encouraging revenues. Of all revenues received by program owners, about 59%–60% comes from rental releases listing for $60 and above. It is predicted that by 1989, the average title will be released at $99.95.

TABLE 8.13
Top Sellthrough and Rental Titles, 1987

Top Sellthrough Titles	Units 0	List	Wholesale $$ (millions)	Retail $$ (millions)	Box Office (millions)	VTR*
Top Gun (Paramount)	2,850	$26.95	$48.30	$76.80	$177.50	$43.20
Lady & The Tramp (Disney)	2,000	$29.95	$37.70	$59.90	—	—
Crocodile Dundee (Paramount)	1,800	$29.95	$33.90	$53.90	$176.00	$30.60
Star Trek IV (Paramount)	1,500	$29.95	$28.30	$44.90	$111.00	$40.40
American Tail	800	$29.95	$15.00	$23.90	$ 46.00	$52.10

TABLE 8.13
(Continued)

Top Rental Titles 1987	Units 0	List	Wholesale $$ (millions)	Retail $$ (millions)	Box Office (millions)	VTR*
Platoon (HBO)	350	$99.95	$22.00	$35.00	$138.00	$25.30
Karate Kid II (RCA/Columbia)	300	$79.95	$14.80	$23.90	$115.00	$20.70
Lethal Weapon (Warner)	280	$89.95	$15.80	$25.10	$ 65.00	$38.60
Dirty Dancing (Vestron)	280	$89.98	$15.90	$25.20	$ 50.00	$50.40
Golden Child (Paramount)	275	$79.95	$13.80	$21.90	$ 80.50	$27.20
Color Purple (Warner)	265	$89.95	$15.00	$23.80	$ 97.50	$24.40
Back to School (HBO)	260	$79.95	$13.00	$20.70	$ 91.00	$22.80
Aliens (CBS/Fox)	250	$89.95	$13.90	$22.50	$ 79.00	$28.40
Secret of My Success (MCA)	240	$89.95	$13.40	$21.60	$ 67.00	$32.20
Peggy Sue Got Married (CBS/Fox)	235	$89.95	$13.30	$21.10	$ 44.50	$47.40
Ferris Bueller's Day Off (Paramount)	230	$79.95	$11.40	$18.30	$ 71.00	$25.70
Heartbreak Ridge (Warner)	225	$89.95	$12.70	$20.20	$ 43.50	$46.40
Color of Money (Touchstone)	220	$89.95	$12.40	$19.97	$ 52.50	$37.50
Outrageous Fortune (Touchstone)	220	$89.95	$12.50	$19.80	$ 53.00	$37.30
Stand By Me (RCA/Columbia)	210	$89.95	$11.70	$18.90	$ 53.00	$35.60
Roxanne (RCA/Columbia)	200	$89.95	$11.30	$18.00	$ 41.00	$48.80
Nightmare on Elm Street II (Media)	200	$89.95	$11.30	$18.00	$ 44.50	$40.20
3 Amigos (HBO)	200	$89.95	$11.30	$18.00	$ 39.50	$45.60
Ruthless People (Touchstone)	200	$79.95	$10.00	$16.00	$ 72.50	$22.00

*Video Theatrical Rating = Percentage of theatrical retail sales achieved at video retail level.
Source: Video Week, January 4, 1988

Videodisc Systems

*I*n the 1920s the dominant instrument for recording sound was the phonograph. It was therefore not surprising that when the question of recording television signals was posed, the first system thought of at the time was identical to that used for recording sound on phonographic recorders.

Introduced in the 1920s, recording television signals by disc was tried several times in succeeding decades. Its importance resurfaced in the 1960s after Ampex's success in videotape recording technology had created needs for expansion into other areas of video recording.

Experiments on magnetic disc continued from Baird's pioneering attempt in 1927 with no apparent success until the mid-1960s when Ampex Corporation made a breakthrough in videodisc technology. Until then, most video manufacturers' long-range product development plans involved the videotape recording concept.

In July 1965, the MVR Corporation of Palo Alto, California, introduced a single-frame videodisc recorder at a meeting of the SMPTE in San Francisco. This system recorded video signals up to 600 single frames on a magnetic disc. Any of the frames could be erased, replayed, or replayed instantly.

MVR later built the model VDR-210CF videodisc for CBS according to specifications in August 1965. This system was used by CBS to record and playback action highlights of football games on CBS Television Network. The unit, which weighed 40 pounds, recorded segments of the action that was then replayed in regular motion, or stopped motion to provide "freeze action" shots. This unit set a stage for other such systems used by other networks.[1]

In 1966, ABC contacted Ampex and requested a system capable of slow speed instant replay of significant moments in sports action for their popular "Wide World of Sports." Ampex decided against the use of magnetic tape in such a venture because repetitive scans during slow motion would cause tape deterioration. A magnetic disc was recommended instead because it would withstand numerous head exposures. The development team tried a new medium—the magnetic metal disc. John Poole, the head of the engineering team for the project, was an authority on the magnetic disc, having managed the development of a metal disc buffer for Ampex's Videofile Information System.

Ampex then developed the HS-100. The disc revolved at 1,800 rpm. During recording or playback, a series of recording heads travelled radially across the disc frame a few thousandths of an inch above the magnetic platter, making 30 tracks per second for normal television. During slow motion, the speed at which the head travelled was reduced to less than 30 tracks per second, as the disc spinned at its 1,800 rpm rate, while during stop motion, the head stopped entirely as the disc continued to revolve.[2] ABC made its first broadcast with this stop-action and instant replay system in March 1967, and the HS-100 became the foundation for its sports coverage from the late-1960s.

The Ampex HS-100 also triggered a new group of products; for example, the HS-200 was a recording system for teleproduction and the DR-10 was used for educational purposes, x-ray technology, and scientific experimentation.

Many manufacturers were encouraged by the prospects evident in videodisc technology as seen in the early 1960s, but most ended up with failures.

Sony announced two videodisc machines in March 1966. Both machines used plastic discs to record and playback monochrome motion pictures and still pictures in color. "Videomat" recorded monochrome pictures for instant playback and contained a camera, lights, discs, and a 19-inch television set. The "video color demonstrator" recorded up to 40 color still pictures on the disc for playback over a standard television monitor. The picture could be erased or repeated as desired.

In 1978, Sony announced further developments on laser-based and optical videodisc systems, and in September 1979 agreed to exchange patents with Philips. But on October 25, 1979, Sony issued a statement, strongly doubting the ability of the videodisc to make any impact on the video market, and Sony thereby withdrew from the videodisc venture.

However, experiments on videodisc systems continued in the 1970s as more companies were convinced that discs would play a major role in the growing home video market. Although their predictions were not correct, many organizations researched and demonstrated newer varieties of videodisc systems, which were not only for commercial purposes but also for home consumers. The major advantage of the videodisc in the home context was its capability of easy and inexpensive replication process. During the 1970s, a major transition from magnetic disc to mechanical and optical disc was evident.

During the 1970s, more VDPs were introduced, including the Teldec (mechanical), Philip (optical), and MCA (optical). After about 15 years of research on videodisc technology, RCA finally commercially introduced its "RCA SelectaVision" (based on Teldec's mechanical disc process) on March 22, 1981.[3] The SelectaVision, a CED format, had a 60-minute playing time on each side based on its 12-inch diameter discs that revolved at 450 rpm.[4] The addition of an FM encoding function enabled it to produce stereo sound. The disc was made of plastic and had 10,000 grooves to the inch. Various models were capable of such effects as visual search, forward, and reverse scanning of programs and rapid access (via a digital time indicator) of desired program segments. The player contained a pause button. The picture and sound were transmitted through a diamond stylus running along the grooved disc. The complete unit weighed about 20 pounds.

RCA made a total investment of about $150 million before releasing its SelectaVision. It also budgeted $30 million for advertising and promotion and signed a number of companies to its licensing agreement.

Initially included were Zenith, J.C. Penny, Montgomery Ward, Sears, Sanyo, Toshiba, Hitachi, Sharp, Nippon Electric of Japan, and Radio Shack. Under a nonexclusive licensing agreement, CBS was to produce videodisc software for the system.

Further programming agreements with Paramount Pictures, United Artists, and Walt Disney Productions among others, involving about 1,000 titles were also signed.

RCA officials claimed that "the machine would make home movie-watching as common as listening to rock records." Unfortunately, there was a major drawback in videodisc's success. The VCR was a direct threat. VCRs not only allowed viewers to play a movie but also enabled them to tape whatever they desired. The videodisc, on the other hand only had playback ability. When RCA launched its videodisc player in 1981, sales of 200,000 players were projected by the end of the year; however, not more than 100,000 players were actually sold. Although a technological success for RCA, SelectaVision was an economic disaster. By 1984, RCA was offering the units at low prices. More problems were created when Hitachi undercut RCA's price (which was over $500) by $200.

By early April 1984, when RCA withdrew from the videodisc market, it was selling players for $199. All told, RCA had lost about $580 million on the project.

Many other companies were involved in the videodisc market. Several manufacturers failed due to technological problems; others were affected

FIG. 9.1. Pioneer LaserDisc Model LD-W1.

economically. Although most consumers still prefer VCRs to videodiscs, some videodisc manufacturers still persist in their continued presence in the market. RCA, for example, does not rule out manufacturing videodiscs made with a different technology base. Victor Company of Japan (JVC) blames RCA for its failure in the videodisc market claiming that "RCA's problem was that they tried to compete with VCR, and focused on one function—playback." Many videodisc players were equipped with random access, which is vital to many industrial and commercial applications—for example video catalogue stores or training aids in industry. Random access

FIG. 9.2. Pioneer LaserDisc Model CLD-1010.

FIG. 9.3. Sony AV Laser. Sony's MDP-200 Laser player offers up to 425 lines of horizontal resolution and can be programmed for up to 16 different videodisc chapter of 99 music selections. It has two drives systems: one turns the spindle for 3-inch and 5-inch CD-videos; while the other turns the spindle for 8- and 12-inch laser vision discs. (*Source:* Courtesy, Sony Corporation of America, Park Ridge, NJ.)

is also important to some home applications such as educational materials for both adults and children. Therefore, JVC contended that its "videodisc player was not an alternative to VCRs, but an addition." It claimed that 80% of the people who buy its videodisc already owned a VCR. With the introduction of Video High Density (VHD), which permitted random access, still frames and a variety of slow and fast speeds in forward and reverse, JVC was optimistic of its videodisc product line.

Special advantages of the VDP player include its ability to store vast amounts of still-frame images (over 54,000 video images per side), quick access to program segments made possible by its radial disc design, continuous playing for a long period without deterioration in playback quality, fool-proof devices for privacy, and interactive programming and data storage application capabilities.

VIDEODISC INTERACTIVE CAPABILITIES

However, some experts nonetheless see the optical videodisc's future in producing "interactive" programs due to a major distinction of disc's radial design that allows rapid movement between any two points on the disc's surface—without moving through every point in between as is necessary with tape. Interactive capabilities of videodisc are already being taken advantage of by industrial and governmental organizations. Discs are used frequently by commercial establishments for training purposes and merchandising. Corporations such as the big three United States automobile makers use interactive discs to provide pictures and specifications of new cars for both salespeople and potential customers. Other companies such as IBM and Apple Computers are among the growing list of manufacturers using discs for product service training, demonstrations, marketing instructions, and point-of-sale support. The Defense Department is one of the major users of videodisc programs used to attract new recruits.

There are many other applications of the videodiscs especially for industrial purposes. For instance, Panasonic has perfected a system whereby information is recorded and stored on videodiscs and used for editing as well as library functions. An on-going research project at the Maryland Center for Public Broadcasting is testing the possibility of broadcasting directly from disc input. A general concensus in the industry is that the random access capabilities and relative hardiness of the disc medium is superior to tape in such direct broadcasting applications. Laser-based optical videodisc disc systems are currently the most durable of all audio-visual storage media with a suggested life of 600 years.

Despite the videodisc's current disappointing performance in the market, some industry experts are predicting an optimistic future due to the prospect of connecting videodisc with home computers. The benefits to be received from this are twofold: providing video content for microcomputer applications and storing digitally encoded data or programming. However, the likelihood of such a system is remote in view of the fact that home computer has already passed its saturation point with only a meagre penetration while videodisc is all but extinct.

Nevertheless, in 1979 MCA and IBM formed a partnership that handled disc production and industrial marketing. This partnership was known as DiscoVision Associates, and it assumed the half interest in the Universal Pioneer venture that had been held by MCA DiscoVision.

Portable Video Recorders

*T*he roots of portable video recorders lie in the development of the helical-scan system. Helical-scan technology contributed immensely to the reduction in size of most video recording equipment. It was the helical technique that made it feasible for videotape manufacturers to diversify into the home consumer market.

From the same helical technology (discussed in chapter 7), a new generation of light-weight (portable) equipment was heralded into the broadcast and home markets. Beginning from the mid- to late-1960s, the changes in shape and sizes of various video recording apparatuses were evident. The first commercial videotape recording machine (VR-1000) manufactured by Ampex weighed 1,350 pounds (console only) and required a floor space of about 89 square feet, whereas the typical portable recorder (the VR-303) manufactured by the same company weighed only 95 pounds and could be carried. Later portable broadcast units such as the Sony BVH-500 and BVU-50 weighed even less at 37 and 14 pounds respectively.

Today, portable video recorders are not only used for broadcast purposes, but they also have industrial and home functions. The broadcast industry in particular has a serious need for light-weight tape recorders for on-location assignments such as sports and emergency news coverage. The advent of helical-scan portables met those needs.

This chapter examines broadcast industry's need for portables and traces their history briefly back to the helical technology that made them possible. Some important types of portables produced to date, including the electronic news gathering (ENG) are examined.

A portable video recorder, as examined in this chapter, is one that weighs no more than 100 pounds. Its features include full portability in size and weight for on-location use and broadcast stability and acceptability. The recent development of consumer portable systems is also discussed.

PORTABLE VIDEO RECORDING EQUIPMENT

In December 1962, Ampex introduced its first portable videotape recording machine. Designated the VR-1500, it weighed only 96 pounds. It was the second helical system manufactured by Ampex (the first being the ill-fated VR-8000). Therefore, it was nicknamed "Junior." In the same year, an improved version of the machine was produced and an additional portable model was also introduced. The two models, VR-1500 and VR-660, were nearly identical portable recorders. Both machines recorded and reproduced sound and picture with good fidelity.[1] They used standard 2-inch tape, resulted in less expensive operation costs, and were capable of recording from one or more television cameras or off-the-air signals.

The VR-660 was designed for broadcast use. Its picture quality (acceptable at the time), compact size, and rugged construction led to television network applications in on-location remote coverage. The VR-1500 was identical in appearance to the VR-660 but was specifically designed for closed-circuit television applications. Features available in both machines included broadcast stability, stop motion, complete 2-channel audio editing capability, full portability in size and weight for on-location use, complete tape interchangeability among other forthcoming Ampex portables, minimum maintenance, long tape life, and ability to withstand rugged, continuous day-to-day use.

Both machines weighed 100 pounds and could be operated on a standard household current of 115 volts AC. Both the VR-660 and VR-1500 were utilized in a variety of ways including teacher training and coverage of specialized research and experiments in schools, colleges, and universities; on-the-job training; management communications; process and quality control; plant security and surveillance; advertising agency commercials and program review; motion picture production quality control and review, entertainment in commerce and industry; flight simulation, surveillance, reconnaissance, security, military training and radar recording in defense; medical and dental training and research in medicine and dentistry; training programs, briefings and information services, examination and testing; criminal investigations; and security and air traffic safety in government.

In March 1965, Ampex announced another portable videotape recorder called the VR-303. This system was a direct response to England's Telcan, which was introduced in 1963 by two English technicians. The VR-303 was a longitudinal scan machine with a fixed head and used $\frac{1}{2}$-inch tape. It could only record up to 50 minutes of program material on a $12\frac{1}{2}$-inch reel and was designed to be used by nontechnical personnel with minimal instructions. This system was short-lived.

The 1967 Ampex VR-3000 was regarded as a professional portable videotape recorder that out-performed other existing portable systems. Weighing only 35 pounds, the system was a combination of videotape and camera. For the first time, a battery was incorporated into the machine. The VR-3000 was capable of recording on either high-band or low-band monochrome tape that could be played on any standard transverse recorder. It also registered high-band color from studio color cameras with no modification. The machine recorded on 20 minutes reels. The accompanying camera weighed 13 pounds and used a Plumbicon tube.[2]

Next, the VR-3000B was introduced. It was special because it boasted an attached time base corrector improving image stability and making full color location playback an option for the first time. A compact 55-pound unit, the VR-3000B was available in NTSC, PAL, or SECAM color standards. In action, the camera operator recorded continuously or intermittently, rewound the tape, and monitored it on the camera viewfinder or on an external monitor.[3] These were features that were seldom available on systems at the time. An automatic backup and restart logic that put recorded segments immediately next to each other on the tape was also available in the unit. With standard carrying case, AC power, an optional two battery system, and a backpack rack, the unit was self-contained.

The advantages of light-weight videotape recorders in the 1960s resulted in the introduction of portable systems by many video hardware manufacturing companies, but most early portables did not measure up to broadcast standards. These machines, although called portables, were often very bulky and almost impossible to carry around. For example, in June 1962, Machtronics Inc. introduced a portable helical-scan system called the Model MVR-10, the world's first commercial 1-inch VTR. The machine weighed 90 pounds, used a 1-inch wide tape, was transistorized, and had a recording time of 90 minutes.[4] Late in the same year, the Model MVR-11 appeared. This was a more advanced machine that weighed only 65 pounds due to the elimination of the self-contained monitor that was a part of the MVR-10. In 1963, the MVR-15 was introduced. It was claimed that it had broadcast capability although there was no evidence of that.[5]

Other important portables that paved the way for modern day systems included Westel Company's Model WRC-150 in 1964, a portable television camera and backpack. Westel was established by Alex Maxey who was on the VR-1000 development team at Ampex.[6] RCA developed the TR-10. Sony's contribution to portable systems was outstanding utilizing the U-matic system.[7] Sony's BVH-500, a 1-inch video recorder was frequently interchanged with the Sony BV-1000 production recorder for excellent professional results.

THE ENG

Backpacked or hand-held cameras were used by networks to cover political conventions as early as 1952 in the United States. However, it would take 20 years before the broadcast industry would have available a light-weight videotape camera and video recording equipment capable of transmitting information between location and studio instantaneously.

ENG was specifically developed for the economic advantages of cost and speed (film was expensive and slow in relation to most needs of modern television news department).[8] ENG was first demonstrated at the Society of Motion Picture and Television Engineers (SMPTE) meeting in Washington, DC, in 1971. ENG equipment also had an ideological function: to give the impression of bringing the audience into direct contact with events. News gatherers hoped to reduce significantly the time between the occurrence of an event and the audience's ability to become "witnesses."

In 1968, CBS Laboratories introduced a light-weight camera that a news-camera operator could carry on one shoulder, connected directly to a network switching or recording system. This portable camera was known as the Mark VI Minicam, a 45-pound unit consisting of camera, lens, and other electronic news gathering accessories. Describing what might comprise a typical ENG system, a correspondent reporting from the NAB panel meeting in April 1975 stated:

A miniature camera, often of foreign manufacture (Ikegami or Fernseh at the top of the line, Akai or Sony in more modest configurations), coupled with a portable tape recorder (almost always a helical-scan unit, and frequently Sony's three-quarter-inch cassette, IVC's one-inch reel-to-reel or Akai's one-quarter-inch model), operated by a three-person crew (two technicians and a reporter) out of a suburban van or panel truck equipped with a top-mounted microwave dish. Signals are beamed back to a prominent landmark at mid-city, atop which four "horns" have been placed to pick up signals from all points of the compass. At the studio, tapes are edited on A and B machines (the Sony VO-2850 is in common use, along with its command unit, the RN-400) to transfer selected segments from original to final form. (SMPTE time codes are applied to the tape before editing to assist in accomplishing this step.) Signals are passed through a time base corrector (CVS and Television Microtime are prominent pioneers in the field) to meet FCC standards for broadcast quality. Edited news segments may go directly to air at that point, or be transferred to two-inch tape "casts" for random insertion into newscasts.[9]

Much portable equipment already used in the industry was later equipped to work as ENG machines once the technology was introduced. Sony System's VO-3800 and its accompanying editing machine, the VO-2850, were specific examples. Other ENG equipment included BVU-100 and BVU-50, produced by Sony and a major force in the development of the technology that made ENG possible. The BVU-100 used Sony's ¾-inch U-matic videocassettes; which eliminated problems formerly associated with handling, threading, and storing videotapes. The BVU-100 produced broadcast quality pictures due to a re-design in Sony's former circuitry. It weighed 30 pounds with batteries and had a record/playback time of 20 minutes. BVU-100 worked hand-in-hand with the BVU-200 studio editing recorder that employed a framing servo that insured stable professional editing. An additional longitudinal track was added to the BVU-100 to accommodate the SMPTE time code. Apart from the BVU-200, the BVU-100 could also be used with the BVP-100 3-plumbicon video color camera, which was ideal for both ENG and studio use, the BVE-500 studio editing console designed for use with the BVU-200, and finally with the BVT-1000 Digital Time Base Corrector, which allowed for broadcasting directly from U-matic videocassettes while holding the video lock even through wider error excursions.[10]

The BVU-50 was another in the series of Sony U-matic portable ENG machines. Developed as a sister machine to the BVU-100, it offered full interchangeability with any standard U-matic recorder or player. Weighing under 50 pounds, it offered easy handling and operational efficiency.

Commercial Use of ENG Equipment

All three networks were busy working at miniaturizing their equipment, to be used primarily for political conventions. The idea was to put a correspondent on the floor, backed up by a live television camera, without problems of weight or being tied to the heavy cables that were normal at the time. The result of this competition among stations and the ideology force of giving the viewers apparent instant access to events was the switch to electronic news gathering, which began in earnest after the 1972 political season. New and more sophisticated equipment included high quality portable cameras. Videotape recorders were improved remarkably and bulky cables gave way to lighter ones or eliminated by substitute short-range transmitters.

In 1972, Ikegami introduced an experimental electronic camera that weighed 34 pounds. The industry was still in need of a standard portable VTR that was capable of meeting the needs of modern day broadcasting. Most television stations were using Sony's ¾-inch U-matic helical-scan VTR that was introduced for consumer and industrial use. At the same time Panasonic introduced a ½-inch VCR called "cartridge vision" to the consumer and industrial market. In 1973, Consolidated Video Systems (now known as Harris Video Systems, or HVS) applied a digital device called time base corrector (TBC) to solve the problem of correcting the inherently unstable time base of the helical-scan small-format recording system. This equipment practically formed the core of the beginning of ENG. By 1974 most stations were interested in the new ENG trend.

One of the television stations that led in the transition into ENG was KMOX-TV in St. Louis. This station was using portable equipment as early as 1973. Although problematic and not meeting with the station's exact demands, it was able to develop new components in conjunction with CBS engineers. In September 1974, KMOX-TV abandoned the use of film for news coverage. At this point, only about 10% of U.S. television stations were using any form of ENG equipment.

By late 1974, CBS had incorporated some ENG equipment into its news team's equipment. Detailing the use of this equipment during President Nixon's visit to Moscow, CBS Vice President Marshall B. Davidson, commented:

> This news-gathering unit operates entirely on its own power sources and, with its excellent portability, is able to cover events at any location at short notice. The recordings were edited in Moscow, using two Sony VO-2850 U-matic cassette recorders and the new Sony RM-400 editor unit. Thus, the second major accomplishment was that all electronic news coverage was fully edited into its final form in Moscow before transmission by satellite to New York.
>
> This was the first time that a portable self-contained 'back-pack' recorder and a portable editing system had been used in overseas electronic news gathering. Because the system worked so well and provided such flexibility, CBS News was able to transmit more unilaterally produced, electronically gathered news stories from Soviet Union than had ever before been available from an overseas location.
>
> With almost half of all the CBS News stories broadcast during the President's visit having been electronically gathered and edited on location, CBS was able to provide more timely reports and topical footage than would have been possible using film cameras alone.[11]

CBS established a close liaison with Sony Corporation resulting in the refinement of techniques and equipment used in ENG technology.

By February 1975, the Japan Broadcasting Corporation (NHK) had developed a new electronic news gathering system that adopted the merits of both the 16mm-film system and the television system. NHK's system consisted of a compact color corrector. The compact color camera consisted of

a single-tube color camera using a single-frequency color-encoding principle. The newly developed saticon tube (developed by NHK) was used as a
pickup to be in the camera. The cassette-type VTR employed ½-inch high-
energy tape for ease of operation. Portability, lightweightness, and reliability were regarded as the major factors in the design.

One organization that closely watched the growth of ENG from its inception has been the Radio Television News Directors Association (RTNDA).
Its observations of ENG have been published regularly in its publication the
Communicator. Constant surveys had been conducted on ENG and its reception in the industry. By April 1977, more than half of the commercial
television stations in the United States were using ENG ranging from major
market operations tending to use ENG mainly for live feeds to smaller
market stations that had totally abandoned film in favor of ENG. By summer
1979, 86% of stations were using ENG. The use of news film on a regular
basis had been halved. The survey also showed that 42% of the respondents were using nothing but ENG, 44% were using both ENG and
news film regularly, and 11% were using only news film.[12] Only 3% of
those surveyed were using neither ENG nor news film and had no plans to
do so. Those in this group were mostly large-market independent stations
with no more than a token news operation.

ENG Versus News Film

Research conducted by RTNDA showed that stations that were not
equipped with ENG believed that they were at a disadvantage. Four out of
every five news directors in the top 50 markets indicated that they were at a
disadvantage without it. About half of those in markets 51–100 felt they had
a disadvantage and about one third of those in smaller markets thought lack
of it would affect them adversely. Film was able to compete strongly in
markets where stations only used tape recordings. However, the professional perception was that when live ENG was involved, film was always
the loser, as it looked outdated when a competitor covered a story live.

Moreover, ENG changed news gathering and reporting practices. Stations with ENG were shooting more stories than those with only news film.
(Cost of film stock and processing was no longer an inhibition.) A general
concensus was that ENG stations would shoot more stories than they could
use, but it was found that they used as many stories as were shot. Although
ENG stations covered more stories, the types of stories were not different
from those covered by news film operators. Results published by the
RTNDA indicated that the types of stories covered by TV news depended
more on the established norms of news processing than on changes in
news reporting technology.

A major difference between ENG and news film was cost. Sophisticated, state-of-the-art three-tube television minicams and microcams (Ikegami, Thompson, RCA, Fernseh) cost about $40,000 per camera. The small cameras (Sony, Akai) cost about $5,000. Portable tape units used in the field (such as Sony's VO-3800) cost $3,000; over $13,000 for a studio editing system; about $10,000 for a time-base corrector; over $20,000 for the microwave link. The overall cost, including vehicle and other assorted minor components, brought the total cost for a complete ENG system to about $100,000.[13]

Nevertheless, ENG produced savings, as against film—the elimination of film stock and processing costs. Operation cost figures from KMOX-TV (a CBS affiliate in St. Louis) put the cost of 1,040,000 feet of 16mm film used before the advent of ENG at $83,000 per year and $8,000 worth of processing chemicals, which brought the total cost of the news film operation to $91,000 annually excluding labor. The station, on the other hand, had spent only $6,000 on videotapes annually once they converted to ENG. Other stations such as WFMY-TV South Carolina were spending about $9,000 per month in film stock and processing costs.[14]

Labor was one area in which ENG's cost reduction scheme was questionable at the initial stage. Most television stations employed only one film cameraperson who easily carried a hand-held CP-16 (the industry norm) with a shot-gun directional microphone for most news assignments. However, because of the bulkiness of videotape recorders, and not so much of the size of the ENG camera, a two-person operation was warranted in ENG (although it was possible for one person to back-pack Sony's ENG equipment; nevertheless, it was quite a heavy load especially for long assignments).

It was also observed that initial downtime and maintenance cost for film was considerably less for film than for ENG. Speaking at the SMPTE, ABC's Isaac Hersly estimated that due to the simplicity of the mechanical film transport system, only 1 spare was needed for every 10 cameras; whereas, in ENG, for every three operating crews, one set of spare gear was needed to allow for downtime and maintenance. Confirming the existence of technical problems in ENG operation's, RTNDA research indicated that of all the ENG station's engineers, only 35% were adapting very well to ENG equipment, 44% fairly well, and 21% were said to be "not well" at all.

Advantages of ENG included speed of delivery, as stories could be microwaved to the station. Although experts were quick to point out the pros and cons of ENG, obviously, the pros (especially economic) out numbered the cons, and increasingly did so as new technological improvements were made on the ENG systems from the early 1970s to the present. Newscasting was able to enhance the illusion of immediacy. It was this ideological imperative that led to the development of ENG and other portable video recording systems.

CAMCORDERS

The aforementioned professional developments were, by the 1980s, being translated into a consumer device—the camcorder, a self-contained portable camera for amateurs. In June 1980, Sony introduced a device that was a combination of a video camera and video recorder and not significantly larger than an 8mm home movie camera, capable of recording images and sounds on a tape cassette not significantly larger than an audio one. Sony called it the "videomovie." Although this was an experimental unit, which would not be marketed immediately, Sony was convinced that the system contained materials that would constitute an industry standard in the future. In 1980 the market for video camera was still small, and according to industry statistics published by the Electronic Industries Association (EIA), sales of consumer video cameras to U.S. dealers were too low to be measured in 1979. Sales of video cameras have continued to be low over the years, with only 16% of VCR households owning video cameras in 1982 and 1983, dropping back to 12% in 1984.[15]

At the spring 1981 conference of NAB, RCA and Panasonic unveiled combination camera/recorders designed to enable television news crews to operate without constricting cords between cameras and recorders. These systems utilized VHS cassettes and recorded up to 20 minutes, using speeded up recorders that were made to record up to 6 hours on consumer machines. One major advantage of this high speed equipment was the resulting quality picture. At the same time, Sony was demonstrating its version of this combination system (using the Betamax format) in a nearby hotel suite near the exhibit floor. Describing this system, David Lachenbruch, editorial director of Television Digest, referred to them as "camcorders." This name has been used since then to describe these new portable devices, including the consumer unit demonstrated by Sony the previous year.

Although electronics manufacturers have since mastered and converted most equipment into solid-state, transistorized circuitry, video cameras continue to be equipped with vacuum tubes that capture images (the only other type of tube still manufactured in large quantities is the display or picture tube). Because camera tubes are large, fragile, and consume relatively large amounts of power, it was therefore a formidable task to produce a consumer camcorder of reasonable size and weight at a reasonable price.

Thus, in 1981, both the cassette size and the drum size (which caused a drop in writing speed) were reduced, which in turn lowered significantly the size of the recorders. In 1982, JVC introduced the VHS-C recorders (the

"C" standing for compact, a term that applied to both recorder and cassette). The cassette, which was able to record only 20 minutes of video and audio, was primarily responsible for the reduction in the size of the recorder. Standard VHS tracks recorded on the tape and the mini-cassette, and placed into an adapter could be played back on a standard home VHS recorder. In 1983, JVC introduced a tiny camera because the HVS-C was only really a VCR, followed by a brace to which both camera and recorder could be attached to form a single continuous unit that would fit on a shoulder. This in turn was the standard camcorder that the industry has been anticipating—one that was adequate in size and weight. Demonstrated at the 1983 NAB convention, it weighed only 8.25 pounds.

In March 1982, the 8mm Video Standardization Conference was formed by 122 companies to determine the specifications of what might become the electronic 8mm movie camera.

An agreement was reached at the 8mm Video Standardization Conference on March 28, shortly before the NAB Convention. The new standard approved was an 8mm-wide tape in cassette a bit larger than a common audiocassette. The drum diameter as well as the writing speed were reduced drastically. As the area of tape devoted to a second of video was lowered in the process, a new mechanism had to be found to recover these quality losses. Improved tapes called metal tapes (metal-powdered and metal-evaporated) instead of the normal oxide tapes used in all VCRs prior to the 8mm standard were recommended. The first of these metal tapes were demonstrated in cassettes late in 1978. "Their magnetic properties (coercivity and retentivity) were roughly two to three times higher than those of even so-called 'high energy' tapes. The relationships between magnetic properties and actual audio and video performance was complex, but higher coercivity tended to allow improved signal-to-noise ratio (less "snow" in pictures) and higher retentivity tended to allow more information recorded in less tape area."[16] However, these improved magnetic tapes generally worked well in machines equipped to deal with them. For instance, it is almost impossible to erase high coercivity tape in a machine designed for normal coercivity tape.

Despite these set standards, Sony also went ahead in promoting its camcorder called "Betamovie," the equipment of JVC's VHS-C. Introduced in January 1983, Betamovie was highly regarded in the industry despite its shortcomings. These included a lack of an electronic viewfinder (which meant that it had no playback capability), no "tape remaining" counter, and there were no rewind or fast forward features. As a result, Betamovie videographers shared the insecurity of 8mm filmmakers, who never rest easy until the developed footage is projected without problems on the movie screen in effect sacrificing a major advantage of video. On the other hand, Betamovie's did utilize a full-sized Beta cassette, which allowed as much as

3 hours and 20 minutes to be recorded, as against only 20 minutes on a VHS-C cassette, or a maximum of 90 minutes on the 8mm video standard. Further, Betamovie's size (5" × 8¾" × 14") and weight (6½ pounds including battery and cassette) were identical to that of an 8mm film camera. A special electronic feature in Betamovie was that unlike all electronic cameras that processed color information and detail information separately, then combined them into a single signal, Betamovie did not combine the signals, thereby saving circuitry, size, weight, power consumption and, in theory at least, the degradation caused by the combining and separating process. (VCRs, it must be noted, record color and detail separately and thus must separate the two forms of information from the single incoming signal.) Betamovie became available to consumers in August 1983.

In 1984, JVC improved upon its 1983 version of the camcorder, introducing an all-in-one camcorder called "videomovie." Videomovie retained most of the features of its predecessor including the VHS-C cassettes but still could not record more than 20 minutes. Like the Betamovie, however, it had a shrunken head drum that helped reduce its overall size. Unlike Betamovie, it featured an electronic viewfinder and tape shuttle modes for truly instant playback. Weighing about 5 pounds (including battery and cassette), it could be used as a camera for separate video recorders. A video output jack was also provided to allow direct connection to a television set or monitor. With a special adapter, the VHS-C cassette could be played in a standard VHS VCR. Zenith was the first American video distributor to introduce videomovie, after acquiring first rights from JVC.

Eastman Kodak was next to enter the camcorder market with an 8mm camcorder. Capitalizing on the shortcomings of Sony's Betamovie and JVC's videomovie, Kodak's 8mm was perceived as the industry's savior. Whereas Sony lacked a viewfinder and playback capability and JVC could not even record a half-hour television program, Kodak's 8mm camcorders featured a built-in recording and playback capability and a standardized maximum tape length of 90 minutes. With the addition of necessary accessories, it could substitute completely for a home VCR.

However, even with its 90-minute recording time, Kodak's 8mm cassettes were too short for pre-recorded movies. Although not included in the 1983 standard, a thinner tape capable of recording for 2 hours was recommended by the standardization conference and may soon replace the 90-minute cassette. Kodak's 8mm camcorder uses a cassette significantly smaller in size than VHS-C cassette and Betamovie cassettes.

Many companies are joining in the camcorder race. In January 1985, Matsushita introduced two full-size VHS camcorders under its Panasonic and Quasar name brands. Sony announced a new line of 8mms, claiming "it bets on 8mm as the complete home video system of the future." It also argued that camcorder was the only first full line of 8mm video products.

FIG. 10.1.   Panasonic's PV-460 Camcorder. Panasonic's new PV-460 Camcorder comes with a new technologically advanced Electronic Image Stabilization (EIS), which helps eliminate jitters caused by movement during recording. This hi-tech unit also offers audio/video dubbing, high-speed shutter, and the index/address search system. (*Source:* Courtesy, Panasonic Corporation, Secaucus, NJ.)

Sony's solid-state imaging device camcorder has been introduced in the United States, and Sony is also introducing a Betamovie with electronic viewfinder.

Tracing the history of portable equipment down to camcorders, it is regretable to notice that the video industry is still far from having the type of "perfect" equipment that will allow for a trouble-free home entertainment. Relentlessly, however, manufacturers are experimenting with lens technology, as lenses already represent a significant proportion of the size and weight of a camcorder. Other recording techniques that will result in longer recording time are also being tested. Maybe one of the drawbacks of the camcorder is not with its technology, but rather with its price. At $1,695, it is scarcely an average consumer item.

There are six different formats of camcorders available for a consumer to choose from. Camcorder owners still make up a minute segment of the home video industry. There are over 110 various models of camcorder available, making it a more difficult task for the consumer to select a choice. Of importance is the size of each of the equipments. Camcorders are available in full size VHS models, compact VHS-C, and the technologically advanced miniture 8mm format.

Of particular interest are the new breed of camcorders. The S-VHS and S-VHS-C (Super VHS-Compact) dominate this group. The difference between these equipment and the conventional hardware is the technological superiority entrusted in them. In terms of picture quality, the S-VHS camcorders surpass their competitors at the meantime. A major contributory factor to S-VHS advancement is its high horizontal resolution. S-VHS optimum performance is estimated at 440 lines with a frequency response of up to 505 MHz. This supercedes Super Beta's 260 (3.24 MHz), 8mm's 266 (3.33 MHz) and VHS 234 (2.92 MHz). However, these qualifications can be misleading at times as most of the models are far from reaching their full potential. With the intense competition, it is hard to foresee the level of innovation each manufacturer is likely to incorporate in each model. However, camcorders are also enjoying the high level of technological impact currently being experience in the video industry (see chapter 9).

The Impact of Video Technology on Related Industries

*T*his chapter is devoted to analyzing the various effects of magnetic recording technologies on other existing related technologies.

CONSUMER ELECTRONICS INDUSTRY

The consumer electronics industry took shape in 1920 with the advent of radio broadcasting in the United States, as the first radio receiving sets were made available to consumers in the market. It was popularly known as the radio industry then. The word "electronics" came into common use in the mid-1940s, as more enthusiasts who were familiar with terms such as "earphones," "B-battery," "cat's whiskers," and "crystal set," would not cease to wonder at these surprising advancements in home entertainment.

Radio penetration was considerably rapid. By 1922, 100,000 radio receivers were sold at factory value of $5 million. The cost for an average unit was $50. By 1924, radio's annual factory value had increased 10 times to $50 million.

ORIGINS IN THE LATE 1800

Many early landmarks contributed to the advent of consumer electronics. Considered to be the most outstanding were Edison's invention of the phonograph in 1877, Fleming's development of the electron tube in the 1890s, Marconi's first wireless transmission in 1895, Poulsen's invention of

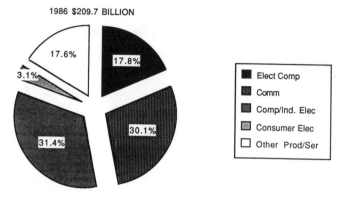

1986 $209.7 BILLION

17.6%

3.1%

17.8%

30.1%

31.4%

- Elect Comp
- Comm
- Comp/Ind. Elec
- Consumer Elec
- Other Prod/Ser

FIG. 11.1. U.S. factory sales of electronics by industry group (%), 1985–1986 (*Source: Consumer Electronics, 1988.*)

the Telegraphone in 1898, and de Forest's development of the vacuum tube in 1906.

The existence of the recording industry as it is today perhaps would not have been exactly the same if not for Edison and Poulsen's successes. In a similar fashion, de Forest's invention of the vacuum tube was a cinch in the development of radio broadcasting and the practical application of television. It might be argued that perhaps radio would not have been completely accepted by the public if not for the fact that the average consumer was conditioned to the type of entertainment provided by the sounds emanating from the phonograph in their living rooms. The phonograph was already 50 years old as a home entertainment device before being accompanied by radio. With the ensuing marriage to radio, Edison's phonograph, a completely mechanical accoustical device, was accepted into the consumer electronic family. Before long, the phonograph was undergoing a rejuvenation process as its antiquated soundbox was replaced by electronic amplification (earlier developed by de Forest), while an electric motor took the place of the phonograph's spring drive.

The importance of radio to the average consumer created an era known as the "radio age"—a period from 1920 through 1941 when the United States entered World War II. During this period, many dynamic innovations were introduced to upgrade the quality of radio performance. Such innovations included the loudspeaker, the superheterodyne circuit, the line-cord radio, the automobile radio, and the AC and battery-operated portable radio.

Magnetic Recording and Radio

Until the outbreak of World War II, recorded music (or canned music as it was called in the United States), was a taboo in American broadcasting. The prevalent recording technology in the United States being extremely inferior, it was ludicrous for stations to permit the airing of recorded programs. Nevertheless, all this changed when the Allied Forces made contact after the war with German radio stations and discovered the advancements made on the Magnetophon. This technology would then introduce a new era in radio broadcasting.

FURTHER DEVELOPMENTS
FROM THE RECORDING
TECHNOLOGY—HI-FI/STEREO IN AUDIO

A common trend in the recording industry has been the continuous development of new technologies that rapidly outdate their predecessors. Many such innovations, although not originally developed specifically to enhance any recording devices, would later find uses in recording units.

As the radio audience became sophisticated, there was a need for quality sound reproduction among this group of engineers and educated laymen. To satisfy their need, the industry introduced the "hi-fi," which turned out to be a major innovation in the radio and recording industries. By 1948, the fidelity of the reproducing medium had surpassed that of the recording medium. The hi-fi equipment market was further revitalized by the introduction of the 45 rpm and 33⅓ rpm long-playing disc.

Initially ignored due to the overwhelming popularity of the television, high-fidelity FM radio grew to become a force to be reckoned with. When tape recording was introduced to American broadcasting during the postwar era, it made a remarkable difference. Soon, hi-fi found its way into homes through a variety of entertainment devices.

Stereophonic phonograph as well as the stereo record was introduced in 1958. Again this popularized the record-playing equipment market. The approval of the FM stereo multiplex system of broadcasting by the FCC made it possible to receive radio programs as well as to listen to records and tapes in stereophonic sound.

Wire-Recording Technology
and the Telephone and Phonograph

At the turn of the century, Poulsen's magnetic recording device although received enthusiastically by the scientific community, was seen as a threat by the telephone industry. It had been designed to receive telephone messages, store them, and later replay the signals. The Telegraphone was not in direct competition with the telephone; therefore, Poulsen and his colleagues expected coexistence between it and the telephone. AT&T, however, concluded that once clients realized that their conversations might be recorded, they would discontinue the phone service fearing for their privacy. However, there is no evidence of any legal action taken by the company against the Telegraphone. No evidence exists either of any of AT&T's clients discontinuing their services for reasons related to magnetic wire-recording devices.

But as evidence later presented at the Hearing before the Senate Committee on Patents revealed, this was not the end of the matter. Testifying before the Committee, attorney George Sullivan who represented the American Telegraphone Company stockholders revealed that Charles Rood, the Chairman of American Telegraphone Company, was collaborating with AT&T to work against the technical progress and commercial exploitation of magnetic sound recording in the United States (see chapter 3).[1] Sullivan accused Rood of colluding with AT&T to suppress the Telegraphone from being made available to the public, "fearing that a readily accessible telephonic recording device could diminish AT&T's members exchanges by a third."[2] The American Telegraphone Company witness testified:

This is an instrument capable of recording both sides of a telephone conversation. It records it so perfectly and clearly that two talking at once cannot hope to successfully deny their own identities. If this were out as a true recording instrument in the hands of the public, so that the truth could be recorded at any time by any body at either end of the line, no man could safely use the telephone to make an illicit engagement with another man's wife or to carry on illegimate business transactions, at least so easily as now, through the use of the telephone.[3]

A New York telephone manager testified that an enormous amount of illicit business transactions were done on the telephone and speculated that if the Telegraphone were commonly available his company would lose 33% of its gross revenues. Further evidence suggested that Rood had several other business relationships with AT&T in the past before joining the American Telegraphone Company. It was later established as well that Judge Lindley, former President of American Telegraphone, was serving AT&T's interest while holding his position at American Telegraphone. Therefore, although he relinquished his post, he made sure he handed it over to someone with similar connections. Rood was introduced to Lindley by Charles F. Miller, Rood's employee at Hamilton Watch Company. Evidence presented before the Senate Hearing Committee has Miller assuring Lindley that, "Mr. Rood has done these things (wrecking other companies) many times and, of course, will not ask for anything that will not go through legally as well as meeting the entire satisfaction of all."[4] Sullivan also claimed that Rood was used by phonograph interests to suppress development and marketing of the Telegraphone out of their fear that the Telegraphone would have a competitive edge. Rood, it was confirmed was a personal friend of Thomas A. Edison. Without the consent of his Board of Directors, Rood had invited Edison's representative to the American Telegraphone factory at Wheeling, showing him all the vital magnetic recording technologies available to his company at the time.

VIDEOCASSETTE RECORDER AND TELEVISION

Recent animosity between the videocassette recorder on the one hand and television as well as advertising agencies and sponsors on the other has been widely publicized. In order to fully understand the core of the problem, it is necessary to briefly define each party's profile in this case. In most cases, the sponsor is a large corporation who sells its products through advertisements shown on network or local television. Most sponsors contract with advertising agencies who produce, place the advertisements on suitable spots on television, monitor its effectiveness, and advise the sponsor accordingly on safe promotion of the products concerned. In some cases, sponsors produce their advertisements in-house, and therefore deal with the television stations by themselves. The television station serves as a go-between for the sponsors/advertisers and the consumers who are influenced to buy the products by the advertisements. The stations own the medium by which the advertisements are carried. The television station gets its revenue through fees paid by advertisers. On the other hand, most VCR owners use their equipment to record programs off the air in many cases for time-shifting purposes. It is the existing relationship between television usage and videocassette recording of television programs that is at the center of this dilemma. The typical consumer uses the videocassette recorder for two primary purposes; first, to watch pre-recorded programs and second, to record programs off-air or off-cable for viewing at a later time (which is called time-shifting). Overall, home recording has been the predominant use. Examining the VCR from a most important perspective, it is easy to notice how its recording capabilities is changing the way consumers entertain themselves at home. By 1984, several media organizations were probing the profile of VCR users. Companies such as A.C. Nielsen, Arbitron, Electronic Media/SRI, Kegan, AGB, etc. and a number of advertising agencies were interested in the uses of the VCR. VCR owners were being asked the importance of different VCR features in the decision to purchase a VCR, and the following rationale were given in order of importance to the VCR owner:

- Ability to record programs off television and to replay at a more convenient time (time-shifting). This was by far the most important

VCR feature cited, being "important" or "very important" to 88% of VCR households.

- Ability to rent pre-recorded programs. This was "important" to 45% of the sample, and the second important reason for owning a VCR.
- Ability to build a permanent collection of favorite movies and television shows.
- Ability to watch, record, and playback television shows without commercials. This reason was cited by 31% of VCR households as being of any degree of importance. Apparently, consumers used a VCR to eliminate commercials, but did not consider this feature a primary reason to invest in a VCR. However, more consumers are now considering this as one of the most important uses of the VCR.
- Saving the expense of going to the movies or paying for pay television services by watching videocassette recordings. Of the sample, 25% felt that this was an important reason.
- Shoot home movies with a video camera. Only 25% felt this was an important reason to own a VCR. In Nielsen's 1984 VCR Usage Tracking Study, only 12% of the VCR households indicated that they owned a video camera. Of those who own a video camera, about 65% use it between once a month to once every 4 months. Only 9% used it once a week or more.
- Duplicate borrowed or rented videotapes. This practice requires multiple VCRs. This practice, however, was listed as important by only 18% of the entire VCR-owning sample, although only 10% were equipped to dub tapes.
- Purchase pre-recorded programs. This practice is almost the most unpopular among VCR owners. Only 11% of the sample considered it an important factor. This contrasts the 45% of the sample who considered renting pre-recording cassettes important.

By far, most people used their VCR to record programs off television for time-shifting purposes. The majority of television recordings are done off network television programming. Network program recording accounted for 74% of VCR recording in 1983. Eight percent of recording was of independent stations programs, 8% was of pay television and 10% of VCR recording was of other programming such as nonpay cable, super stations, Public Broadcasting Service, and Satellite Television. Recording is highest during prime time (8 p.m. to 11 p.m.), followed by daytime (12 noon to 5 p.m.). On the average, 42% of all recordings occur during prime time, and 38% during daytime. Three studies conducted on VCR by Nielsen in 1982, 1983, and 1984 revealed that when a percent of households making one or more recordings is examined, movies are the most recorded program type. These studies revealed that on the average, 50% of the sample households recorded a movie in an average month. Daytime soap opera on the other hand is the most frequently recorded program. The logic here is that although 50% of the sample record movies in an average month, only 23% record soap operas, whereas, although 39% of this sample record soap operas as frequently as possible, only 18% record movies as frequently. Drama–mystery–suspense was the third (25%) most recorded category, and comedy and sports came in at the fourth and fifth positions. However, in 1984, sports was the fourth recorded program, with 26% of VCR households recording. This was due to the Los Angeles Olympics, which was watched by a majority of households. Therefore overall, movies account for 18% of all recordings. Soap operas account for 10 of the 11 most recorded programs. Women are considered primary recorders, and they tend to be overall heavier users of television. Heavy recorders are categorized as those households recording 21 or more times a month. They account for 23% of VCR households and 63% of recording activity. It is believed that "heavy recorders" are also heavy television users. Women taping daytime drama (soap operas) account for a significant portion of these "heavy recorders." As VCR penetration increases, these individuals will continue to be a significant group that would view above-average levels of time-shifting programming, probably daytime dramas, and consequently eliminate the majority of commercials in these taped programs during playback. Therefore, "heavy recorders" it seems, will constitute a segment of the VCR population that will be increasingly difficult to reach through traditional television advertising.

The average VCR household is larger, has more children, and younger heads-of-house than the total U.S. households. VCR owners are most likely to be college educated. Their population skews heavily to the 35- to 49-year-old bracket, although the base is fast changing to a much younger age bracket. The average VCR owner has an annual income of $20,000 or more, and lives in the urban area, although there is an indication of a change from urban to suburban among newer VCR owners.

Soap operas are among the top-recorded programs by VCR users. In 1984, for instance the top 10 recorded programs on a regular basis were: "All My Children," "Days of Our Lives," "As the World Turns," "The Guiding Light," "The Young and the Restless," "Magnum P.I.," "Remington Steele," and "The A-Team."

How VCR Usage Affects Television Commercials

An examination of attitudes of VCR owners indicated various behaviors while recording any given program. In 1985, market studies revealed that

75% of all recordings were made while no one was present to watch the recorded program when it aired. Of this, 21% of households were watching a different program while recording, and 54% were not watching television. While recording, only 25% of the households were watching the same program. If a program is watched while recording, it is played back 45% of the time. However, only 79% of those who record actually playback the tape, and if during playback they choose to skip over commercials, this audience is lost to the advertiser, although various ratings (Nielsen and Arbitron) would indicate otherwise. Overall, tapes that are played back are viewed an average of 1.4 days after recording. Fifty percent of recorded tapes are viewed on the same day, 80% within 1 day, 94% within 5 days, and 98% within 10 days. The frequency and threat of commercial elimination has been a major concern for network television and their affiliates, advertising agencies, and sponsors. The term commercial zapping has been used frequently in the industry to define this problem. Commercials can be deleted either by stop or pause features while recording, or by speed search or fast forward during playback of recorded programs (see Tables 11.1 and 11.2).

Commercial deletion activities differ by program source. When viewers simultaneously view and record a network affiliate, they tend not to delete most commercials. Network affiliates also have the highest amount of recording activity without viewers, amounting to 75%.[5] Investigation of commercial deletion by program type indicates that movies, mini-series, musical variety, and science fiction are most likely to have commercials deleted. Recordings of soap operas are five times less likely to have commercials not deleted. Of the two forms of commercial zapping, the use of speed search and fast forward during playback is of most concern to advertisers. The rational behind this statement is that deletion of commercials during recording demands the most attention; if the individual recording the program is cooking or doing some other chores, he or she stands the risk of "chopping" the program immediately following the commercial break. Even if commercials are successfully deleted, the individual recording the

TABLE 11.1
Frequency of Elimination of Commercial Using Either Stop
or Pause While Watching and Recording that Program
at the Same Time

Usually (more than 75% of the time)	36.4%
Frequently (50%–74% of the time)	9.7%
Occasionally (25%–49% of the time)	10.1%
Seldom (less than 25% of the time)	17.1%
Never	14.2%
Do not view while recording	12.5%

TABLE 11.2
Frequency of Use of Speed Search or Fast
Forward to Skip Over Commercials
When Playing Back a Program
Recorded From Television

Usually	48.9%
Frequently	10.0%
Occasionally	11.3%
Seldom	14.0%
Never	15.8%

program has already been exposed to the advertisement, although such commercials might not have been recorded. In a recent development, advertisers have intensified their fear in commercial zapping since Vidicraft, a small manufacturer of home video accessories, introduced and shipped hundreds of their new commercial zapping machine called the CCU-120. This machine automatically edits out television advertisements during home recording of as many as nine events for as long as 9 weeks in advance.

However, there are two encouraging signs to advertisers at the moment. First, the Vidicraft device costs $399, and it is not likely to be purchased in large quantities by consumers until there is a considerable decrease in price. Second, because this machine functions by distinguishing commercial breaks through such signs as "fade to black," "differing audio levels," and so on, telecasters could conceivably combat this automatic zapping by eliminating these "signposts." However, there are other equipments being introduced by various manufacturers to zap commercials. And this is a serious threat to television.

Commercial deletion during playback of commercials placed in daytime/women programming is usually high, with commercials being skipped during playback an average of 73% of the time. Actually, the 22% of VCR owners (heavy recorders) that tape daytime dramas are probably only exposed to one-fourth of the normal level of commercials. This did not cause any alarm among advertisers in the past when VCR penetration was only in the teens. However, it is beginning to create some concern as penetration increases.

In order to understand the usefulness of these analyses, it is important to comprehend the method of measurement in the industry. Television audience measurements were conducted by two major companies in the United States, A.C. Nielsen Company and Arbitron, until the arrival of Audit of Great Britain (AGB) a few years ago. The base from which negotiations between advertising agencies and the broadcasters bargain are the Nielsen audience figures. Nielsen gets these figures almost instantly from its monitors (autimeters) wired to a national sample of 1,700 television sets.

(This figure has since been increased to compete with AGB, which seriously doubted the accuracy of Nielsen's data collected from such a minute representation of U.S. television households.) However, its figures include the videocassette recorders that are recording programs that may or may not ultimately be viewed, and the number of sets tuned in to programming, that are also switched to eliminate commercials as soon as it is time for commercial breaks. The problem is how best to measure this "time-shifted" audience. It is a complex issue. The audience for a given program was clearly defined by time in the past; they were simply those watching a particular program on a specific station. Time-shifting blurs the time factor, and more so, as VCR penetration increases, the definition of "audience" becomes less clear. Due to the presence of the VCR, an audience's program is spread over the course of a day, week, or month. How then could this be measured? The two major audience measurement companies, Nielsen and Arbitron, including the new comer, AGB, have all adopted similar policies to combat this controversial issue.

Another company, BARB, partly devised a solution beginning June 6, 1985, whereby viewing via the VCR will be measured by remote detection units that will be installed in every video-owning BARB panel member's home. However, this process involved only instances in which a program is being viewed and recorded simultaneously. The issue of how time-shifting viewing of recorded programs should be included in any data remains unresolved. The present system introduced by BARB is expected to raise viewing figures by 2% to 3% that is an advantage to advertisers.

Nielsen's VCR Usage Report, however, gives a more reliable result simply because it is a diary-based study as opposed to a metered study. The result of this report is not included in Nielsen's daily figures. Viewing diaries used for audience measurement result in fairly straightforward procedure. Diaries allow viewers to record the names of the programs they watch, whether the programs' immediate sources are a broadcast signal or a videocassette. To account for videocassette viewing, time-shifted viewing within the week is simply added back into viewing that took place when the program was aired. Off-air recording is entered into the diary only when the program recorded was viewed at the same time. The problem created by VCR in metered measurement is a complex one. A television set outfitted with a VCR has two tuners, one in the set and the other in the VCR. Nielsen and AGB meter both tuners. Arbitron on the other hand is modifying its tuner to report VCR tuning. Meters record only channel and time, therefore they can only indicate when a VCR is in use, not what it is playing back. For this reason, the rating services do not include VCR playback viewing in their calculation of rating from metered sample. Nielsen and AGB treat VCR recording in the metered sample as actual viewing. Advertisers are against this principle because analysis of playback behavior shows that while 25% of the programs taped are viewed at the same time, some 75% are time-shifted. Only 80% of them are indeed played back "usually within 1 to 3 days." Among those that are played back, 50% have their commercials "zapped."

Two proposals would therefore be suitable for this problem. The first proposal, which has also been examined by the advertising industry, suggests that Nielsen exclude VCR recording from their viewing statistics. Further complication and misunderstanding could be avoided through this proposal although, it does not in itself solve the problem. The second proposal is the most ambitious attempt to measure not only VCR playback, but also viewing of individual commercial messages. This method involves Nielsen's device called "Smart" boxes, which are capable of reading the automatic measurement of lineups (AMOL) codes. The AMOL is invisibly broadcast along with the program material, and identifies the program being aired. Currently being used by ABC, CBS, and NBC, it identifies the network, month, day, hour, minute, and seconds the program was originally telecast by the network. The "Smart" box would assign a rating to the coded telecast regardless of when it is viewed, be it immediately, or a week later via a VCR. It is programmed to ignore any code that presents itself in an accelerated fashion, as in the fast-forward mode of a VCR, and this means that "zapping" would be measured.

Apart from the problem of how to best measure the commercial viewing audience (as apposed to the program viewing audience) that has been identified earlier in this section, the major area of concern to advertisers remains how to stop viewers from skipping over commercials during playback. This is indeed a challenge because VCR owners have the option to "zap" out commercials at will.

In order to stop viewers from skipping over commercials during playback, a great deal of creativity has to be introduced so that advertising messages, rather than being "tuned out," must be at least as welcome as the program itself. In fact, most advertising agencies are beginning to consider television as a less captive medium, and more as a medium whose audience is allowed the freedom to view or not to view their commercial messages, as VCR penetration increases. This has been the system in use with nonbroadcast advertising, so as VCR becomes a mass medium, advertisers are incorporating areas of nonbroadcast experience to its television advertising. Just as a print advertisement is constructed to attract and hold a totally voluntary audience, so must broadcast commercials be magnetic to viewers.

Most advertisers have already adopted the creative advertising strategy previously mentioned. An example are the Pepsi-Cola commercials that introduce such stars as Michael Jackson and Lionel Ritchie. These commercials, although only 30 seconds long, make lasting impressions. Pepsi advertised the Michael Jackson commercials as any network would its forthcoming programs. Of course the response has been encouraging. Using celebrities who appear on television to introduce a specific product is not enough in this case, rather the use of a most popular celebrity with talent, be it musical or comedic, could make a difference.

The next option is to make the product to be advertised a part of the program on which it is to be advertised. A Coca-Cola commercial in this case would be a scene in which an actor or actress in a program is seen drinking Coke as the program continues, or a family is using A-1 Sauce during a dinner scene in the regular program. Devising a creative means that would integrate this system into actual programs without public outcry from certain quarters or legal actions from governing bodies rather than its effectiveness would be a concern. If blended creatively, it would be impossible for a viewer to skip over any particular scer.e in which a product is demonstrated or "advertised." In some countries, the United Kingdom for example, such strategy is totally prohibited. Commercials could be turned into a mini-program, or wrapped around a news brief, or interesting daily tidbits. At the present VCR penetration level, no single factor could stop the growth of VCR, and as it continues to grow, commercials would continue to be skipped. The effect could be detrimental to advertisers unless adequate precautions are taken.

Advertising on Videocassettes

Most sponsors disagree with Nielsen as to the effectiveness of their commercials in VCR homes. Many believe that a large number of VCR users zap through commercials most of the time, contrary to Nielsen's contentions. Such fears have generated alternative strategies among most manufacturers and sponsors.

At current pre-recorded cassette prices of $85–$95, it is difficult to generate a considerable number of sales among average consumers. The rationale is therefore to decrease the price of cassettes in order to penetrate the market. It was predicted that almost half the cassettes that will be sold between 1988 and 1989 will be priced at less than $20 each however, high prices still prevail. Some box office hit cassette prices have been reduced to $29.95 from $89–$95 in the hopes of boosting the purchase rather than the rental market.

Advertising on Pre-recorded Tapes

A joint promotion between Pepsi-Cola and Paramount Pictures has made it possible for the price of the 1987 box office hit *Top Gun*, released on cassette, to be sold at a considerably low price of $26.95. The cassette begins with a 30-second Diet Pepsi commercial. This cooperative trend is just the beginning. At the release of Paramount's 1986 smash hit *Crocodile Dundee* on August 5, 1987, for $25.95, Quantas Airways Limited helped promote it by offering about 120 free trips to Australia. Such promotions, unheard of since the start of this industry, are becoming commonplace.

The video recorder is and will continue to be a major problem for the television industry.

VIDEO RECORDERS
AND CABLE TELEVISION

The cable television industry has been haunted by the advent of video recorders as a mass consumer durable. This issue has been controversial in the industries for years. However, no solid evidence exists that the allegation against VCRs is true. Although when one compares statistics for these two technologies, it is possible to see why the cable industry would be concerned about a possible threat. Yet it is not clear how soon or how video recording will affect cable. At present, VCR penetration is at 58.1% and cable penetration is at 51%. In 1986, it was estimated that by 1990, VCR penetration will supersede cable penetration. It happened in 1987. But contrary to views held by most cable executives, this does not necessarily constitute any massive problems for cable.

In fact, industry research revealed that videocassette recorder usage is higher in cable television households, especially in those with pay services, than in homes with only broadcast television. Forty-nine percent of the VCR households indicated that they also subscribed to cable television in 1984. Moreover, older VCR owners (those who have owned their VCRs for over 2 years) were most likely to subscribe to cable. Forty-eight percent of those owning a VCR for less than 1 year subscribed to cable compared to 51% of those owning for 3 or more years. The perceived explanation for this is that cable delivers uninterrupted movies, and movies constitute the most recorded program type. This is encouraged by the fact that pay cable companies are not advertising-based, and therefore, VCR owners enjoy commercial-free movie/programs.

Several studies also indicated that recording pay cable programs has decreased in recent years from the 1982–1983 level. This positive sign for cable companies might have been due to an increase in videocassette rentals. This trend constitutes the most important threat to cable from video recording.

Statistics indicate that 60% of VCR owners rated the value of rental or

pre-recorded cassettes higher than pay subscription (18% reverse the ranking and 22% rated them equal). Among pay television subscribers who
were VCR owners, a majority (38%) agreed that rental of videocassettes was
higher in value than a pay television subscription (as compared to 33% who
rated the opposite).[6] Part of this is due to the release patterns for recent
movies. It generally takes between 4 to 6 months after theatrical exhibition
before a film is available on pre-recorded cassettes, whereas the time period is between 7 to 11 months for pay television.

VCR is an Advantage to Cable

At the 10th Annual Cable Television Administration and Marketing Society
conference held in New York in 1984, the VCR was singled out as "the most
feared competitive technology on the horizon." Thomas Willet, senior vice
president of marketing and programming at Continental Cablevision asked
"Is the VCR a formidable opponent or just a trendy gadget?" The concensus
of the panel was that VCRs might actually encourage consumers to subscribe to a pay service—a reasonable if somewhat self-serving assessment of
current trends. Recalling industry VCR studies, one notes good evidence to
support this argument. For one thing, more VCR owners are subscribing to
pay services. Therefore, VCRs must be performing an important role in pay
households, one that is complementary rather than harmful. In fact, VCR
owners without pay subscription television seem to indicate that one reason is lack of pay television availability rather than an active choice to not
purchase it. This means that if properly promoted, most VCR households
might be potential pay subscribers. Fifty-four percent of VCR households
have, at one time or another, subscribed to pay television service. Twenty-
four percent were once subscribers, but later discontinued their services.
Most former subscribers attribute relocation and unavailability of cable or
pay in their new communities to their nonsubscribing status. However,
46% of those without pay service, indicated that it was very likely that they
would subscribe if cable/pay services were available.

Some Multiple-Cable System Operators (MSOs) are now concluding that
VCRs are no longer the threat they were once considered to be and are
developing strategies that take advantage of the relations between VCRs
with cable systems. A new phenomenon in the industry is the marketing of
VCRs alongside cable systems. Group W Cable introduced "VCR hookup
marketing" in a number of franchises. Hookups were offered free for subscribers as part of the installation and at a charge to current households.
Ability to tape the various movies/programs on cable television contributed to household retention of services. Time-shifting in cable households
is what makes cable subscription vital to most VCR owners.

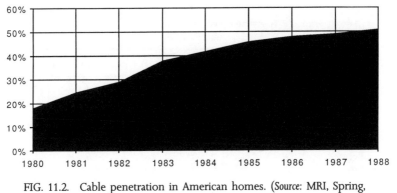

FIG. 11.2. Cable penetration in American homes. (*Source:* MRI, Spring, 1987.)

VCR Penetration Doubles Pay TVs

More households with cable television are purchasing VCRs. As of February 1988, 58.1% of all U.S. television households had VCRs. At the same token, pay television subscribers amount to only 28.3% of U.S. television households. Overall, total cable television penetration in the United States stands at 51% (see Fig. 11.2).

When translated into raw numbers, VCR population is at 51,476,600. Cable is at 45,274,600, and pay television 25,073,800. These figures are based on January 1988 estimates of 88.6 million television households (98% of total U.S. homes).

Of all television designated marketing areas (DMAs) in the United States, Anchorage and Fairbanks lead in VCR penetration at 78% and 76.2% respectively. Las Vegas comes in third with 74.5%. Sioux Falls and Laredo are the only two DMAs with low penetrations of 39.5% and 39.1% respectively.

Ironically, Laredo has the highest pay television penetration in the United States (53.5%) as of May 1988. Other major pay markets include: Victoria, Texas, 44.9% (57.6% VCR); Honolulu, 43.3% (60.3%); Norfolk–Portsmouth–Newport News, 42.2% (58.9%); New Orleans, 41.6% (55%); Biloxi–Gulfport, 40.9% (59.4%); San Angelo, 40.4% (53.1%); Jacksonville, 39.6% (53.8%); Hartford–New Haven, 38.4% (61.8%); and San Antonia, 38.2% (54.7%).

VCR and Pay Per View

Most American prefer watching movies at home on their VCR according to a recent study conducted by the Electronic MEDIA/SRI Research Center. They would rather rent movies at their local video store than view it

TABLE 11.3
Markets with Above-Average VCR Penetration and Pay Cable Penetration
and Ranking

Market	% VCR	% Pay	Pay Rank
Anchorage	78.0	33.4	35
Fairbanks	76.2	33.2	36
Las Vegas	74.5	26.5	127
San Francisco–Oakland	68.3	24.9	150
L.A.	67.5	23.5	164
Reno	66.9	34.5	25
San Diego	66.9	34.4	27
Baltimore	65.5	22.3	127
Rockford	65.9	26.9	117
Sacramento–Stockton	65.8	24.2	158
Presque Isle	64.9	24.2	158
Santa Barbara	64.9	27.7	101
Chicago	64.7	26.9	117
Dallas–Ft. Worth	64.6	27.2	111
N.Y.	64.3	29.1	78
Boston	64.0	34.7	24
Seattle–Tacoma	63.3	24.3	155
Lake Charles	63.2	29.9	67
Washington	63.0	25.1	145
Bend, Ore.	62.5	24.6	152
Cheyenne–Scotts Bluff	62.5	38.1	11
Monterrey–Salinas	62.2	20.2	187
Chico–Redding	62.0	18.5	200
Burlington–Plattsburgh	61.9	26.1	133
Hartford–New Haven	61.8	38.4	9
Phoenix	61.7	25.3	142
Idaho Falls–Pocatello	61.3	24.5	153
Detroit	61.2	31.4	54
Salt Lake City	61.1	23.0	166
Fresno–Visalia	60.9	25.0	148
Bangor	60.8	16.7	205
Ft. Wayne	60.8	26.3	130
Atlanta	60.5	26.3	135
Providence–New Bedford	60.4	34.2	28
Tucson	60.4	34.2	182
Honolulu	60.3	43.3	3
Houston	60.2	27.8	98
Philadelphia	60.2	29.5	72
Bakersfield	60.1	29.5	72
Minneapolis–St. Paul	60.1	22.1	175
Albany–Schenectady–Troy	60.0	35.2	22
Austin	59.7	32.4	40
Denver	59.5	29.2	74
Biloxi–Gulfport	59.4	40.9	6
Portland, Ore	59.4	26.8	122

TABLE 11.3
(*Continued*)

Market	% VCR	% Pay	Pay Rank
Yakima	59.3	25.4	141
Colorado Springs–Pueblo	59.2	32.2	43
Norfolk–Portsmouth–Newport News	58.9	42.2	4
Toledo	58.7	23.8	163
Portland–Auburn	58.6	28.4	89
Waco–Temple	58.6	27.2	111
Beaumont–Pt. Arthur	58.5	28.9	83
Flint–Saginaw–Bay City	58.5	21.1	183
Kansas City	58.2	29.8	69

Source: Video Week, May 9, 1988

through a pay per view (PPV) service or in a movie theater. When given a choice of watching a movie on rented videotape or on a pay-per-view channel, 55% of the respondents preferred to rent a video, whereas only 32% chose PPV (see Fig. 11.3). Further demographic breakdown indicates that younger respondents are more likely to favor home video, while older respondents were more likely to favor PPV.

Cable growth is contingent on (a) the quality of programs available to viewers and (b) franchiser's ability to curb subscription fee to a minimum. It is no longer enough to lure subscribers with a premise of advertising-free programs. However, once subscribed, cable households remain heavy cable viewers. They devote about 34% of their time to watching cable as opposed to 35% broadcast network programs. During prime time, cable viewing increases sharply to 64%, whereas network affiliates viewing declines to minus 9% (see Fig. 11.4 and 11.5).

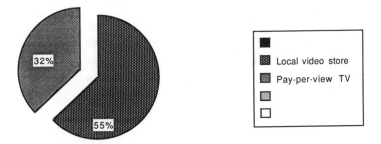

FIG. 11.3.   Likelihood of viewing movie through PPV or renting/buying at local video store at same cost. (*Source:* Electronic Media, December 14, 1987.)

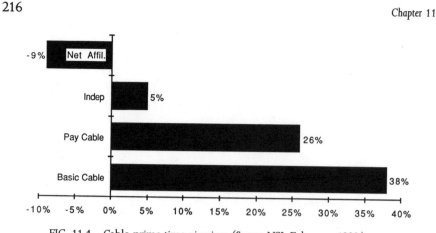

FIG. 11.4.   Cable prime-time viewing. (*Source:* NSI, February, 1988.)

The growth of VCR in cable household reflects increase cable viewing in these households.

VIDEO RECORDERS
AND THEATRICAL MOVIES

Hollywood, which at first underrated videocassettes as a means of distributing movies to the public and feared them as a potential drain on movie theater attendance, is now realizing their economic potential.

A question frequently asked is: "Will VCRs render movie theaters obsolete?". Evidence indicates that in the short-term and as with television and cable, video recorders are complementary to movie theaters, not a

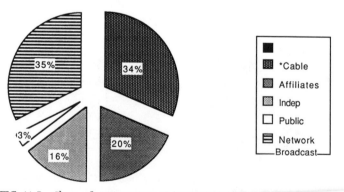

FIG. 11.5.   Share of viewing time: Television and cable. (*Source:* NSI, February, 1988.)

threat. Furthermore, an examination of the attitudinal data from industry studies revealed that people in VCR households frequently viewed movies in theaters. Overall, 38% of all members of VCR households went to the movie theaters six or more times in a period of 1 year as compared with 17% who did not view any movies in the theater. Movie theater attendance tended to be high among households that purchased pre-recorded cassettes during the year, rented during the month, or were among the pay television households. Forty-one percent of these households attended movie theaters six or more times during the year. Movie theater attendance was highest among adults 18–24 years of age in VCR households. Overall, individuals in this age bracket went to the movie theater an average of 16 times during the course of the year. Pay television household members had the highest average attendance of 18 times. Among this age group, only 5% of total households indicated that they never saw a movie in the theater during the year. Interestingly, heavy videocassette renters viewed movies at the theater more than any other group in this category. Only 1% of these renters said that they did not go to the movie theater in the past year.

Why then would individuals who are exposed to so many movie titles in their homes want to see movies in the theater? The answer may be more psychological than economic. First, the various reports on home movies, pay cable, and movie theaters,[7] indicate a skewed trend toward new titles. A survey of rental stores reveals that new titles are completely rented out before consumers rent old titles. It seems that "freshness" and novelty are strong factors in viewing practices, aided, of course by promotion and peer discussions. The second answer may be the irreplacable pleasure of the movie theater environment. The movie theater is a social institution as well as a business.

Not immediately harmed by VCRs, Hollywood is gaining profit through them. By 1982, a typical movie was earning 8% of its revenues from cassettes and disks, and in 1983 that figure increased to 13%. Hollywood studios have now placed more emphasis on the meagre one-time-only "first sale doctrine" than they did some 5 years ago. For example, in 1984, U.S. and Canadian videocassette rights to the movie *Silkwood* were sold for about $1.5 million. Soon afterward, a similar right to *Santa Claus—The Movie* brought about $2.6 million, with the sale occurring several weeks before production on the movie began. An average of $400,000 was paid for such rights in 1982, and about $500,000 in 1983. At a price undreamed of even in 1983, the videocassette rights to George Lukas' *Empire Strikes Back* were sold in 1984 for $12 million. Lukas, who had earlier vowed that "*Empire Strikes Back* would never be available in America's living rooms" because he planned to keep releasing the movie to theaters, later realized that the home movie is bringing Hollywood's revenues second only to theatrical box offices.[8]

The problem, however, is to convince consumers to purchase rather than rent pre-recorded movies. Because pre-recorded videocassettes were costing about $79.95 (until 1984), but can be rented out for as little as $1.50 a night, almost all movies that are sold are sold to retail stores rather than directly to the users.

One strategy to cash in on the rental returns by the movie industry, represented by the Motion Picture of America Association (MPAA), has been to seek compensation through percentages or taxes on rentals. Another strategy has been to reduce the purchase price.

For instance, Paramount experimented successfully with a reduction price program during the Christmas 1984 season, with prices reduced to as low as $25. Others followed suit, including Warner Brother's *Purple Rain* for $29.98, CBS' *Star Wars* for $39.98, and CBS-Fox Video's *Empire Strikes Back* for $79.98.

A factor in Hollywood's problem has been the legal difficulty of the "first sale doctrine," part of the U.S. copyright laws. This doctrine denies copyright owners any rights over the disposition of a work after its initial sale. Thus, Hollywood studios cannot control what a purchaser such as a rental company does with a videocassette. As a result, studios cannot differentiate in their sales between the final consumer and the rental markets, although they are entirely different markets in terms of returns to the studios. In a sales scenario, each videocassette sold at the low retail price of $40 returns approximately $4.70 to the copyright holder.[9] (Theatrical exhibition returns about 50¢ per viewer. Thus, even if 10 people viewed the purchased tape, the studio's revenue would not fall far below box office returns.) However, rental returns are much lower. Dealers can easily recover their costs and proceed to take in more profits, with the studio achieving no gains beyond the first sales income.

Home Video Preferred Over Theaters

Presented with a choice of viewing a movie on rented tape and viewing it in the theater, 62% of respondents in a recent survey preferred to rent a tape, whereas only 34% chose to go to the theater (see Fig. 11.6). This does not, however, translate into doom for the movie theaters. There are still ardent fans of new theatrical (movie) releases as well as lovers of the irreplaceable theater atmosphere. With the current slow down in the sales of videocassettes, there might be some good days ahead for movie theaters.

In 1985, the cassette business added $2 billion a year in revenue to Hollywood coffers. At present, cassette rentals and sales total $7.2 billion annually and that number is expected to grow at a sluggish rate of less than

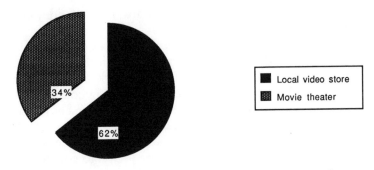

FIG. 11.6. Likelihood of viewing movie in theater or renting/buying from local video store at same cost. (*Source*: Electronic Media/SRI Survey, December 14, 1987.)

10% worldwide. Although this might be interpreted as a classic sign of a market that has attained maturity, the cassette market is still in its infancy and will continue to grow into the 1990s.

Although cassette sales might be less popular among VCR owners, rentals will continue to show a marked increase. Broadcast and cable television program recording by VCR households will eventually have an adverse effect on the cassette sales market unless the prices of cassettes are lowered drastically from what they are now.

HOME VIDEO AND COPYRIGHT LAW

In November 1976, MCA and Disney Studios instituted a lawsuit against Sony Corporation, its advertising agency, and four videocassette recorder retailers, charging that Sony and its agents induced infringement of copyright. It was the first major litigation to confront the home video industry.

As the case developed, it joined the whole Motion Picture Association of America (MPAA) and its lobbyists on one side and Sony, VCR retailers, and consumers on the other. The basic argument centered around the fact that VCR's unique capability to make copies of copyrighted materials directly from broadcast or cable television or to make copies of pre-recorded video cassettes, without paying those who own the copyrights in these creative works, posed serious questions of equity and fairness which also debased the essential protections of copyright. Noting that the principal use of VCRs was to record and playback copyrighted materials, the MPAA asserted that the practice of recording these copyrighted materials was unfair to copyright owners who were deprived of control over their products and who were also deprived of direct compensation for the additional unauthorized uses of their materials.

It was further argued by the MPAA that the chances of distributing their works in favorable markets such as subsequent television showing, theatrical re-release, prerecorded cassette and disc markets were jeopardized by incessant recordings of these materials. Recording commercial television programs off-the-air was said to have been adversely affecting the audience rating system," reducing the value of advertising time, and preventing copyright owners from earning appropriate revenues from licensing to the broadcast medium. It was therefore logical to conclude that the threat posed by VCRs would adversely affect motion picture and video works, thereby "jeopardizing the ability and incentive to create. Thus, the American consumer was, in the long run, going to be denied diversity of programs, while the adverse effects of uncompensated home video would continue to increase as the VCR market expanded. The MPAA asked that the court rule that the recording of off-air programs was unconstitutional, invoking the copyright law.[10]

Originally filed at the U.S. District Court in Los Angeles in 1976, the suit was won by the defendants with the court arguing that neither the 1909 nor the 1976 copyright laws "gave copyright holders monopoly power over an individual's off-the-air copying in his home for private noncommercial use."[11] Two years later on October 19, 1981 this decision was reversed by a three-member U.S. Court of Appeals in San Francisco. The Federal Appellate Court ruled that "Videotape recording of copyrighted television programs, even if done at home only for private use, was in infringement of the rights of those who own the programs."[12] The court further held that "the millions of consumers who use videotape machines to record programs off their living room television screens could be sued for damages, along with the companies that manufacture or distributed such devices, the stores that sold them and their advertising agencies that encouraged their purchases."

Yet the court failed to make any binding statement regarding damages. It was apparent that it would be almost impossible for owners of the shows (TV network and production studios) to determine who was recording or how much each recording was costing them on a case-by-case basis. Acknowledging the complexities of the relief question, the Court of Appeals suggested that a possible solution was to have the VCR manufacturers make royalty payments to the owners of the shows. The Court also noted that an injunction against further manufacture and sale of videotape recorders should be reconsidered as a possible remedy.

An appeal was made to the U.S. Supreme Court. Led by Jack Valenti, President of the MPAA, the Hollywood forces compiled a memorandum that among other things accused the defendants of making an excessive profit on VCRs over a short period of time; building unnecessary libraries of copyrighted video works amounting to some 84 million copies of television transmissions over a 1-year period; excluding TV commercials while recording on VCRs, which threatened the incentive for advertisers to engage in TV advertising; using VCRs for time-shifting, harming copyright owners and others who depended on copyright protection; and harming the public by contributing to a long-range loss in product quality and diversity of copyright works.

In proposing what they termed "A fair solution to the home video recording dilemma," the MPAA cited two proposed legislations that they helped formulate: S.31 introduced by Senator Charles McMathias (R–MD) and H.R. 1030 introduced by Representative Don Edwards (D–CA) and Carlos Moorhead (R–CA). These bills were directly asking manufacturers and importers of VCRs and blank tapes to pay royalty fees to the copyright owners.

On January 17, 1984, the Supreme Court ruled that noncommercial, private home videotaping of off-the-air copyrighted programs was legal and did not constitute copyright infringement. The majority opinion, which was read by Justice John Stevens and joined by Chief Justice Warren Burger and Justices William Brennan, Byron White, and Sandra O'Connor ruled that "time-shifting, recording a program for later viewing does not harm the copyright owners in the movie industry, and therefore falls under the fair use statute of present copyright law." Justice Stevens noted that prohibition would "merely inhibit access to ideas without any countervailing benefit."

He pointed out:

One may search the Copyright Act in vain for any sign that the elected representatives of the millions of people who watch TV everyday have made it unlawful to copy a program for later viewing at home, or have enacted a flat prohibition against the sale of machines that make such copying possible.

He continued:

It may well be that the congress will take a fresh look at this new technology, just as it so often has examined other innovations in the past. But it is not our job to apply laws that have not yet been written.

Following Justice Steven's comments, several bills are now pending in Congress on this subject. Among them are S.31 and H.R. 1030. Also in consideration are S.175 by Senator Dennis DeConcini (D–AZ), which would exempt hometaping from copyright liability, a companion bill (H.R. 175) by Representative Stan Parris (R–VA) and Thomas Foley (D–WA) and H.R. 1027 and H.R. 1029, which would modify the "first sale doctrine."

EMERGINING NEW TECHNOLOGIES
FOR THE FUTURE

Since 1981, there has been a dramatic growth in videotape recorder technology, the VTR industry, and most remarkably in its nonbroadcasting and consumer-oriented sector. The expansion of the videocassette recorder, and its related industry during this relatively short time span has enabled it to play one of the leading roles in the worldwide electronic industry today. The highly complex nature of the art of VTR engineering has often subjected it to state-of-the-art levels of related peripheral technologies such as the precision of machine work, material selections, and chemical process rather than a direct and simple skill levels of the electrical and electronic design engineering. Therefore, consumer VTR owes much of its development to these various collateral technological developments, especially with respect to components such as heads and tapes as well as improvements in the VTR proper. However, as the potential of the VCR continues to stir widespread interest and activity as that created by color television, the overall improvement and quest for new developments continues.

The Digital Era

The home entertainment industry has added another important feature to most of its products. Digital effect seems to be the answer to the industry's definition of a "convenient product." Imagine being able to take total control of a VHS VCR that can perform multi-screen freeze, strobe, channel scan, and intro search. With digital effect, the screen can be divided into 4, 9, or 16 segments, so that a variety of programs on other channels can be viewed on the same screen. The digital circuitry also enhances overall picture quality as well as quality of still, doublespeed playback, five-speed slow motion, and variable fast-motion playback.

Apart from these special effects, digital circuitry also improves the overall picture quality and the ability to view pictures during searches. Digital-effect VCRs use versatile microprocessors to compliment the signal proceeding circuitry of conventional analog machines. Video signals are converted by these chips into electrical pulses. These pulses represent the numbers 0 and 1, which make up the binary map of the video signal. In computers, diskettes can be copied several times with the thousandth copy remaining identical to the first one. In VCR digital-effect it is not true, because the video signals are recorded as analog. It is also possible to change the map with no damage to the original signal, allowing for a variety of enhancement and special effects. The microprocessors that store the digital information are called Dynamic Random Access Memory (DRAM).

Most digital VCRs use DRAM microprocessors accommodating 256 kilobytes of binary data each. The industry is just beginning to see an integration of the digital effect with other new technological trends such as High Quality (HQ), S-VHS, S-VHS-C, and compact disc. The home entertainment center of the future has a lot to offer indeed by way of superior technology.

Digital Audiotape (DAT)

Digital audiotape (DAT) is the most recent technological achievement in the audio industry. It represents the collective engineering abilities of leading audio hardware and tape manufacturers. DAT uses a sophisticated ultra-compact cassette, about half the size of the analog cassette, providing up to 2 hours (4 house in the EP mode) of continuous digital recording with specifications that rivals professional studio digital recorders performance.

The quality of DAT sound is unbelievably superior, and compared to Compact Disc (CD). Its frequency is flat from 2 to 22,000 Hz, while its dynamic range is 96 dB, above the entire audio band Distortions, hiss and modulation noise, wow and flutter are nonexistent. This translates into the fact that any recorded material assumes an original quality when played back on DAT. Equipped with exceedingly tight cassette and disk mechanism tolerance, DAT utilizes a highly advanced error correction system. Data that would have otherwise be degraded are reconstructed by a built-in hardware circuitry.

How DAT Works. DAT's unique ability to store so much data is due to its helical-scan recording format derived from VCR technology. In streaming tape drive and conventional music cassettes the tape moves past a stationary head as data are recorded from one end of the tape to another along a long track. Tapes can be joined together or laid on parallel tracks if increased capacity is needed.

In helical-scan recording used in VCRs and DAT, the information is stored in diagonal stripes from the bottom of the tape to the top. The tape and head move simultaneously in nearly perpendicular directions. DAT uses two heads, which take turns in laying tracks. Although the magnetic orientation of the track is slightly different, the tracks are parallel. The tracks are closely knitted, without conferring with each other. Its ingenuity lies in each head recognizing and reading the track it recorded without distraction from adjacent track.

DAT devices for computer storage is expected to make its debut in the market in 1988. In the United States, a joint venture between Sony Corporation and Hewlett-Packard Company has resulted in a standard format proposition and a staunch promise to introduce machines using the format in

Digital audio tape.

A digital audio tape, or DAT, system records data in helical tracks
like candy cane stripes, using two heads. Data bits from track A are
oriented differently from those of track B, allowing close packing of
tracks without interference. In conventional streaming tape technology
data bits are oriented similarly from track to track leading to more:
interference

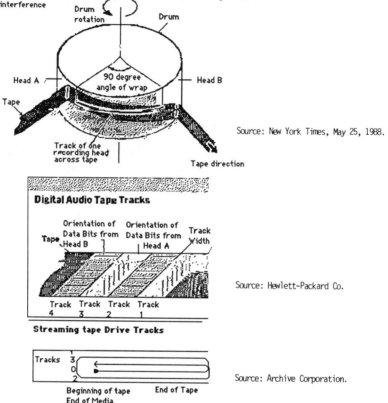

Source: New York Times, May 25, 1988.

Source: Hewlett-Packard Co.

Source: Archive Corporation.

FIG. 11.7. Digital audiotape. (*Source:* New York Times, May 25, 1988.)
Digital audiotape tracks. (*Source:* Hewlett-Packard Co.) Streaming tape
Drive tracks. (*Source:* Archive Corporation.)

1989. Moreover, two leaders in streaming tape drive technology, Archive
Corporation of Costa Mesa, California, and Wangtek, a subsidiary of Rexon
Inc., have endorsed the Sony/Hewlett-Packard plan. This move has been
interpreted as a hint that DAT may take over as the predominant recording
method in the near future.

If DAT makes it into the computer industry, it will be the second consumer electronic device that has found solace there. An important use was
found for musical compact disk as CD-ROM's optical disk for storing disk

data bases. In these two instances, the manufacturers are counting on economy of scale resulting from huge volumes on the consumer side to render the computer product less expensive. Without this success on the consumer side, it might be difficult for DAT to be successful on the computer side. DAT's overall success on the computer side however, depends on a universal agreement on standard. At this point this is still uncertain, for although Sony and Hewlett-Packard have agreed to a 3.5-inch floppy disk drive, some manufacturers including Hitachi Ltd., support a different format.

A typical DAT system uses a drum 30mm in diameter that rotates at 2,000 RPMs as the tape makes contact with a quarter of its circumference. Despite the minute size of the tape (3.81mm wide), it is able to meet the required recording density of 3 million bits per second. DAT's tape is threaded around a rotating head drum in a similar fashion to the VCR's. DAT is not selfish either, although sounds recorded from modern digital sources give the best result, a significant improvement in sound reproduction can be received from LPs, tapes, and other analog sources.

DAT is considered the best in consumer audio technology. Its exemplary quality is the reason key audio industry policy makers as well as politicians have been fighting to limit its progress.

Legal Implications. DAT has generated its share of controversy in the audio industry. VCR had its ordeal in the law court as the movie industry fought for copyright compensations from manufacturers. Dual cassette players were not free from such industry problems either, as fear of consumers being able to record from side A to B gripped industry policy makers in the United States. No doubt then, that DAT with all its excellent qualities, has been the center of recent political uproar in the United States. The problem is that the Recording Industry Association of America seems threatened by DAT's excellent qualities. The industry's case is that reproductions made by DAT are as good as the original, enough to increase consumers preference in duplicating on friends' or relatives' DAT units rather than purchasing new pre-recorded compact discs and audiotapes.

CBS was quick to developed an anti-taping device (blackbox) called Copycode System that is designed to prevent consumers from making high quality copies of compact discs using their DATs. As usual, DAT's fate was left for the politicians to decide. Fortunately, DAT seems to be winning. The National Bureau of Standards (NBS) has recently ruled against the introduction of the Copycode System after 5 months of testing, which was ordered by several Congressional committees as a result of intense lobbying by the Recording Industry Association of America. NBS found, among other things, that Copycode causes distortion in sound, and that it could be bypassed by using cheap external signal conditioning components.

The case against DAT, however, is not completely over yet. The Recording Industry Association of America (RIAA), reacting to the disappointing verdict issued by NBS, vows to resolve the problem through negotiation, legislation, or litigation. Issuing a warning, RIAA promises to sue any manufacturer who tries to introduce DAT recorders to the American market before a genuine solution is reached on the issue.

New Function for DAT.   Although the verdict seems to be in favor of the DAT manufacturers, it is not certain when the technology will be made available for consumer use. It is, however, going to be introduced under a different guise—as a computer storage device. As an audio hardware/software, DAT has the ability to store music as digital bits, producing distortion and hiss-free tapes. But, DAT's digital signal recording ability has made it appropriate for storing computer data that already exist in digital format. A DAT cassette is three-eighths of an inch thick, the size of a credit card, and can hold 1.3 gigabytes, or 1.3 billion characters of data, the equivalent of two encyclopedia.

Until now, the primary means of storing information in computers has been with tape drives. However, the major disadvantage of a tape drive is the length of time it takes for the tape to wind to the desired position. But, tapes have the advantage of being an important backup storage to preserve data in case a disk "crashes." Tapes are also used as an inexpensive way of distributing bulky software programs that are too large to distribute on floppy disks. Reel-to-reel tape has long been used as backup storage for mainframe computers by large corporations.

The market for disk drives has been expanding in recent years, with the surge in personal computers. Some personal computers are equipped with disk drives with storage capacity of 40, 60, or over 100 megabytes. This amount of data cannot be backed up on floppy disk. Currently, the streaming tape drive comes with cartridges using ¼-inch wide tape. As of now, the streaming tape drives are considered slightly faster than DAT drive.

The DAT cassette used for computer storage purposes would be the same used for music, although the players require extra features. DAT computer units would need extra error correction circuits as a single mistake in a computer program can be disastrous.

Digital Videotape Recorder

The digital concept, as it relates to television and the videotape recorder, has been known to engineers for almost two decades. However, although technical merits have been anticipated in principle, there have always been great concern and reservation as to its practicality. The digital concept has

FIG. 11.8. Panasonic prism Model-45905 projection television. The Panasonic prism projection television Model-45905 is technologically advanced. It is equipped with a newly developed hybrid Internal Magnetic Focus (IMF) gun, impregnated-cathode tubes, an aspherical fine-element lens system and black level correction circuit. Other features include a menu driven, intelligent remote control, a colorful on-screen menu package, stereo system with graphic equalizer and a 10w-per-channel amplifier and ultra-stylish cabinet. (*Source:* Courtesy, Panasonic Corporation, Secaucus, NJ.)

already been used in television. Toshiba America, Incorporated, was the first to unveil its $1,200 digital television set at the 1984 Summer Consumer Electronics Show in Chicago. This technology was based on the Digit 2000 chip set developed by ITT Intermetall GmbH, of West Germany.

The Digit 2000 consists of a five-chip kit of very large-scale integrated circuits that digitize all audio and video functions between the tuner and the output stages. Although its performance was far below expectations as evidenced from the initial poor picture quality of Toshiba's set,[13] it immediately attracted the attention of several other manufacturers. Among the firms producing color television sets using Digit 2000 circuits are Sony, Matsushita, Toshiba, and ITT Consumer Products Group in West Germany. Others, including RCA and General Electric Corporation, were skeptical until 1985, citing a desire to be sure of offering digital sets with performance level "equal to or better than those of their analog counterpart." Moreover, the main factor that seemed to divide the industry was the justification of whether digital television could offer consumers the value that its initial premium price would command. Initially, digital was no match to its analog counterpart. However, with the introduction of new improvements such as the two-chip kit, it is capable of implementing add-on features such as videotex, ghost compensation, and convergence correction at little extra cost.[14]

The concept of digital VTR has not been as easy as digital television. General thinking concerning the practicality of digital VTR has always been unfavorable mainly due to the fear that a large quantity of tape would be consumed. However, with the introduction of a new idea by John Baldwin, digital VTR has captivated an intense interest in the industry that has led to the development of several prototypes and an effort to adopting an optimum method of signal coding worldwide, as well as the possibilities of adopting final technical standards. These advances concern only the commercial and industrial videotape recorders. Its application has been successfully implemented in consumer video recording, however, the price tag is still astronomical. At present, the few digital VCR units available are sought after by "videophiles." By 1989, almost every VCR manufactured will be equipped with digital system. Broadcasters are optimistic about this technology. "The generally recognized principal merit of the digital system is in facilitating less degradation of the program material quality, even after the repeated editing operations which are usually required in broadcasting productions; but this would not be likely to occur often with consumer VTRs."[15]

Perpendicular Recording

A majority of video engineers agree that the main stream of development for the future of the VTR is in the high diversification of signal recording, and to this end have supported the proposal of an interesting technological concept. This system that is not completely new (but rather once forgotten) has been revived and improved upon by Professor Iwasaki of Japan, who, with his colleagues, have proved that self-demagnetization of signals perpendicularly recorded in media is small compared with that of signals recorded in the usual transversal mode. An attempt to arrive at hardware designs that would meet the requirements for practical applications has been in progress.

Magneto-Optical Recorders

This technology is triggered by the read-only-memory disc named Direct Read After Write (DRAW), which was introduced a few years ago. The Magneto-Optical Recording invention is the Magnetic-Laser-Optical reusable Direct Write and Read Memory system using Kerr rotation. Although it is most literally part of the videotape family, it will have possible applications that will be common with VTRs in the future. It will have a strong impact on ready and random accessibility of recording.

Simply, this new technology permits a linkup through a single unit of compact disk recorders, VCRs, and personal computers. It is viewed as an all-in-one home entertainment and information center; and because its total implementation is complex to meet in the near future, the industry is committed to introduce the technology in bits and pieces. The introduction of individual magneto-optic disks that will improve performance of personal computers and home audio systems as well as new units to play these disks were expected in the market by 1987. Optimem, a subsidiary of Xerox is expected to introduce a machine that uses the new computer disk by 1988.

Basically, magneto-optic technology encodes information in the form of patterns of magnetic particles on a plastic or other solid surface. However, the prototype machines under development use laser lights to read the encoded information as opposed to magnetic heads used by standard magnetic tape or disk systems now in use. Although modern compact disks and certain computer disks use laser light, magneto-optic disks have an advantage of being able to erase and re-record signals.

The magneto-optic technology industry is expected to grow to more than $11 billion by 1995. The American companies involved in this new technology are 3M, IBM, Control Data, Eastman Kodak, and Xerox. Although pioneers in the field, they now face a competition from the following Japanese corporations, Hitachi, Fujitsu, NEC, and Matsushita.

Due to its flexibility, magneto-optic disks are expected to provide a heady competition for manufacturers of high-density hard-disk computer drives such as IBM Winchester 3380.[16] The new disks are expected to have little impact on the compact disk market, as they primarily will be used to record radio and television broadcasts or other home recordings, whereas compact disks are usually pre-recorded music.

HIGH DEFINITION TELEVISION (HDTV)

Most viewers in the 87.4 million television households in the United States probably would not find anything wrong with the picture quality they receive from their television. This of course is not the case with few dedicated and innovative television enthusiasts. The latter group of course, perceive our present television system as an anachronism at best, and anxiously await its condemnation. As a component of a field that has captured an enormous attention, and recorded extensive new technological outputs since the advent of the VCR, improvement on the television has indeed taken a back seat. The guilt in the media technology circle is even intensified when one is reminded that our present television system has been in existence since 1953 when our present U.S. color television standard was approved by the National Television Systems Committee (NTSC).

During the past two decades, researchers have recorded a significant progress in achieving what many regard as an ultimum standard in television imagery. Spearheaded by the Japanese, "a new and improved" television standard, simply called high definition television (HDTV) was demonstrated in 1981. Ever since, it has been regarded by advocates as a standard that should be accepted all over the world.

What Is HDTV? High definition television is known for its bright and vivid color; with picture quality whose resolution almost equals that of 35mm film; a much larger but proportionately wider screen—the same aspect ratio as a movie theater screen; and complete with compact disk quality digital stereophonic sound.

HDTV has (1,125 lines, 60 Hertz), twice as many lines as the 525-line U.S. standard television. When compared to the present color and luminance degrees, poor horizontal resolution and narrow 4 : 3 aspect ratio, the HDTV is "immaculate." If HDTV is all that it is said to be, then why has it not been widely accepted internationally since its first demonstration in 1981? It has received a variety of praise from industry experts, as well as skepticism from others. The debate continues.

HDTV Issues

Since NHK (Japanese Broadcasting Corporation) unvailed the 1,125-line/60 Hertz HDTV at the Society of Motion Picture and Television Engineers' Conference in San Francisco in 1981, the television industry has been divided into two groups—proponents and opponents of the HDTV.

Although proponents seem to be the majority, several elements in this group differ on how to achieve an acceptable HDTV as well as a suitable modus operandi. Over the years several committees and task forces have been set up worldwide to tackle problems inherent with the HDTV. At issue are the method of transmission and compatibility.

Method of Transmission

A major issue facing the acceptance of the HDTV is whether it can be transmitted to individual viewers' homes in the form of conventional broadcasting while still maintaining its quality. During the past decade, the search for a system of transmitting a new and improved form of television has intensified. Three distinct approaches to the problem have been proposed. They are MUSE, single-channel approach, and two-channel compatibility.

MUSE.   Opponents of the Japanese HDTV's 1,125-line/60 Hertz that operate with an aspect ratio of 16:9, argue that a vast information is lumped in HDTV signals. In fact, HDTV requires 30 megaHertz of spectrum space—five times the six megaHertz bandwidth needed to transmit the present U.S. standard NTSC 525-line/60. With an aspect ratio of 4:3. NHK's success in developing the HDTV was based on their bandwidth-compressing techniques that were instrumental to the development of the MUSE system. This system allows 1,125/60 pictures to be cramped into a bandwidth of 8.1 megaHertz.

However, the MUSE system is the only HDTV transmission system that has been genuinely tested under actual broadcast conditions as opposed to other methods that are still considered in the laboratory stage. A demonstration of MUSE was co-sponsored by the NAB, and the Association of Maximum Service Telecasters (AMST) in Washington during an over the air transmission test.

Single-Channel Approach.   NBC is spearheading the single-channel transmission approach. Their system known as the Advanced Compatible Television System (ACTV) is a joint project of the David Sarnoff Research Center and General Electric/RCA Consumer Electronics. The objective is to improve TV transmission within the 6 megaHertz limit of the NTSC channel. In their computer simulation demonstration at an HDTV colloquium in Canada in October 1987, a 1,025-line picture with a 5:3 aspect ratio was shown. ACTV system proposes time compression and expansion techniques to broadcast a four-part signal in a single channel. Special ACTV wide screen receivers would be employed to decode the four parts, resulting in quality images, and NTSC sets would receive the normal 525-line image.

Two-Channel Compatibility.   This concept is based on the premise that signals from two channels, probably a normal 6 megaHertz of bandwidth and 3 megaHertz from an UHF band, should yield quality pictures. The signal would be received by the existing conventional NTSC sets. This system would adopt 1,125 lines with an aspect ratio of 5:3, and a possibility of utilizing a 16:9 ratio if necessary. Deeply involved in this research is the New York Institute of Technology's Science and Technology Research Center in Fort Lauderdale, Florida.

Similarly, North American Philips Corporation has proposed a two-channel system called HD-NTSC. Their two channels are defined in terms of NTSC and augmentation signal package (NTSC-SP and A-SP). Philips equates its NTSC-SP with the conventional 525/60 NTSC signal. A-SP is able to boost side panels the extra parts of the high-definition TV picture, with data thereby increasing aspect ratio from 4:3 to 16:9. With the high standard (1,125 lines) set by NHK, it is hard to accept such systems transmitting low 525 lines as HDTV.

Compatibility

A major concern in the industry in terms of a general acceptance of HDTV is compatibility. First, given the importance of television in our society, and its present high penetration level in the U.S. (over 130 million sets), uniformity among hardware then becomes a priority. Although the television industry is concerned about compatibility in the industry, it is also concerned about competiting industries such as the VCR and cable industries.

The main problem is the uncertainty as to whether MUSE transmission would ever be accepted as a U.S. terrestrial transmission standard. Despite compressing MUSE into 8.1 magaHertz, MUSE is still incompatible with NTSC's 6 megaHertz limit. Currently, it is impossible for any television unit in the United States to receive the MUSE signal. Opponents have used this deficiency as a major weapon against the system.

NHK seems to have a keen foresight into possible future acceptance of its system. A joint venture between NHK and Broadcasting Technology Association of Japan (BTA) is determined to make available a variety of HDTV production equipment and accessories on the international market by 1989. Hardware and software would include high-sensitivity cameras, base-band cassette VTR, digital video recorders, and so on. Consumers would be able to purchase special projection display units and MUSE to NTSC converters that would be attached to conventional television sets. MUSE television receivers, VCRs, and video disks would be available for sale by 1990.

In his report submitted to the House Telecommunication Subcommittee, Masao Sugimoto, NHK's chief engineer noted that his company intends to make available 100,000 receivers in 1990 and 500,000 in 1991 to consumers in Japan and the United States respectively. By then, NHK would be expected to be able to send MUSE signals to the United States by satellite.

The political impasse involved in the acceptance of this vital technology has already been noticed at length since the early 1980s. Opposition to the HDTV is rather strong in Europe. The Advanced Television Systems Committee (ATSC) is one of the series of bodies formed to study the HDTV issue. ATSC correctly sympathizes with the Europeans. It is argued that the technology does not allow for compromise standards at a higher field rate such as 100 Hertz, nor is it conducive with 50 Hertz, which is considerably lower than the 60 Hertz field rate. ATSC has guided the United States during the 1985–1986 international debate on the problems of HDTV. The group, however, recommended to the State Department that the United States adopt the 1,125/60 HDTV system as the world standard. It also noted that the system is gaining rapid acceptance in television and cinema production. Another organization that is exploring the same subject is the International Radio Consultative Committee (CCIR), a United Nations-sponsored body responsible for setting world television and other technical standards. In a conference convened at Dubrovnik, Yugoslavia in May 1986, CCIR postponed decision on HDTV until late 1988 due to European opposition to the U.S.-supported 1,125/60 technology.

SUPER VHS

Super VHS or S-VHS is the latest generation of the Video Home Systems format. Until its introduction, the Betamax was considered to have the best picture in the industry. Not any longer. S-VHS is sharper than Betamax and more powerful than broadcast television. It outperformed any previous consumer video format and off-the-air reception.

FIG. 11.9. RCA Super-VHS VPT 640. (*Source:* RCA Consumer Electronics Division, Indianapolis, IN.)

FIG. 11.10.   Sony 8mm VCR Model EV-S800. EV-S800 is Sony's third 8mm
VCR. It has a jog/shuttle dial that makes it easy to select precise editing
points. The deck can be used as a player for assemble editing or as the
recorder for insert editing with its flying head that creates relatively clean
edits. It delivers 260 lines of horizontal resolution and is one of the most
versatile 8mm around. (*Source:* Sony Corporation of America, Park Ridge,
NJ.)

The advent of the S-VHS has added to the certainty that VHS can un-
equivocally be regarded as the world standard for home video as the market share for Beta continues to decline. For years, although the most popular in terms of sales, VHS has always been the underdog, accused of
technical inferiority to both Beta and 8mm. VHS manufacturers took the
first step toward bringing their product to par by intergrating high quality
(HQ) picture enhancement circuits, which resulted in sharper pictures, and
eliminated noisy video signals. Super VHS takes the technology a step further by enhancing picture resolution by about 80%. With 425 lines of
horizontal resolution (nearly double the 240-line capability of standard

FIG. 11.11.   Sony's ED Beta VCR—EDV-9500. Sony's ED Beta VCR Model
EDV-9500 boasts an incredible picture quality. It is equipped with Hi-Fi
sound system and has an improved signal-to-noise of 3dB over Super-
Beta. It has 500 lines of horizontal resolution. (*Source:* Sony Corporation of
America, Park Ridge, NJ.)

VHS), it delivers dramatic improvements in both color and clarity, a quality comparable to professional 1-inch videotape recorders.

JVC, the VHS format licensor, introduced the Super VHS in fall of 1987. JVC guaranteed home video users picture quality in the extended play (EP) mode. In conventional VHS, tape recorded in the EP mode results in considerably poor image than those recorded in the standard play (SP) speed. Super VHS guarantees reduced interference and the elimination of distortion of color and brightness.

Software

Super VHS requires an improved high-density oxide tape in a standard cassette shell notched to tell the recorder whether a standard or super tape is being used. Super VHS therefore uses Super VHS cassettes that meet short wave-length recording requirements such as high output, high frequency response, and smooth tape surface.

Compatibility

Super VHS has a limited compatibility with standard VHS. Due to the fact that Super VHS uses a higher frequency bandwidth to record the video signals, Super VHS recordings made on the new VCRs cannot be played on conventional VHS VCRs. However, conventional VHS tapes can be recorded, played, and freely interchanged between Super VHS and conventional VHS equipment. When Sony introduced its new Super Beta format in

FIG. 11.12.   RCA Super-VHS VPT 695. (*Source:* RCA Consumer Electronics Division, Indianapolis, IN.)

FIG. 11.13. Panasonic Super VHS Model PV-S4880. One of the highly acclaimed Super VHS equipped with a variety of Hi-tech components. S-VHS is noted for its superior picture and sound quality. (*Source:* Courtesy, Panasonic Corporation, Secaucus, NJ.)

1985, JVC was quick to criticize, noting that it was incompatible with existing Beta machines. This time JVC is at the receiving end of the criticism. JVC's limited compatibility may have an impact on sales of the S-VHS.

A complete S-VHS package consist of a Super VHS VCR, a high quality video monitor, preferably equipped with an S-Video (or Y/C) connector, and for live taping, a Super VHS camcorder, and a supply of Super VHS cassettes. Super VHS can be used with conventional televisions and camcorders that do not have S-Video connectors, however, the resolution will be limited to the specifications of the TV or camcorder. S-Video allows Super VHS to achieve superior performance. S-Video cables and connectors separate the luminance and chrominance components of the video signal, which are usually mixed in conventional video connections. The result therefore is cleaner, pure color pictures as well as elimination of interference, and greater audio fidelity.

When Super VHS is used to record broadcast signals, a difference in picture quality is evident. The reason is that the incoming TV broadcast

FIG. 11.14. JVC Super VHS HR-S7000U. (*Source:* Courtesy, JVC Company of America, Elmwood Park, NJ.)

FIG. 11.15. JVC's S-VHS VCR Model HR-S8000U. JVC's Super VHS Model HR-S8000U is equipped with a full digital-effect capability, flying erase heads, Hi-Fi sound and sophisticated LCD remote controlled programming. It comes with a flip-up remote. Through the digital-effect clips, freeze frames, and 4, 9 or 16 box picture-in-picture grids with strobes solarization, mosaic, and the latest digital zoom effect can be created. This digital-zoom effect enables one to blow up a quarter of the screen to full size. (*Source:* JVC Company of America, Elmwood Park, NJ.)

signal is higher in horizontal resolution (336 lines) than conventional VHS recording. The difference in picture quality depends on the resolution ability of the television set or monitor. Recording live with a Super VHS camera or camcorder gives an excellent picture quality as the equipment takes full advantage of Super VHS' 425-line resolution capability.

JVC's first generation Super VHS (HR-S7000U) received maximum attention in the industry. JVC at that point placed higher emphasis on picture quality, thereby ignoring other considerably essential effects. Months later, new JVC VCR boasts an assortment of digital effects. The Super VHS is an expensive unit, suggesting that it would only be made affordable to a handful of consumers.

TIME-SHIFTING BY TELEPHONE

The term *time-shifting* has been synonymous with VCR almost from the beginning. The excitement that came with consumers' ability to record in absentia still lingers. With the increase in the workforce especially among women, time-shifting made it possible for consumers to work, and as well, return to enjoy their favorite daytime soap operas. In other words, the average VCR owner was able to "beat" television's own programming system. Time-shifting, however, is only good if one remembers to program the VCR before leaving home. Not long ago, answering machine manufacturers were able to add an interesting addition to its features whereby owners could switch it on by remote if they forgot to do so before leaving home. A similar technology has been extended to include the VCR.

Panasonic has introduced an innovative technique called the telephone answering programming in their PV-4826 4-head VCR (see Fig. 11.16). This

FIG. 11.16. Panasonic's Telephone Programming VCR. The PV-4826, four-head VCR manufactured by Panasonic enables a majority of VCR users who are accustomed to forgetting to program their VCR's before leaving home to do so by telephone. With the PV-4826, one can easily program the VCR by telephone to record any program on any channel on the television. (*Source:* Courtesy, Panasonic Corporation, Secaucus, NJ.)

equipment enables one to call his or her VCR from any touch-tone phone (or rotary dial phone, using a touch-tone generator) with instructions to record a specific program. Recording can be done instantaneously or later, for any amount of time up to 8 hours.

An estimated 75% of VCR owners who frequently depend on time-shifting also forget to program their VCRs before leaving home. To individuals in this group, the PV-4826 is a lifesaver. An important habit that they have to formulate now is that of leaving a blank tape in the deck each time the machine is not in use.

The set up of telephone programming is actually very simple (see Fig. 11.17). It requires only one extra connection to a standard VCR set up. The PV-4826 is equipped with a modular telephone cable and jack. The VCR's phone cable should be connected to any phone jack, and it can also be

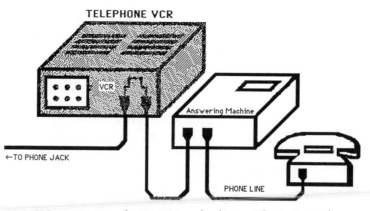

FIG. 11.17. How the PV-4826 works. (*Source: Video,* June 1988.)

connected to a telephone answering machine. When calling to program the VCR, the answering machine will likely pick up, but it can be turned off by entering a two-digit identification code that then switches the signal to the VCR.

The following is how a typical telephone programming sequence might be performed:

Step 1. Dial your home phone number. After 10 rings the VCR picks up.

Step 2. Enter the VCR's two-digit identification number; for example, 23.

Step 3. Type TAPE to inquire if there is a blank tape in the deck.

Step 4. Select a channel; C07#, for example, represents Channel 7.

Step 5. Select the required length of recording; L 230#, for instance, represents 2 hours and 30 minutes.

Step 6. Select the start time, such as T 1100p# for 11P.M.

Step 7. Rewind the tape if necessary by typing REW#.

Step 8. Sign off by typing "*".

Step 9. Hang up. (Each time a phone command is keyed in, the VCR beeps once if the command is accepted, or four times if it perceives a mistake.)

Features

On-Screen Display Programming.   The on-screen display programming feature allows PV-4826 users to program directly from their wireless remote. With this function, commands are verified in bold on-screen video graphics as they are transmitted from the remote. For further assistance, it also features auto prompter, which provides step-by-step instructions for each phase of programming automatically, each time the remote programming button is pressed. The on-screen programming feature also can be used to verify functions such as auto set, stand-by one-touch record, tape counter, time and various tape functions (play, rewind, fast forward, still).

Hi-Tech 4 Video Head System.   The PV-4826 is equipped with Hi-tech 4 video head system, which is based on the recently developed double azimuth head design. It improves on special effects in both SP and SLP modes resulting in excellent still frame and picture search. The hi-tech 4 uses a new sampling method that reads twice as much information as previous Panasonic 4-head systems. In this case, every field of video information is read, as opposed to every other field, so the "step-action" effect is eliminated from slow motion.

Additional Features. Besides the telephone and on-screen programmability, the hi-tech 4 PV-4826 features 155-channel digital quartz tuning with auto set. This new auto set devise enables users to add a secretly activated channel to their unit in proper numerical sequence by pressing a single button. Its audio/video noise-making system replaces noise from blank segments of tape and varied channels with a quiet, blue screen. Other PV-4826 features include high-speed omnisearch, one-touch record, and 43-function wireless remote control.

SUPER CAMCORDERS

The latest in camcorders, the S-VHS and S-VHS-C are rather identical, but unique. Their general feature is no different from any camcorder, with the four major components—a lens, a head assembly responsible for record-

(a)

(b)

FIG. 11.18. The EDC-55 ED Beta Camcorder is an ultra-tech machine. It weighs over 15 pounds and costs about $7,700 (1988). This camcorder is a cross between a professional and consumer equipment. Unlike other camcorders, it can be broken down into three parts—the variable-speed 10× zoom lens, the camera, and the VCR section. It is a ideal hardware for advanced consumers. (*Source:* Sony Corporation of America, Park Ridge, NJ.)

FIG. 11.19. JVC S-VHS Camcorder-GF-S1000H. The JVC Super VHS Camcorder Model GF-S1000H is loaded with new technological advances that include High Quality (HQ) System circuitry and luminance signal comb filter, Super Double-Azimuth 4-head (Super DA-4) System, ⅔-inch CCD Image Sensor, Hi-Fi VHS Stereo Sound, Audio Switching Noise Reduction Circuit, Multiple-Speed Electronic and Shutter, with horizontal resolution of over 400 lines, the GF-S1000H offers an improved picture quality. (*Source*: JVC Company of America, Elmwood Park, NJ.)

ing, a tape transport system, and an image-sensing device which comes either as a CCD or MOS chip. The most important component can be considered the image sensor that reads the image of the subject, breaking it down into an electronic message. With an impressive pixel (picture element) count of 350,000 to 400,000, S-VHS microprocessors have been able to improve on its resolution over others. Conventional units such as full-size VHS and VHS-C, Beta and 8mm have maintained pixels bordering 210,000, and 250,000 since the introduction of solid-state image sensors in 1983. The sudden yearn for high resolution microprocessors has had an impact in the market. The introduction of the S-VHS and S-VHS-C was delayed due to this high resolution consciousness.

The addition of hi-fi stereo audio recording capability to some VHS camcorders has further given them added sonic superiority impetus. 8mm has gained much favor through its audio frequency modulation (AFM) recording system. Simply, it uses a similar principle as FM radio to produce "mono-aural" high fidelity with 80 dB dynamic range. A major drawback, however, is in size. Hi-fi VHS and S-VHS are heavier than a typical 8mm camcorder.

During 1988, an estimated 2 million consumers in the United States will opt to purchase a camcorder. A record increase from the infinitesimal number that owned camcorders in 1986. The Electronic Industries Association estimated that about 1.6 million units was sold in 1987, translating into a 33% increase from the previous year. Being a high ticket item, an average consumer camcorder costs up to $1,500, with models equipped with the latest developments going almost as high as $2,000. According to the 1986 Simmons Market Research Bureau, Inc., owners of camcorders were reported to be college graduates, professional/nonprofessionals, with incomes of $35,000 and above. Their average age group was 35 to 44 with the average family having children 2 to 5 years of age. They are also considered as early innovators, and will pay an extra cost just to acquire some extra features.

Compact camcorders are gaining popularity. It is estimated that by 1991, compact VHS camcorders would have a 77% market share, whereas the full-size unit will maintain a 23% shore, and 8mm having no share whatsoever.

SUMMARY CONCLUSIONS

In its early history, magnetic sound recording suffered greatly from technical imperfections and economic mismanagement, which rendered it commercially impotent for a long period of time. Its acceptance later for motion picture sound recording, its expansion in European broadcasting in the 1930s, and the arrival of the two German industrial giants ensured an acceptable quality. The appropriation of German technology and the introduction of magnetic sound recording to the United States after World War II opened up a new era for the magnetic recording technology. It was now accepted as a superior recording medium especially by radio, and therefore given top economic priority in Europe as well as the United States. Investment in its development in the United States further expanded its uses into the home. Video recording technology began in the 1920s and by offering "close to live" images and solving the problematic 3-hour differential between the East and West coasts in the United States attracted the necessary research and development to reach a high degree of diffusion. Economically, videotape cut costs and saved time. Video technology continues to reap its profits as evidenced by the rapidly growing videocassette recording field.

FIG. 11.20. Sony Video 8 Pro Camcorder has been said to be a perfected version of Sony's previous Model CCD-V110 Video 8 Pro. The CCD-V220 add PCM (Pulse Code Modulation) stereo sound with meters for each channel, a push button-selectable narration MIC near the operators mouth and superior video quality. The added features makes the CCD-V220 23 ounces heavier than its predecessor. (*Source:* Sony Corporation of America, Park Ridge, NJ.)

Epilogue

Looking back to 1877 when Thomas Edison first mesmerized listeners by the sounds emanating from his electro-mechanical phonograph, and 1897 when Valdemer Poulsen made audio recording and instant playback on magnetic wire a reality; to the introduction of the digital audiotape (DAT) and Super VHS in 1987, it is quite easy to see the effect of those primary inventions on today's recording technology. Early recording inventions have paved the way for similar modern equipment, and the overall effect reaches far beyond the recording industry. The result has been a continuous development of superior consumer electronic products that are mostly compatible with major magnetic recording units for home or commercial use.

EMERGENCE OF THE VIDEO ERA

Color Television Standardization

The incessant rumors of color television pictures had been spreading since the introduction of black-and-white television. Finally, in 1950, the Federal Communications Commission chose a color television system that was incompatible with existing black-and-white receivers as the national standard. As it became necessary to explore an alternative, the National Television System Committee (NTSC) was appointed to study all color TV proposals. In 1953, the committee recommended a compatible method that was eventually approved by the FCC as the new standard.

An average television set in 1964 cost more due to the incorporation of all channels (both VHF and UHF) into all receivers. This was a gesture by the FCC that was meant to aid ultra-high frequency broadcasters (UHF channels 14 through 83). Added cost notwithstanding, manufacturers were able to market TV sets at considerable low prices due to efficiency in operation. Demand for color television sets skyrocketed in the 1960s.

Christened "home video terminal," the color television set has gained a new definition in the average home. The television screen has been put to use in a variety of ways apart from the conventional broadcast television. First, nonbroadcast services such as cable television and subscription or pay television shared the screen with broadcast television. Then a number of other services such as the videogame, which allowed viewers' interaction was introduced in 1972. By the mid-1970s, the videocassette recorder (VCR) was introduced. Its market penetration was initially gradual, but since the early 1980s, has increased rapidly.

The abundance of new sources of program turned the television screen into an all-purpose device. The consumers' ability to produce their own programming further made the VCR an invaluable device in the home. Pre-recorded tapes supplied by a number of video software manufacturers and many Hollywood movie companies were available in the market. Videodisc players also provided a less expensive program choice. Personal computers and videotex system encouraged owners and subscribers to interaction through the television screen. Finally, with the availability of direct satellite reception the viewer now has a wide array of choice in terms of programs.

The increasing expansion in the home video industry is an indication of how important society has come to accept the variety of products available to them. The exceedingly rapid evolution of various new generation home video formats such as Super VHS, 8mm Hi-Band, ED Beta, Super VHS-Camcorder is proof that this growth is a part of a larger trend. A major change is in progress in the media/communications industry. At the center of this evolution is the VCR.

There seems to be a "change of guard" in the media field with power being handed over to individuals in their living rooms rather than being based in the control room of network television or large movie corporation boardrooms as it has been for decades. More and more, the public is anticipating an emancipation from this long-standing media control. The trend that was developed almost a century ago with the wire audio recording, which later developed into the magnetic audio recording, and finally magnetic videotape recording has set a chain reaction.

What was once regarded a radical view of future electronic technology is now vastly becoming a common sight in most households in the United States. "Dreams" of an entire room being allocated to high technology receiving, recording, storing and playback; of large video screens, un-polluted video reception with superior sound quality and choice of hun-dreds of stations, of software; and finally the ability to create ones own programs have long become reality. The ensuring competition between the media and public is vastly leading to an interactive state. Compatibility seems to be the key to the enhancement of modern communication.

QUALITY COMMUNICATION

The revolution that started in the home entertainment industry in the 1970s stirred a considerable amount of public interest in the industry. The gradual change from broadcast television to other forms of nonbroadcast services and pre-recording programmings created a competition that forced the media to focus its attention on the home. Improvement in all aspects of media has been evidenced especially during the 1980s. Quality programs have been made possible by experience newscasters and creative person-nels as well as sophisticated technological hardware. The communication industry has aided in the progress achieved so far in media. The availability of a variety of telecommunication equipment that includes fiber-optic tele-phone systems, microwave delivery systems, complex satellite connections and computers have contributed to media's success.

COMMUNICATION OF THE FUTURE

The communication industry has continued to record an impressive growth over the past two decades. This trend has further attracted extensive attention toward the industry. This success is based on the impact of tech-nological innovation in commercial and consumer electronics that encom-pass the field of entertainment. Not too long ago, new technology enthusi-asts who foresaw an end to conventional broadcasting, predicting instead an integration of computers, satellites, television sets, fiber-optic hardware for information storage and various commercial and entertainment pur-poses were termed "radical." Pessimists, most of whom belong to the old school believed that an era for such "radical" change was decades, if not centuries away. However, that era is now.

More households are quickly assuming looks that were only known to exist in science fiction novels and movies. It is not unusual to see families designating the living room, basement, or attic as the "communica-tion/entertainment room." Assigned to the entire room are sophisticated electronic and video equipment such as the video screen, disc, tape, and stereo recorders/players, cable television hardware, camcorders, videotex and other interactive hardware programs. Furthermore, an earth station would be located at the backyard or on the roof and would be capable of receiving multiple channels from a great distance.

This is a far cry from the turn of the century, when a few wealthy living rooms were graced with the presence of an Edison phonograph or Berliner gramophone. The introduction of radio sets in 1920 soon changed the whole concept of home entertainment. The mechanical units gave way to electronic designs in radio.

A major reason for the advancement of the communication industry to the present level is the introduction of "electronics." Electronics is known to be the most influencial technology of the 20th century. So far, its ability seems to be limitless. Latest developments in microelectronics technology now make it possible for the consolidation of hundreds of thousands of electronic circuits on a dime-sized chip of silicon. This, in effect, has quickly developed into the driving force behind everyday functions at banks, offices, supermarkets, mail delivery, and other services. Almost every essential piece of accessory in our home, office, or surroundings has a bit of electronics embedded in them—phones, cars, clocks, radio, TV, microwave oven, and so on. The electronics revolution will continue to have a pervasive and deep-rooted effect on entertainment, communication, international trade, industrial productivity, national security, and our way of living.

Growing from a $200 million U.S. industry in 1927, the electronic industry was in 1986, a $201.4 billion industry, surpassing the chemical, steel, and automobile industries in sales volume. This growth has in effect stimulated interest and curiousity in the industry resulting in a massive research in an attempt to shape the future of the industry. No single month passes without an introduction of a significant equipment in the electronic field. This has been part of a wide-spread trend described as a interactive, fully integrated worldwide communication system. The quest for innovative technology, capable of leading the industry into the 21st century is in progress. Such foresight into the future has been the sole objective behind the establishment of the Media Laboratory at the Massachusetts Institute of Technology in Cambridge, Massachusetts. The Media Laboratory is sponsored by organizations that either jointly or individually sponsor these giant projects.

The Media Lab seems to be the center of hope for the future of the media industry. Back in the late 1970s, the three industries, broadcast and motion picture; print and publishing; and computer (viewed as overlapping one another), were predicted to almost merge by the year 2000. Following along this line of thinking, various divisions of the Media Lab were created, each responsible for researching a particular area. As of the beginning of 1987, the lab was divided into 11 sections whose primary tasks were to invent new ways of communicating. The divisions are:

1. Electronic Publishing—sponsored by IBM. This group investigates electronic books, newspapers, magazine and TV broadcast of the future.

2. The Speech Group—sponsored by the Defense Advanced Research Project Agency (DARPA), and Japan's Nippon Telephone and Telegraph concentrates on inventing sophisticated talking telephones.

3. The Advanced Television Research Program—sponsored by ABC, NBC, CBS, PBS, HBO, RCA, 3M, Tektronic, Ampex, and Harris. This group is trying to achieve the best quality picture that any television can provide by integrating into it some computer intelligence. Media Lab is researching its own version of HDTV.

4. Movies of The Future—sponsored by Movie Conglomerates such as Warner Brothers, Columbia, 20th Century Fox and Paramount. With the advent of the VCR revolution, the movie industry, a once mechanized industry, would compete with computer digitalization. How to service the impending threat by new technology is the focus of this study.

5. The Visual Language Workshop—sponsored by Polaroid, IBM, and Hell, a German printing firm. Their responsibility is to investigate how best computer can improve art.

6. Spatial Imaging—also known as holography, is sponsored by General Motors and DARPA. This group researches and invents various forms of three dimentional holograms.

7. Computers and Entertainment—sponsored by Apple Computer. This team explores ways in which computer could be used to entertain kids and adults alike by way of games, puzzles and other mind buggling activities.

8. Animation and Computer Graphics—sponsored by Japan's Television, NHK, and Bandai. Bent on inventing realistic animation, the group is bringing life into various computer generated graphics and animation as we know them today.

9. Computer Music—sponsored by the Science Development Foundation to explore the interaction of computer with various facet of music. Some might call it synthetic or interactive music.

10. The School of the Future—sponsored by IBM, LEGO, Apple Computer, MacArthur Foundation, and the National Science Foundation. This school investigates the result of grade school

students' interaction with the computer after being exposed to it for quite sometime.

11. Human–Machine Interface—sponsored by DARPA, the National Science Foundation, and Hughes Corporation. Their objective is to perfect a computer capable of responding to ones eyes and voice commands.

Other sponsors of these futuristic ventures, include: Mead, Dow Jones, Time Inc., Hewlett-Packard, Kodak, Polaroid, Schlumberger, Digital Equipment Corporation, *The Boston Globe*, *The Washington Post*, NEC, Hitachi, Sony, Sanyo, BBN (Bolt, Beranek & Newman), Asahi Shimbun, Fujitsu, Fukutake, Mitsubichi, and so on. Participating in the program are 100 government and corporate sponsors.

The diversified background of these organizations is testimonial to the objective of the media lab viz-à-viz the future communication industry—to unify or form an alliance between all media and communication. Being a proponent of the so called radical view, events at media lab then symbolizes my view of the communication of the future.

A LINK FROM THE PAST

The history of magnetic recording as traced from the late 1800s continues to have a tremendous impact on today's industry. Today, DAT and S-VHS, have replaced Edison's Phonograph and Poulsen's Telegraphone, but still maintain the basic recording principles invented a century ago. Currently, Media Lab and numerous other research outfits are hard at work perfecting inventions in television, optical fiber technology, "conversational desktop," interactive CDs. They are achieving results that are still not conceivable by a vast majority of the public. They are in effect breaking down the various boundaries and merging the various technologies in such a way that they could function in a three-way tie—independently, interdependently, or interactively.

These technologies are invented with the individual in mind. Today's consumer is an educated consumer. He or she is as fast as the society surrounding him or her. Therefore the consumer's model technology should be all-purpose, interactive, and portable. The consumer should be able to be in all continents of the world at the same time if need be. The satellite, telephone, computer and videoscreen fulfill this purpose. The VCR revolution has taken the whole broadcast evolution one step further.

The fate of broadcasters now more than any other time in history lies in the consumers' hands. The consumer is exposed to choices of programs.

He or she records what he or she wants, zaps through commercials, and can even create his or her own program if so desired.

Actually, we are now witnessing the dreams denied those early travellers who pondered Memnon's "voice," and experimenter's whose talking heads were anything but what they were supposed to be. We can now document every sound and movement made by our day-old infant until he is of age. We can now record any aspect of nature surrounding us, and above all we do it at will.

What a freedom! It must have been terrible for Friar Roger Bacon whose 13th-century talking head was nothing but a fraud. I bet he would be amazed by our television, tape and disc system, satellite earth stations, videotex, audio components, radio and car stereo, personal computers, game consoles, telephone, telecommunications and communications equipment, watches, calculators, electronic games, toys, security systems, appliances, and musical instruments. We have it all at home.

Notes

CHAPTER 2
REPRODUCING THE SOUND OF THE LIVING
WORLD

1. The Story of the Phonograph, *The Phonogram*, May 1900, p. 22.
2. *Ibid.* p. 23.
3. Duane H.D. Roller, The De Magnete of William Gilbert, Menno Hertzberg. The University of Oklahoma, March 1959, p. 14.
4. Epistle of Peregrinus of Maricourt Fl. 1269 AD. NP.
5. Sir William Snow Harris, Rudimentary Magnetism, J. Wkeale, London. 1850–52. p. 1.
6. The Story of Phonograph, *The Phonogram*, Nov. 1900. p. 27.
7. Emile Berliner, *The Gramophone: Etching, The Human Voice.* A paper read at the meeting of the Franklin Institute, May 16, 1888. p. 7.

CHAPTER 3
THE ORIGIN OF MAGNETIC RECORDING

1. Oberlin Smith, "Some Possible form of Phonograph," *The Electrical World*, September 8, 1888, p. 116.
2. *Ibid.*
3. *Ibid.*
4. "Poulsen Telegraphone," *Scientific America*, September 22, 1900, p. 78.
5. U.S. Patent 661,619.
6. Poulsen, "The Telegraphone": The equipment consisted of a board on

which was mounted a steel wire (piano wire) about five feet long and $\frac{1}{50}$th of an inch in diameter stretched on it. An electromagnet was slid along it, embracing the wire with one of its poles. The core of the electromagnet was a piece of soft iron wire about $\frac{1}{3}$ of an inch long and $\frac{3}{100}$ of an inch in diameter, and the electromagnet itself was in series with a battery and a microphone, or connected to a transformer in the microphone circuit. The wire remained completely unmagnetized at the beginning of operation. When the microphone was spoken into while the electromagnet was sliding along the wire with a velocity of about 1 meter per second, the current fluctuations produced registered themselves by means of the electromagnet on the steel wire. When the electromagnet was hooked up to a telephone, and made to run over the wire again, the telephone repeated what was spoken into the microphone. The main contributory factor here was the coercive nature of the steel wire on which magnetization had been impressed upon in undulations, causing permanent kinds of writing, and also recording the articulation of the voice. "When the electromagnet was connected to a moderate power battery and made to pass once more over the wire, the magnetic writing was obliterated under the influence of the constant magnetic force, which was great compared with the intensity of the writing magnetic forces." Parallel to the axis of the drum was a rod on which a kind of sleeve could slide. The electromagnet was fastened to this sleeve. The electromagnet embraced the steel wire with one or both of its poles when the equipment was in motion, and during the rotation, the steel wire pushed the electromagnet and the sleeve along the rod. Poulsen warned that every component in his apparatus had been carefully formulated, in terms of dimension, and construction of the electromagnet to correspond with the telegraphic application at hand, and cautioned that reliability depended on efficiency of application with other components." p. 208.

7. "Recording Telephones," *Nature*, August 16, 1900, p. 371.

8. Basil Lane, "75 Years of Magnetic Recording," *Wireless World*, March 1975, p. 104.

9. U.S. Patent 873,083.

10. *Hearing Before the Committee on Patents, United States Senate, 72nd Congress, 1st Session, on S. 1301, A Bill to Renew and Extend Certain Letters Patent.* March 10, 1932 (Washington D.C.: U.S. Government Printing Office, 1932), p. 39.

11. *Ibid*, pp. 24–25; Before World War I, the United States maintained two short-wave stations, one at Tuckerton, New Jersey, and the other at Saville, Long Island. Both stations formed part of the transatlantic network linked to a station outside Hamburg, Germany. The Tuckerton station was built and operated by Telefunken of Germany, while the Long Island station was operated by the Atlantic Communications Company, a corporate establishment in the United States. Later in 1914, the U.S. Navy raided the Tuckerton station, having received substantial evidence that it was being used to inform German U-boats of shipping movements on the U.S. coast. Among the list of inventory at Tuckerton were two telegraphone machines delivered by American Telegraphone in 1914, and were said to have been operating "with great success." In 1915, attention was once more drawn to the coast of New York and New Jersey as amateur radio operators complained of disturbing "musical buzzing noise" every night from 11:30 p.m. to the early morning hours. One ham radio operator, Charles E. Apgar of Westfield, New Jersey, later recorded

these noises consistently on his homemade wax cylinder recorder. Meanwhile, the news of the mysterious signal activities got to Chief Radio Inspector L. R. Kruman of the Bureau of Navigation in New York, who then summoned W. J. Flynn, Chief of the U.S. Secret Service, and Apgar to a meeting in New York. Apgar was asked to playback his recordings. Based on this, and other general suspicions, the German-operated station was seized on July 10, 1915, on the grounds that it was being used to transmit secret codes to Germany. At least one telegraphone was seized with Morse code messages recorded on it at standard speed. "The tape was then played at high speed, recorded in Germany, and played back at the original recording speed. There was no code to be broken after all."

Further testimony against Rood claimed that just before the United States entered World War I, the press was invited on a goodwill tour of a German submarine named "Deutschland," and while below deck, a photographer took pictures that clearly showed two telegraphones.

12. British Patent 331,859; Curt Stille.

13. See J.C. Adams, *The Development of a Magnetic Tape Recorder* (unpublished BS Thesis, Massachusetts Institute of Technology, 1938); R.G. Adams, *Magnetic Recording of Sound* (unpublished BS Thesis, MIT 1938); Curtis Hillyer, *The Development of a Magnetic Tape Recorder* (unpublished BS Thesis MIT, 1938).

14. James B. Darragh, Jr., "Flight Test Data Mechanically Recorded," *Aero Digest*, September 1940, p. 96. William Lafferty, Jr., *The Early Development of Magnetic Sound Recording in Broadcasting and Motion Pictures, 1928–1950.* (Unpublished Ph.D. dissertation, Northwestern University, Evanston, Illinois, 1981), pp. 7–8.

15. G.E.'s Model 20A used 11,500 feet of steel wire 0.004 inch in diameter and recorded for 30 minutes at 5 feet/seconds and 1 hour at 2.5 feet/seconds; "Voice Recorded on Hair-Like Wire," *General Electric Review*, December 1943, p. 694.

16. Magnecord was formed by four men, (John S. Boyers, J.L. Landon, Russ Tinkham, and Spec Barker). The latter two worked for Amour before establishing Magnecord; Mooney, Jr., p. 4.

17. "Sound Recording, The Blattner System of ElectroMagnetic Recording and Reproduction," *The Electrician*, October 18, 1929, p. 472.

CHAPTER 4
INTRODUCTION OF TAPE DEVELOPMENT AND
THE GERMAN MAGNETOPHON

1. AEG located in Berlin at the time, was the second largest electronics company in Germany next to Siemens Company.

2. Peter Hammar and Don Ososke, "The Birth of the German Magnetophon Tape Recorder 1928–1945." Reprinted from db, *The Sound Engineering Magazine*, March 1982, n.p.

3. Captain James C. Manard, *Fiat Final Report No. 708*, "High Frequency Magnetophone Magnetic Sound Recorders," January 1946, p. 47.

4. Richard H. Ranger, *Fiat Final Report No. 923*, "Further Studies in Magnetophones and Tapes," May 1947, p. 5.

5. William C. Lafferty, Jr., *The Early Development of Magnetic Sound Recording in Broadcasting and Motion Pictures, 1928–1950,* (Unpublished PH.D. Dissertation, Northwestern University, Evanston, Illinois, August 1981), p. 131.

6. Basil Lane, "75 Years of Magnetic Recording 2—The Dark Years," *Wireless World,* April 1975, p. 161.

7. Peter Ford, "The History of Sound Recording, III. The Evolution of Magnetic Recording," *Recorded Sound,* April/July 1963, p. 118.

8. Paul A. Zimmerman, Magnetic Tapes, *Magnetic Recorders, Electrodes* (Ludwigshafen/Rhein: Badische Anilin & Soda Fabrik AG, 1969) p. 7; The "K" meaning Koffer, the German word for portable case.

9. Lane, p. 222.

10. Peter Hammar and Don Ososke, "The Birth Of the German Magnetophon Tape Recorder 1928–1945." Reprinted from *The Sound Engineering Magazine,* March 1982, n.p.

11. Lafferty, p. 138; Lane, p. 222; K. C. Raynor, *German Magnetic Tape Recorders,* PB 1027 (Washington, DC: Office of the Publication Board, U.S. Dept. of Commerce, 1945), pp. 1–24; Peter Ford, "History of Sound Recording, III, p. 121.

12. Hammar & Ososke, n.p.

13. All magnetic recording equipment discussed so far in this study utilize the direct current biasing.

14. Hammer and Ososke, n.p.; Joel Tall, *Techniques of Magnetic Recording* (New York: The Macmillan Company, 1958), pp. 12, 18.

15. Ibid.

16. British Intelligence Objectives Subcommittee, p. 61.

17. Tall, p. 127; U.S. Patent 1,640,881.

18. Kenzo Nagai et al., "Experimental Consideration of A.C. Biasing in Magnetic Recording and Proposition of the New Recording Method" (in Japanese), *Denki Gakkawi,* March 1938 n.p.c.

19. BIOS, *Final Report,* p. 16.

20. Hammar and Ososke, n.p.

21. Robert Angus, "75 Years of Magnetic Recording," *High Fidelity Magazine,* March 1973, p. 47.

22. S.J. Begun, *Magnetic Recording* (Murray Hill Books, Inc., New York, 1949), pp. 165, 167.

23. Lafferty, pp. 153–156; "Patents Siezed from Aliens Now Abstracted," *Science Newsletter,* April 7, 1945, p. 220.

24. C. Lester Walker, "Secrets by the Thousands," *Harper's Magazine,* October 1946, p. 330. Due to its popularity, a copy of the Tonschrieber confiscated by Col. Ranger at Radio Luxembourg was demonstrated and placed on public display in Washington DC.

25. "Patents Siezed . . . , p. 220.

26. "Scientific Cleanup", . . . pp. 19–20; "German 'Know-How' . . . , p. 105.

27. John T. Mullin, personal interview with the author in Redwood City, CA, April 24, 1984.

28. John T. Mullin, "Creating the Craft of Tape Recording," *High Fidelity,* April 1976, p. 62.

29. "The Birth of . . ." p. 56.

30. *Ibid.*

31. Harold Lindsay, "Magnetic Recording, Part II," *db, The Sound Engineering Magazine*, December 1977, p. 39.

32. *Ibid.*

33. Edmund G. Addeo, *"The Story of Ampex,* (Unpublished Internal Document, Ampex Corporation) n.d., p. 11–40.

34. Alexander M. Poniatoff, "History of Ampex," *Engineering Meeting*, Unpublished Internal Document, Ampex Corporation, August 13, 1952, p. 1. In registering the company, Poniatoff chose the name "A.M.P." Standard for his initials—Alexander Matthew Poniatoff, incidentally, the initials were his nickname. Unfortunately, another company, Aircraft Marine Products, which had been registered shortly before Poniatoff's company, had taken the name "AMP." Poniatoff then added "ex" to his initials, making it AMPEX. A journalist writing on the company shortly after opening, explained that the suffix "ex" stood for "excellence," thus indicating the type of products Ampex intended to make. Poniatoff and his employees liked the explanation, and have gone along with it since then.

35. Myron J. Stolaroff, "Early Development of Ampex Model 200," *Engineering Meeting* (Unpublished Internal Document, Ampex Corporation), August 13, 1952, p. 1.

36. Harold Lindsay, "Mechanical Development of First Two Ampex Models." *Engineering Meeting* (Unpublished Internal Document, Ampex Corporation), August 13, 1952, p. 2.

37. "Wire Recorders for Army," *Electronics*, October 1943, pp. 234–235; Ross L. Hollman, "Sound Trapped by Wire," *American Mercury*, June 1946, p. 655.

38. Arnold Krammer, "Technology Transfer as War Booty: The U.S. Technical Oil Mission to Europe, 1945," *Technology and Culture*, January 1981, p. 765, Laferty, p. 161.

39. "ABC's $300,000 Blueprint to keep Day and Night Shows on Same Time Schedule via Recorded Broadcasts," *Variety*, March 27, 1946, p. 39.

40. "ABC Sees Daylight on 300G Solution," *Variety*, April 10, 1946, p. 93.

41. Mullin, p. 79.

42. Lindsay, p. 40.

43. Mrs. Margery Lindsay (wife of the late Harold Lindsay) personal conversation with the author at Redwood City, CA, April 24, 1984.

44. *Presenting the New-Ampex Magnetic Recorder*, Promotional Leaflet, Ampex 200, Ampex Corporation, n.d., n.p.

45. *Ibid.*

46. Mullin, p. 79, Personal interview.

47. Lindsay, p. 44.

48. "History of Ampex Recorder Development," based on a Conference held on April 30, 1958, pp. 1–5; Addeo, p. 11.

49. *Presenting the New Ampex Magnetic Recorder*, promotional leaflet, Ampex 200, Ampex Corporation, n.d., n.p.

50. Bigwood, pp. 31, 33, 38; James R. Cameron and Joseph F. Cifre, *Cameron's Encyclopedia, Sound Motion Pictures*, n.p.

51. Addeo, pp. 11–40.

52. *The History of the Development of Ampex and General Description of its Operation and*

Facilities, Unpublished Internal Document, Ampex Corporation, n.d., n.p., While the networks and recording studios were installing the Ampex tape recorders, film companies were also studying the situation, later following suit by replacing the traditional optical sound recording that had been used for over two decades with magnetic tape recording.

CHAPTER 5
NONMAGNETIC METHODS OF RECORDING TELEVISION

1. British Patent 288,680, B. Rtcheouloff, June 7, 1928.

2. Joe Roizen, "The History of Videotape Recording," Shoenberg Memorial Lecture, Television (Journal of the Royal Television Society) January/February 1976, p. 16.

3. Arthur H. Jones and Keith E. Mullinger, "Multiplexing Film Cameras to Minimize Television Program Failures," Tele-Tech, 1949, p. 1.

4. Albert Abramson, "A Short History of Television Recording," Journal SMPTE, February 1955, p. 72.

5. A. Dinsdale, "Television Sees in Darkness and Records its Impressions," Radio News, June 1927, pp. 1422–1423.

6. Abramson, p. 72.

7. Rtcheouloff.

8. British Patent, 297,078, R. Hartley and H. Ives, 1927.

9. British Patent 386,183, American Television Labs, Inc. Jan. 12, 1953.

10. Lee de Forest, Father of Radio, The Autobiography of Lee de Forest. Chicago: Wilcox & Follett Co., 1950, pp. 418–422.

11. John L. Baird, "The Kerr Cell and its Use in Television," Journal of Television Society, Jan. 1935–Dec. 1938, pp. 110–124.

12. E.L. Traub, "Television at the Berlin Radio Exhibition," Journal of Television Society, Jan. 1935–Dec. 1938, p. 56.

13. London Times, November 29, 1934.

14. W.D. Kemp, "A New Television Recording Camera," British Kinematography, July 1952, p. 39.

15. H.W. Baker, and W.D. Kemp, "The Recording of Television Programmes," BBC Quarterly, Winter 1949–50, p. 236.

16. D.A. Smith, "Television Recording," Wireless World, Aug. 1949, p. 305.

17. W.D. Kemp, "Television Recording," Journal of the Society of Motion Picture and Television Engineers, April 1953, p. 573.

18. Ibid.

19. W.D. Kemp, "Video Recordings Improved by The Use of Continuous Moving Film," Tele-Tech, Nov. 1949, pp. 32–35, 62–63.

20. Abramson, p. 74; W.D. Kemp, "Television recording," An abstract (75% of the original paper, presented at the Convention of the British Contribution to Television, April 28–May 3, 1953), Journal of the Society of Motion Picture and Television Engineers, April, 1953, pp. 367–384.

21. D.S. Bond and V.J. Duke, "Ultrafax" RCA Review, March 1948, pp. 99–115.

22. Thomas T. Goldsmith, Jr. and Harry Mulholland, "Television transcription

by motion picture film," *Journal of the Society of Motion Picture and Television Engineers*, August 1948, p. 107.

23. M.A. Trainer and W.J. Poch, "Television equipment for aircraft," *RCA Review*, Dec. 1946, p. 469.

24. R.E. Shelby, F.J. Somers and L.R. Moffet, "Naval airborne television reconnaissance system," *RCA Review*, September 1946, p. 303.

25. Robert M. Fraser, "Motion picture photography of television images," *RCA Review*, June 1948, pp. 202–217.

26. Polaroid Corporation, Report on optical plastic synthesis fabrication and instrument design, Office of Scientific and Research Development, Report No. 4417, 1945.

27. W.R. Fraser and G. Badgley, "Motion picture photography of color television images," *Journal of the Society of Motion Picture and Television Engineers*, June 1950, p. 135.

28. Charles R. Daily, "Progress Committee Report," *Journal of the Society of Motion Picture and Television Engineers*, May 1955, p. 240.

29. Lloyd Thompson, "Progress Committee Report" *Journal of the Society of Motion Picture and Television Engineers*, May 1956, p. 258. Lenticular film was developed by the French in the 1920's, and revived by Eastman Kodak decades later.

30. C.H. Evans and R.B. Smith, "Color kinescope recording on embossed film," *Journal of the Society of Motion Picture and Television Engineers*, July 1956, pp. 365–372. Whereas on kinescope recordings could be played back at any station, it was impossible to playback initial videotape on other machines.

31. Leo Levi, "High-fidelity video recording using ultrasonic light modulation," paper presented at the Society of Motion Picture and Television Engineers, Convention at Los Angeles on April 24, 1958.

32. Lewis R. Blair, and Louis Behrmann, "16mm color kinerecording for theater projection," Paper presented on April 24, 1958, at the Society of Motion Picture and Television Engineers, Convention at Los Angeles.

33. Lloyd Thompson, "Progress Committee Report for 1957," *Journal of the Society of Motion Picture and Television Engineers*, May 1958, p. 304.

34. Vernon J. Duke, "A status report on current experimentation in color kinescope recording," *Journal of the Society of Motion Picture and Television Engineers*, Sept. 1963, p. 711.

35. Adolph Radzdow, "The BRYG system of photographic color projection for television," Paper presented on April 24, 1958 at the SMPTE Convention at Los Angeles.

36. Lloyd Thompson, p. 304.

CHAPTER 6
THE ADVENT OF THE VIDEOTAPE RECORDER

1. *RCA demonstrates magnetic tape recording of television pictures in color and in black and white—hailed as major step toward era of electronic photography*, Unpublished RCA Release, New York, December 1, 1953, p. 1; Mullin p. 79.

2. "Videotape" was Ampex's trademark for their original videotape recorders. *Key Dates In Magnetic Recording*, Unpublished Document, Ampex n.d., n.p.

3. United States Patent 661,619, Valdemar Poulsen.

4. George B. Goodall, Videotape Recorder, *International Projectionist* (Report), April–August, 1959, p. 2.

5. Ibid.

6. J.F. Robinson, *Videotape recording, theory and practice:* Communication Arts Books, Hasting House, Publishers, 1975, p. 19.

7. H.F. Olsen, W.D. Houghton, A.R. Morgan, J. Zenel, M. Artzt, J.G. Woodward, and J.T. Fisher, "A system for recording and reproducing television signals," *RCA Review*, March 1954, p. 2.

8. H.F. Olsen, W.D. Houghton, A.R. Morgan, M. Artzt, J.A. Zenel and J.G. Woodward, "A magnetic tape system for recording and reproducing standard FCC Color Television Signals," *RCA Review*, September 1956, pp. 333–334.

9. Robinson, p. 48.

10. *Principle of magnetic tape recording*, Unpublished Document, Ampex Corporation, n.d., n.p.

11. *What's a videotape recorder*, Ampex Corporation, Unpublished Document, n.d., n.p.

12. Ibid.

13. Ibid; Skipwith W. Athey, "Magnetic tape recording," National Aeronautic & Space Administration, Washington D.C. 1966, p. 40.

14. Mark Sanders, "The development of the Ampex AST system. An exclusive report on the development and technology behind the Off-Tape, broadcast quality, slow motion, still frame system," *Video Systems*, April 1980, p. 47.

15. British Patent 288,680, B. Rtcheouloff, June 7, 1928.

16. John T. Mullin, "The birth of the recording industry," *Billboard*, November 18, 1972, p. 79.

17. Ibid.

18. John T. Mullin, "Video magnetic tape recording," *Tele-Tech and Electronic Insdustries*, May 1954, p. 77.

19. Ibid; Joe Roizen, "A history of magnetic recording," *Broadcasting and Television*, March 7, 1963, p. 29.

20. Hiroshi Sugaya, "Recent advances in video tape recording," IEEE Transactions on Magnetics, volume MAG-14, No. 3, September 1978, p. 632.

21. "RCA demonstrates system for recording color television programs on magnetic tape," *Collection of David Sarnoff's Speeches*, RCA, p. 891.

22. "RCA demonstrates magnetic tape recording of television pictures in color and in black-and-white . . . ," RCA release, December 1, 1953, pp. 1–10. Olsen, et. al. "A system for recording . . . ," pp. 3–17.

23. Ibid; H.F. Olsen, W.D. Houghton, A.R. Morgan, J. Zenel, M. Artzt, J.G. Woodward and J.T. Fischer, "A system for recording and reproducing television signals," *RCA Review*, March 1954, p. 16.

24. Ibid; *New York Times*, November 8, 1953, p. x–5.

25. "RCA Demonstrates Magnetic Tape . . . ," p. 3.

26. *Newark Evening News*, December 2, 1953 quoted from RCA Release, December 11, 1953, pp. 1–20.

27. *New York Times*, December 2, 1953, quoted from RCA Release, December 11, 1953, pp. 1–20.

28. *New York Times*, December 13, 1953, p. x 19.

29. *Ibid.*

30. Sugaya, pp. 632–637.

31. Edmund G. Addeo, *The Ampex Story*, Pioneering video recording, Ampex Corporation, p. 11; Charles P. Ginsburg, "The birth of videotape recording," Ampex Corp. 1981, n.p.

32. Ginsburg, n.p.

33. *Ibid.*

34. *Ibid.*

35. *Ibid.*

36. Dwight Newton, "Day and night," *Redwood City Tribune*, April 15, 1956, Reprint, n.p.

37. Addeo, p. 13.

38. *Ampex Monitor*, March 1966, pp. 6–7.

39. Addeo, p. 13. The research process leading to the introduction of Ampex's first VTR was very economical. During the four year period of experimentation on the Videotape project, Ampex approved a total sum of $106,000 for research purposes, while only $96,000 was used by the research team.

40. "Twenty years of videotape," Unpublished Document, 3M Company, St. Paul Minnesota, p. 9.

41. Interview with Charles P. Ginsburg at Ampex Museum, on February 24, 1984 at Redwood City, California.

42. Virtually all television stations were operated with monochrome equipment.

43. Joe Roizen, "The History of Videotape . . . ," p. 21.

44. A.H. Lind, "TV tape recording—A review of techniques and equipment," *RCA Engineers*, Feb.–March 1964, p. 64.

45. "Historical highlights and development," 1944–1969, Ampex Corporation, n.p.

46. "Black and White, and full Color VTR," By Ampex Corporation, Redwood City, California, n.d., n.

47. Robert A. Minter, "The videotape recorder and its application to educational television," Ampex, Unpublished Document, Feb. 17, 1959, pp. 1–7.

48. "Getting it tapped," *Time*, January 1957.

49. "VERA: The BBC . . ." *Journal of the Society of Motion Picture and Television Engineers* April–June 1958, p. 399.

50. Interview with Charles P. Ginsburg at Ampex Museum on Feb. 24, 1984 at Redwood City, California.

51. A.C. Luther and R.N. Hurst, "The TR-22 . . . A Deluxe, all transistor television tape recorder," *Broadcast News*, Nov. 1962.

52. A.H. Lind, "The TR-22 . . . RCA's transistorized television tape recorder," *RCA Engineer*, October–November 1961, p. 30.

53. A.H. Lind, "TV tape recording . . . ," pp. 44–47.

CHAPTER 7
THE HOME VIDEO REVOLUTION

1. Albert Abramson, "A short history of television recording, part II" *Journal of the Society of Motion Picture and Television Engineers* March 1973, p. 191.

2. N. Sawazaki, M. Yagi, M. Iwaski, G. Inanda and T. Tamaoki, "A new videotape recording system," *Journal of the Society of Motion Picture and Television Engineers*, December 1960, pp. 868–871.

3. Personal interview with Peter Hammer, Curator/Consultant Ampex Museum, Redwood City, California, April 24, 1984.

4. "Two-Head color VTR," *Japan Electronics*, Jan. 1961, p. 21.

5. Mark Sanders, "Recent advances in helical-scan recording," Unpublished release, Ampex Corporation, no date, n.p.

6. "Advantages of the two-head videotape system," *Int. TV. Tech. Review*, July 1961, pp. 19–21.

7. Edmund G. Addeo, *The Ampex Story*, Ampex Corporation, Unpublished Document, n.d., n.p.

8. "Historical highlights and development 1944 19–69," Ampex Corporation, (Unpublished Document), n.d., n.p.

9. L. Merle Thomas, A Report on the broadcast use of helical-scan videotape recorders," *IEEE Transactions on Broadcasting*, December 1977, p. 107.

10. A format becomes eligible for standardization when two or more manufacturers build, or plan to build.

11. "Home Video Recording Arrives," *Amateur Cine World*, *Associated Press—Cutting Services Ltd. (APCUT)*, July 11, 1963 n.p.; "A Sound and Vision Recorder—its here," *Evening Press* (Dublin), *APCUT*, July 10, 1963, n.p.

12. "New Video Process," *Broadcast Management/Engineering*, October 8, 1967.

13. Although EVR was a failure, it contributed by providing an insight to what would later become home video cassette recorders.

14. "Toward compatible VTRs," *Electronics*, November 10, 1969, p. 236.

15. "And another VTR from Sony," *Electronics*, November 10, 1969, p. 236; *Television Cartridge and Disc Systems: What are They Good For?*, 1971, n.p.

16. Tape recording magazine, June 1970, p. 189; "A European standard," *Radio Electronics*, Dec. 1970, p. 4.

17. "Portable VTR reproduces color," *Electronics*, Sept. 14, 1970, pp. 155–158.

18. Roger Kenneth Field, "In the sixties, It was TV; In the seventies, videocassettes," Quoted from the *New York Times* in *Television Cartridge and Disc Systems: What Are they Good For?*, 1971, n.p.

19. John M. Bishop and Naomi H. Bishop, *Making home video*, Wideview Books, 1980, p. 7.

20. Motion Picture Association of America, *Videocassette recorder and the law of copyright*, Washington DC, 1984, pp. 1–30. North American Philips was the first company to introduce the VCR in the domestic market, but their system was more of industrial/educational oriented than home-oriented.

21. Mark Dunton & David Owen, *Complete home video handbook*, Random House New York, 1982, pp. 1–60.

22. Roderick Woodstock, "Zenith's ultimate video switch," *Video Magazine*, Jan. 1984, pp. 69–70.

23. Originally, Sony had an impressive list of followers, having licensed the Beta format to Zenith, Toshiba, NEC and Sanyo. Other licensees included Teknika, Aiwa, Nakamichi, Marantz and Sears although they were not involved in the manufacturing processes.

24. Unlike Beta, over 18 manufacturers and major marketers were VHS licensees. The included RCA, Panasonic, Akai, Hitachi, JVC, Magnavox, MCA, Sharp, Quasar, Canon, Pentax, Sylvania, Montgomery Ward, J.C. Penney and others.

25. Panasonic VHS also offered 9-hour programmable mode in UK.

26. "An about-face at Philips ends the VCR war," *Business Week*, Dec. 5, 1983, p. 88.

CHAPTER 8
VCR MARKET GROWTH

1. *Video Week*, March 18, 1985, p. 2.

2. "Home video & broadcast television, impact and opportunities," *Com/Tech Report*, Vol. 3M No. 3, 1984, p. 8.

3. *Nielsen Home Video Index*, VCR Analysis 1983–84, p. 11.

4. *TV Digest*, January 14, 1985, p. 1.

5. Kaniaki Miura, Yoshinori Okada, Isao Fukushima, Naoto Yoshida and Masaaki Hirano, "HiFi VCR system," *IEEE Transactions on Consumer Electronics*, Volume CE-30, No. 3, August 3, 1984, p. 360.

CHAPTER 9
VIDEO DISC SYSTEMS

1. Albert Abramson, "A short history of television recording," *Journal of the Society of Motion Picture and Television Engineers*, February 1955, p. 72. "Varying Capacitance Creates TV Playbacks," *Digital Design*, October, 1975.

2. Mark Schubin, *An overview and history of videodisc technologies in video discs. The Technology, The Applications and the Future*, White Plains, N.Y. Knowledge Industry Publications, 1980, p. 13.

3. "Broadcast & Technologies, industry experts see 1981 as turning point for videocassette recorder, Videodisc Market," *TV/Radio Age*, Jan. 12, 1981, pp. 5, 126.

4. *RCA Reviews*, Volume 39, No. 1, March 1978; Number 3, September 1978, entire issues devoted to the SelectaVision Videodisc System.

CHAPTER 10
PORTABLE VIDEO RECORDERS

1. *Ampex Data Sheet*, 1964, n.p.

2. New Products, *Journal of the Society of Motion Picture and Television Engineers*, July 1967, p. 726.

3. "Portable broadcast system," *Ampex Products Release*, n.d., n.p.

4. "Portable videotape recorder," *Electronic Products Magazine*, June 1962, p. 43.

5. "Portable TV tape recorders," *Broadcast Management/Engineering*, February 1965, p. 38.

6. Authors conversation with Peter Hammar, Curator and Consultant for Ampex Museum of Magnetic Recording, Redwood City, April 22, 1984.

7. "Color videocassette recorder/player—U-matic," *Sony's Product Release*, 1974, n.p.

8. Philip O. Keirstead, "ENG 'live' news from almost anywhere," *The Quill*, May 1976, p. 26.

9. "State of the Art," *Broadcasting*, April 14, 1975, p. 63.

10. *Sony Broadcast Product Release*, n.d. n.p.

11. *CBS Newsletter*, August 6, 1974, n.p.

12. Vernon A. Stone, *Radio and television news directors association communicator*, April 1977, p. 7.

13. "State of the . . . ," p. 32.

14. Steve S. Ryan, "The State of the Art": Film vs. ENG, *Journal of the University Film Association*, Spring 1978, p. 54.

15. Nielsen Home Video Index, analysis, 1983–84, p. 7.

16. Mark Schubin, "High technology—Camcorders," Unpublished paper for Hi-Fi Magazine, July 1985, pp. 2–3.

CHAPTER 11
THE IMPACT OF VIDEO TECHNOLOGY ON RELATED INDUSTRIES

1. *Hearing Before the Committee on Patents, United States Senate, 72nd Congress, 1st Session*, on *S. 1301, A Bill to Renew and Extend Certain Letters Patent*, March 10, 1932, Washington D.C.: U.S. Government Printing Office, 1932, p. 41.

2. William C. Lafferty, Jr., *The early development of magnetic sound recording in broadcasting and motion pictures, 1928–1950*. Unpublished Ph.D. Dissertation, Northwestern University, Evanston, Illinois, 1981, p. 24.

3. *Hearing Before the Committee on Patents . . .* , p. 41.

4. *Ibid.* p. 14.

5. *Nielsen Home Video Index* (NHI) *VCR Usage Report*, November 1983–January 1984, p. 242.

6. NHI, July–September 1984, p. 60.

7. Research studies and publications by A.C. Nielsen, Paul Kegan, Videoweek, National Association of Broadcasters and Electronic Industry Association.

8. NHI, July–September, 1984, p. 75; The Fairfield Group, a home video industry research and consulting group calculated that there were 150 million videocassette rental transactions in 1983 valued at $750 million. For 1985, they predicted 350 million transactions with a value of $1.75 billion. This is almost half of the $4 billion that is expected to be received at movie theater box offices in 1985.

9. Rental of pre-recorded videocassettes currently outpace sales by over twenty to one. Average rental prices are $2.00–$2.50 per night exclusive of club membership fees.

10. *VCR and the Law of Copyright*: MPAA, Washington D.C., 1983, pp. 1–29.

11. "Sony betamax victory likely to ignite Hill Copyright Activity," *Broadcasting*, Jan. 23, 1984, p. 34.

12. Barnaby J. Feder, "Private videotaping of copyrighted TV, ruled infringement," *New York Times*, Oct. 20, 1981.

13. Toshiba claimed that the fault was in the particular prototype used for the demonstration, and that production receivers would be of better quality.

14. "Digital circuits begin to show up in TV receivers, but stereo sound is the hottest new Feature," *Electronic Week*, October 15, 1984, pp. 48–53.

15. Shigeo Shima, "The evolution of consumer VTRs—technological milestone," *IEEE Transactions on Consumer Electronics*, May 1984, pp. 66–71.

16. Gordon Graft, "Ever-better home entertainment," *New York Times*, March 30, 1986, p. 23.

Glossary

The following is a list of vocabulary that are often encountered in the study of video recording technology some of which are as advanced *verbation* by RCA. (Reprinted with permission from *Living With Video—The Complete Guide To Video Lifestyles*, pp. 56–57.)

AFT (Automatic Fine Tuning): An electronic circuit that automatically locks a TV's or VCR's tuner precisely onto a channel. This feature helps you tune in stations easily.

AGC (Automatic Gain Control): While you make a recording this circuit automatically adjusts the volume of the sound and the brightness of the recorded picture.

Ambient: Background sounds or light. The noise of traffic is the ambient sound of a busy street corner.

Aperture (also called iris or f-stop): The adjustable opening in a lens that allows more or less light to pass through it and into your camera.

Assemble edit: To record one scene after another in chronological order on a tape, until you complete your TV show.

Audio: The sound portion of a video recording or a TV signal.

BTSC (Broadcast Television Systems Committee): The committee that recommends the standards for multichannel television sound transmission and audio processing as defined by the Federal Communications Commission.

Basic service: The cable TV channels you get when you pay the minimum fee. You can subscribe to additional channels (typically movies and sports) for additional fees.

Beta: One of the two popular video recording formats using ½-inch video cassettes. About 25% of home video users have beta recorders, while the other 75% use the VHS format. The two formats are incompatible; you cannot play a beta tape on a VHS machine of vice versa.

Burn-in: A permanent dark scar or after-image left on a camera tube when the camera is aimed at something too bright for too long. Aiming most TV cameras at the sun will burn a streak across the picture that never goes away.

CATV (Cable TV): TV signals that enter the home via rented cables, as opposed to wires from you rooftop antenna.

CCD (Charge coupled devise): A transistorized device capable of sensing a picture in some TV cameras.

CED (Capacitance Electronic Disc): One of two popular videodisc systems. This one uses a tiny needle in a groove to sense the picture. The other, laservision, uses laser light to sense the picture on the disc.

Channel: The TV frequency assigned to a broadcast TV station to which you tune your TV to watch a show. Cable TV companies send many channels down the same wire, representing many TV stations.

Chroma: The color part of a video signal. The black-and-white part is called luminance. A color picture has both parts.

Coax (Short for coaxial): A round shielded, single cable used to carry video or antenna signals.

Comb Filter: An electronic circuit that makes color TV pictures sharper.

Convergence: Color TV pictures are actually made of three pictures, one red-and-black. The three pictures must overlap exactly (converge) to make a sharp picture of many colors. When white objects on a TV screen have colored outlines, the set's convergence needs adjustment.

Converter: A special tuner supplied by cable TV companies that can tune in cable channels that normal TV sets don't get. Cable-ready TVs and VCRs usually don't need converters.

CRT (Cathode Ray Tube): A TV picture tube, or oscilloscope screen, or computer display screen.

DAT: Digital audiotape.

dB: A unit used to measure the strength of audio or electrical signals.

DBS (Direct Broadcasting Satellite): A powerful satellite that receives up to four TV broadcasts at once and retransmits them to earth where the signals can be picked up.

Decoder: see Descrambler.

Demagnetizer: An electronic devise that erases magnetism. Some demagnetizers are used to remove residual magnetism from tape recorder heads; others erase a whole videocassette with the press of a button.

Descrambler: Some pay TV services scramble their TV signals, making them unviewable by nonsubscribers. You rent a descrambler and connect it to your TV or VCR to make the programs viewable.

Dish: A bowl-shaped reflector that is part of the antenna used to receive satellite TV signals.

Dubbing: To remove the old sound from a recorded videotape and substitute new sound. Also, to copy a videotape.

Dupe: A copy of a videotape, or the act of making a copy or copies.

F-Connector: Standard plug used for connecting coax cables to your TV set or VCR.

F-Stop: The number etched on a lens telling how far open the lens iris is. Low F-stops are best when working with low light and high F-stops are best for bright light.

Fade: Gradually dimming a picture's brightness down to black (as in "fade to black") or vice versa. With sound, gradually raising the volume (as in "fade up the music") or gradually turning it all the way off.

Field: One second of any TV picture is made of 30 frames, or still pictures. Each frame is made of 525 lines, like lines of print on the page of a book. Each frame is first made from the $262\frac{1}{2}$ odd-numbered lines, and is called the odd field. Then the $262\frac{1}{2}$ even-numbered lines are projected on the TV screen making the even field. The two fields totalling 60 fields per second, create 30 frames per second.

Flagging, or flagwaving: The flutter or pulling to one side of the top of a TV picture when a stretched video tape is played. Sometimes it's the VCR's fault. Adjusting the horizontal control on the TV can reduce flagging.

Frame: One of the 30 single, still TV pictures that make up 1 second of motion.

Frequency synthesis tuning: A method of electronically tuning a TV channel.

Freeze frame: A TV picture held still. Most VCRs and videodisc players can "freeze" a TV picture.

Gain: The brightness and contrast of a picture, or the loudness of a volume.

Glitch: A momentary disturbance or breakup of your TV picture.

HDTV (High Definition Television): A high quality television that is expected to revolutionize home video in the 1990s and beyond. With quality picture and sound, it is expected to be the television of the future.

Head: The top part of a tripod that holds the camera, or, the parts of the VCR that records the picture and sound on tape. Inside the VCR is a spinning drum around which the tape is threaded. There are one or two pairs of tiny electromagnets (video heads) attached to the drum. As the drum spins, the heads sweep across the tape, recording a picture and sound with each sweep. A second set of audio heads are stationery and record longitudinally, like an audio tape recorder.

Head clog: Very snowy or grainy picture caused when a particle of dirt gets stuck to the video head, obstructing it. Often you can play a "video head cleaning cassette" in the VCR to remove the dirt.

Helican-scan: The method home VCRs use to record a picture on a tape by laying down many diagonal tracks from a pair of spinning video heads.

Hertz: Cycles or vibrations per second. A kiloHertz (1 KHz) is 100 Hz, and a megaHertz (1 MHz) is one million Hz.

Hiss: High-pitched noise, audible when a tape is played.

Hum: Low-pitched noise coming from audio equipment, usually a 60 or 120 Hz tone.

Infrared: Invisible red light useful for signalling equipment by remote control.

Insert edit: To record a scene in the middle of an already recorded tape, erasing the old scene in the process.

Interactive: Gives the viewer the power to participate in or change the progress of a program. An interactive videodisc, for instance, could display a question, wait for your response (which you punch into a keypad) and then show you a particular demonstration based on your answer.

Jack: An input or output socket for electrical signals on equipment.

KHz: kiloHertz, 100 Hertz.

LED: A tiny, light-emitting device that uses very little power. Often used as a status or warning light.

Luminance: The black-and-white component of a TV picture. See also Chroma.

MDS (MultiPoint Distribution Service): Means of broadcasting pay TV signals via microwave to subscribers with special antennas.

MOS (Metal Oxide Semiconductor): A light-sensitive device used in some cameras instead of vidicon tubes. The CCD can "see" the picture and convert it to a video signal.

mHz (megaHertz): One million Hertz.

Mini-plug: Small plug used on home video equipment for connecting earphones or microphones to a VCR.

Modulator: See RF adapter.

Monitor: A TV set without a tuner of its own. It therefore can't receive antenna signals, but it can display a video signal directly from a VCR, computer, or videodisc player.

NiCad: Minature, high-powered rechargeable battery usually capable of operating a portable VCR and camera for an hour or more.

Noise: Unwanted sound or picture disturbances, often caused by electrical interference.

Pan: To aim a camera from left to right or vise versa.

Pause: To stop the motion of a tape momentarily. Pausing a tape during the advertisements while recording a TV show will result in a copy of the program without the ads. Pausing a tape during playback of a show generally holds the picture still.

Pay-per-view: Pay television where you are charged for the shows you actually watch.

Pickup tube: The light-sensitive part of a TV camera that "sees" the picture and turns into a video signal.

RCA plug, or phono plug: Popular plug used on home video equipment. Video inputs and outputs usually take RCA plugs and coax wire. Common audio equipment also used RCA plugs for its audio inputs and outputs, but the wire used there isn't coax.

Random access: Ability to view a particular segment of a recording without watching surrounding material.

RF Adapter: An electronic devise that converts audio and video (as from a VCR or computer) into antenna signal (usually channel 3) for a normal TV set to receive.

Saturation: The intensity of the color in a TV picture.

Scramble: See Descrambler.

Signal-to-noise (S/N) Ratio: A measure, in dB, of how much desired signal a devise gives you compared to how much undesired noise it makes while doing it. A high S/N ratio means high quality sound and picture.

SP/LP/SLP (Standard Play, Long Play, and Super Long Play): The 2- 4- and 6-hour speeds on a VHS videocassette recorder (using a common T120 cassette).

S-VHS: Super Video Home System.

Tiered services: Different cable TV service packages. Each tier offers more deluxe (and expensive) programming, including more movies, sports, and other features.

Teletext: A means of invisibly encoding words onto a TV signals. A Teletex decoder can make the words visible on your TV screen, perhaps displaying sports scores or news.

Timer: A device built into a VCR that, if you program it ahead of time, will automatically start your VCR recording a show while you are away.

Tracking: Precise control of VCR's motors to assure that the video heads "read" the signal off the tape accurately. Also, the control that adjusts the way in which a VCR does this. When playing a tape, if you see a grainy or snowy band across the picture, try adjusting the tracking control.

Tweeter: A hi-fi speaker built to reproduce high-pitched tones.

UHF (Ultra High Frequency): TV channels 14–83.

VHF (Very High Frequency): TV channels 2–14.

VCR: Videocassette recorder.

VHS (Video Home System): One of the two popular (but mutually incompatible) types of VCRs. Three out of four home VCR buyers choose VHS.

Vidicon: The light-sensitive tube in many cameras that "sees" the picture and converts it into video signals.

Woofer: A hi-fi speaker built to reproduce low-pitched tones.

Zoom: An adjustment on a camera lens allowing you to make a picture look closer or farther away.

Bibliography

BOOKS CITED

Athey, S.W. (1986). *Magnetic tape recording.* Washington, DC: National Aeronautic & Space Administration.

Begun, S.J. (1949). *Magnetic recording.* New York: Murray Hill Books.

Bensinger, C. (1982). *The home video handbook.* Indianapolis: Howard W. Sams.

Bishop, J.M., & Bishop, N.H. (1980). *Making home video.* New York: Widenview Books.

Briggs, A. (1965). *The history of broadcasting in the United Kingdom, Vol. II, The golden age of wireless.* London: Oxford University Press.

Cameron, E.W. (Ed.). (1980). *Sound and the cinema, The coming of sound to American film.* Pleasantville, NY: Redgrave Publishing.

de Forest, L. (1950). *Father of radio: The autobiography of Lee de Forest.* Chicago: Wilcox & Follett.

de Lauretis, T., & Heath, S. (1980). *The cinematic apparatus.* New York: St. Martin's Press.

Dunton, M., & Owen, D. (1982). *Complete home video handbook.* New York: Random House.

Ellis, J. (1982). *Visible fictions, cinema, television, video.* London: Routledge & Kegan Paul.

Mee, C.D. (1964). *The physics of magnetic recording.* New York: Wiley.

Pawley, E. (1972). *BBC engineering, 1922–1972.* London: BBC Publications.

Robinson, J.F. (1975). *Videotape recording, theory and practice.* New York: Communication Arts Books, Hasting House.

Robinson, R. (1974). *The video primer.* New York: Links Books.

270

Shier, G. (Ed.). (1977). *Technical development of television*. New York: Arno Press.
Tall, J. (1958). *Techniques of magnetic recording*. New York: Macmillan.
Williams, R. (1975). *Television: Technology and cultural form*. New York: Schocken Books.

SIGNED PERIODICAL ARTICLES CITED

A(dous), D.W. (1939, June 29). Equipment for reproducing dictation and telephone conversations. *Wireless World*, pp. 611–612.
Aliamet, M. (1900, June 2). Le Telegraphone de M. Poulsen. *L'Electricien*, pp. 337–338.
Angus, R. (1973, March). 75 years of magnetic recording. *High Fidelity Magazine*, pp. 42–50.
Balbi, C.M.R. (1930, June 20). Talking pictures-I. *The Electrical Review*, pp. 1145–1147.
Balbi, C.M.R. (1930, June 25). Talking pictures-IV. *The Electrical Review*, pp. 129–130.
Begun, S.J. (1937, August). Magnetic recording-reproducing machine for objective speech study. *Journal of the Society of Motion Picture Engineers*, pp. 216–218.
Begun, S.J. (1940, November). A new recording machine combining disk recording and magnetic recording, with short reference to the present status of each. *Journal of the Society of Motion Picture Engineers*, pp. 507–521.
Bigwood, R.F. (1948, July). Applications of magnetic recording in network broadcasting. *Audio Engineering*, pp. 31–33, 38, 40.
Bishop, H. (1925, July 10). Electro-magnetic sound recording machines. *The Electrical Review*, pp. 45–47.
Blain, R. (1944, June 10). Sound recording. *Telepohony*, pp. 20–21.
Carey, L.I., & Moran, F. (1952, January). Push-pull direct positive recording—An auxiliary to magnetic recording. *Journal of the Society of Motion Picture Engineers*, pp. 67–70.
Chinn, H.A. (1947, May). Magnetic tape recorders in broadcasting. *Audio Engineering*, pp. 7–10.
Clarke, W.H. (1952, April). Magnetic recording—A progress report. *British Kinematography*, pp. 106–113.
Darragh, J. Jr. (1940, September). Flight test data mechanically recorded. *Aero Digest*, pp. 96–87, 180.
De Forest, L. (1914, March). The audion-detector and amplifier. *Proceedings of the Institute of Radio Engineers*, pp. 15–36.
Drenner, D.V.R. (1957, October). The magnetophone. *Audio Engineering*, pp. 7–11, 35.

Duke, V.J. (1958, May). A status report on current experimentation in color kinescope recording. *Journal of the Society of Motion Picture Engineers*, p. 304.

Ford. P. (1963, April/July). History of sound recording, III. The evolution of magnetic recording. *Recorded Sound*, pp. 115–123.

Ford, P. (1963, October). The history of sound recording, IV. Motion picture and television sound recording. *Recorded Sound*, pp. 146–154.

Goodall, G.B. (1959, April–August). Videotape recorder. *International Projectionist (Report)*, p. 2.

Gunby, O.B. (1949, June). Portable magnetic recording system. *Journal of the Society of Motion Picture Engineers*, pp. 613–618.

Hamilton, H.E.S. The blatterphone—Its operation and use. *Electrical Digest*, pp. 347–351.

Hammar, P., & Ososke, D. (1982, March). The birth of the German magnetophon tape recorder 1928–1945. Reprinted from *The Sound Engineering Magazine*, n.p.

Heiss, M. (1984, January). 1984 VCR guide. *Videography*, p. 39.

Hickman, C.N. (1933, June). Delayed speech. *Bell Laboratories Record*, pp. 308–310.

Kolb, O.K. (1950, November). Magnetic sound developments in Great Britain. *Journal of the Society of Motion Picture Engineers*, pp. 496–508.

Kramer, A. (1981, June). Technology transfer as was booty: The U.S. technical oil mission to Europe, 1945. *Technology and Culture*, pp. 68–103.

Lane, B. (1975, March). 75 years of magnetic recording. *Wireless World*, pp. 102–105.

Lane, B. (1975, April). 75 years of magnetic recording—The dark years. *Wireless World*, pp. 161–164.

Lind, A.H. (1964, February–March). Television tape recording—A review of techniques and equipment. *RCA Engineer*, pp. 44–47.

Lind, A.H. (1961, October–November). The TR22 . . . RCA's transistorized television tape recorder. *RCA Engineer*, pp. 30.

Luther, A.C., & Hurst, R.N. (1962, November). The TR22 . . . A deluxe, all transistor television tape recorder. *Broadcast News*, p. 1.

Mennie, D. (1978, January). Technology '78 consumers as programmers. *IEEE Spectrum*, pp. 54–56.

Miura, K., Okada, Y., Fukushima, I., Youshida, N., & Hirano, M. (1978, August). HIFI VCR system. *IEEE Transactions Consumer Electronics*, pp. 468–472.

Mooney, M., Jr. (1958, February). The history of magnetic recording. *Hi-Fi Tape Recording*, pp. 21–37.

Mullin, J.T. (1976, April). Creating the craft of tape recording. *High Fidelity Magazine*, pp. 62–67.

Mullin, J.T. (1954, May). Video magnetic tape recording. *Tele-Tech and Electronic Industries*, pp. 77.

Mullin, J.T. (1972, November 18). The birth of the recording industry. *Billboard*, p. 56.

Nagai, K. (1938, March). Experimental consideration of AC erasing in magnetic recording and proposition of the new recording method. (in Japanese), *Denki Gakkwai*, n.p.

Nagai, K. (1937, August). Studies of noise and recording materials for magnetic recording. *Nippon Electrical Communication Engineering*, pp. 218–224.

Oliver, L. (1900, June 30). One revolution en telephonie. *Revue Generale des Science Pures et Appliquees*, pp. 770–775.

Power, R.A. (1946, June). The German magnetophon. *Wireless World*, p. 198.

Rust, N.M. (1934, January/February). The Marconi–Stille recording reproducing equipment. *The Marconi Review*, pp. 1–11.

Sanders, M. (1980, April). The development of the Ampex AST system. An exclusive report on the development and technology behind the off-tape, broadcast quality, slow motion, still frame system. *Video Systems*, p. 47.

Sawazaki, N., Yagi, M., Iwaski, M., Inanda, G., & Tamaoki, T. (1960, December). A new videotape recording system. *Journal of the Society of Motion Picture Engineers*, pp. 868–871.

Shima, S. (1984, May). Videotape—Its impact on consumer electronics design. *IEEE Transactions on Consumer Electronics*, pp. 66–71.

Shiraishi, Y., & Hirota, A. (1984, August). Videocassette recorder development for consumers. *IEEE Transactions on Consumer Electronics*, pp. 360–361.

Smith, O. (1888, September 8). Some possible form of phonograph. *The Electrical World*, pp. 116–117.

Spellerberg, J. (1977, August). Technology and ideology in the cinema. *Quarterly Review of Film Studies*, pp. 288–301.

Sugaya, H. (1978, September). Recent advances in videotape recording. *IEEE Transactions on Magnetics*, pp. 632–637.

Sugimuto, M., Ogusu, C., & Ikegami, H. (1975, March). Electronic newsgathering system. *IEEE Transactions on Broadcasting*, pp. 15–19.

Walker, R.H. (1971, August). Videotape—Its impact on consumer electronics design. *IEEE Transactions on Broadcasting and Television Receivers*, pp. 160–163.

UNSIGNED PERIODICAL ARTICLES CITED

A European standard. (1970, December). *Radio Electronics*, p. 4.

ABC's new big league status? Crosby deal seen clincher. (1946, July 10). *Variety*.

ABC sees daylight on 300G solution. (1946, April 10). *Variety*, p. 93.

ABC's $300,000 blueprint to keep day and night shows on same time schedule via recorded broadcasts. (1947, March 27). *Variety*, p. 39.

Advantages of the two-head videotape system. (1961, July). *International TV Technology Reviews*, pp. 19–21.

An about-face at Philips ends the VCR war. (1983, December 5). *Business Week*, p. 88.

And another VTR from Sony. (1969, November 10). *Electronics*, p. 236.

And now a vision receiver. (1963, July 10). *Amatueur Photographer*, n.p.

Broadcast & technologies, industry experts see 1981 as turning point for videocassette recorder, videodisc market. (1981, January 12). *TV/Radio Age*, pp. 5–126.

Color videocassette recorder/player—U-matic. (1974). *Sony's Product Release*, n.p.

Crosby's clinko wax radio network. (1946, October 23). *Variety*, pp. 1–30.

Crosby's distress signal up. (1947, November 13). *Variety*, p. 31.

Digital circuits begin to show up in TV receivers, but stereo sound is the hottest new feature. (1984, October 15). *Electronics Week*, pp. 48–53.

French taping shows a la Crosby's; Nazi pushed'em into it, Lewin says. (1947, October 15). *Variety*, p. 37.

German "know how" to probe German technology. (1946, May 4). *Science Newsletter*, p. 279.

Home video & broadcast television, impact and opportunities. (1984). *Comtech Report*, 3M(3), p. 6.

Home video recording. (1963, July 11). *Amateur Cine World*, n.p.

How the VCR spree has new technology on hold. (1983, October 17). *Business Week*, p. 184L.

Industries asked to probe German technology. (1946, May 4). *Science Newsletter*, p. 279.

Industrial research progress at Armour Research Foundation. (1946, January 25). *Chemical and Engineering News*, p. 120.

MBS recorder in D.C. precedent. (1946, February). *Variety*, p. 27.

New products: A VCR surge that defies the recession. (1980, September 1). *Business Week*, p. 28F.

News then and now. (1983, December). *Millimeter*, p. 168.

Patents siezed from aliens now abstracted. (1945, April 7). *Science Newsletter*, p. 220.

Portable VTR reproduced color. (1970, September 14). *Electronics*, pp. 155–158.

Portable videotape recorders. (1965, February). *Broadcast Management/Engineering*, p. 38.

Poulsen telegraphone. (1900, September 22). *Scientific America*, p. 178.

RCA's rivals still see life in videodiscs. (1986, April 23). *Business Week*, pp. 88.

Recorders coming. (1945, December 29). *Business Week*, pp. 54–56.

Recording telephones. (1900, August 16). *Nature*, p. 371.

Scientific cleanup. (1946, May 18). *Business Week*, pp. 19–29.

Sound recording, the Blattner system of electromagnetic recording and reproduction. (1929, October 18). *The Electrician*, p. 472.

State of the art. (1975, April 14). *Broadcasting*, p. 63.

Summary-index of week's news. (1984, May 7). *Videoweek*, p. 2.

The story of the triumph of tape. (n.d.). *Tape Recording and Reproduction Magazine*, p. 6.

The videodisc strikes out. (1984, April 16). *Newsweek*, p. 69.

Toward compatible VTRs. (1969, November 10). *Electronics*, p. 236.

VERA: The BBC vision electronic recording apparatus. (1958, April–June). *Journal of the Society of Motion Picture and Television Engineers*, p. 349.

Videotape: Options for the buyers, (1978, March). *IEEE Spectrum*, pp. 37–41.

Video tape recording. (1958, August). *Wireless World*, p. 362.

Videotape player update. (1970, May). *Broadcast Management/Engineering*, p. 8.

Voice recorded on hair-like wire. (1943, December). *General Electric Review*, p. 119.

Wire recorders for army. (1943, October). *Electronics*, pp. 234–235.

NEWSPAPER ARTICLES CITED

A sound and vision recorder—Its here. (1963, July 10). *Evening Press* (Dublin), *APCUT*, n.p.

Daily N.B.C. show will be on tape. (1957, January 18). *New York Times*, p. 45.

Day and night. (1956, April 15). *Redwood City Tribune*, Reprint, n.p.

Drama in decline, state of live shows is called disheartening. (1958, May 18). *New York Times*, p. 11.

Ever-better home equipment. (1986, March 30). *New York Times*, p. F23.

History Museum of Modern Technology, tale of tape: It's on public record. (1983, January 15). *Los Angeles Times*, Reprint, n.p.

Live TV vs. "canned." *New York Times*, p. 20.

NBC to record with video tape. (1957, November 5). *New York Times*, p. 63.

New museum records history of tape. (1983, January 24). *The Peninsular Times Tribune*, Reprint, n.p.

RCA shows tape recorder. (1956, January 31). *New York Times*, p. 20.

TV in the can vs. TV in the flesh. (1957, November 24). *New York Times*, p. 49.

Tale of tape: Its a public record. (1983, January 15). *The Peninsular Time Tribune*, n.p.

Tape comes of age. (1958, October 5). *New York Times*, p. 17.

Taped television commercial use of new device offers great possibilities and problems. (1956, April 22). *New York Times*, p. 13.

Use of television tapes coming to get stars into commercials. (1957, December 13). New York Times, p. 55.

Wonder of tape, how television shows are recorded without the necessity for film. (1958, May 4). New York Times, p. 11.

THESES AND DISSERTATIONS CITED

Adams, J.C. (1938). The development of a magnetic tape recorder. Unpublished BS thesis, Massachusetts Institute of Technology, Cambridge, MA.

Adams, R.C. (1938). Magnetic recording of sound. Unpublished BS Thesis, Massachusetts Institute of Technology, Cambridge, MA.

Camras, M. (1942). Magnetic recording on steel wire. Unpublished master's thesis, Illinois Institute of Technology, Chicago, IL.

Gomery, J.D. (1975). The coming of sound to the American cinema: The transformation of an industry. Unpublished doctoral dissertation, University of Wisconsin, Madison, WI.

Hillyer, C. (1938). The development of a magnetic tape reorder. Unpublished BS thesis, Massachusetts Institute of Technology, Cambridge, MA.

Lafferty, W.C. (1981). The early development of magnetic sound recording in broadcasting and motion pictures, 1928–1950. Unpublished doctoral dissertation, North Western University, Evanston, IL.

Staiger, J. (1981). The Hollywood mode of production: The construction of divided labor in the film industry. Unpublished doctoral dissertation, University of Wisconsin, Madison, WI.

GOVERNMENT PUBLICATIONS CITED

Abstracts of Mechanical and Electrical Vested Patents, Volume IV Classes 226–315. (n.d.). Washington, DC: Office of the Alien Property Custodian, Division of Patent Administration.

Brush Development Company. (1943). Fourth Report on the development of a high frequency stain analyzer, PB 24884. Washington, DC: Office of the Publication Board.

Crawford, J.W.C. (1945). Plastic in German sound recording systems. London: British Intelligence—Objectives Sub-Committee, Final Report No. 1379.

Harcourt, W.M. (1946). AGFA colour, BIOS Final Report No. 397; Item No. 9. London: British Intelligence Objectives Sub-Committee.

Hearing Before the Committee on Patents, United States Senate, 72nd Congress, 1st Session, on S. 1301, a Bill to Renew Certain Letters Patent. (1932, March 10). Washington, DC: U.S. Government Printing Office.

Manard, J.C. (1946, January). High frequency magnetophone magnetic sound recorders, FIAT Final Report No. 708.

Polaroid Corporation. (1945). *Report on optical plastic synthesis fabrication and instrument design.* Office of Scientific and Research Development, Report No. 4417.

Ranger, R.H. (1947). *Fiat Report No. 923, Further studies in magnetophones, May 13, 1947.* Washington, DC: Office of Technical Services.

Renewing certain letters patent. (1932, June 1). Calendar No. 812, U.S. Senate, Report No. 763, pp. 1–3.

Schuster, R.R. (1943). *Recorder (AN/ANQ-X-A) and recorder reproducer ANQ-1 (XA-1) "Aerobserver," PB 6232.* Washington, DC: Office of the Publication Board.

U.S. War Department. (1945). *Magnetic wire recorder, PB 37072.* Washington, DC: Office of the Publication Board.

U.S. War Department. (1945). *Magnetic wire recorder, PB 48304.* Washington, DC: Office of the Publication Board.

U.S. War Department. (1945). *Magnetic wire recording, P.B. 48934.* Washington, DC: Office of the Publication Board.

PATENTS CITED

United States Patents

341287 Recording and Reproducing Sounds. Sumner Tainter. May 4, 1886.

342214 Recording and Reproducing Speech and Other Sounds. Chichester A. Bell and Sumner Tainter. May 4, 1886.

661619 Method of Recording and Reproducing Sound or Siginals. Valdemar Poulsen. November 13, 1990.

836339 Magnetizable Body for the Magnetic Record of Speech. P.O. Pedersen. November 20, 1906.

873078 Electromagnet For Telegraphone Purpose. Peder P. Pedersen and Valdemar Poulsen. December 10, 1907.

900392 Sound Recording and Reproducing Instruments. George Kirkegaard. October 6, 1908.

1142384 Telegraphone. George S. Tiffany. June 8, 1915.

1213150 Method of Producing Magnetic Sound-Records for Talking-Motion-Picture Films. Henry C. Bullis. January 23, 1917.

1639060 Magnetic Talking, Dictating, and Like Machine. Gustav Scheel (System-Stille GmbH). August 16, 1927.

1640881 High Frequency Biasing. W.L. Carlson and G.W. Carpenter. August 30, 1927.

1883560 Electromagnetic Sound Recording and Reproducing Machine. Harry E. Chipman. October 18, 1932.

1883561 Magnetic Sound Recording and Reproducing Head. Harry E. Chipman. October 18, 1932.

2248790 Sound Recording Device. Arnold Stapelfeldt. (C. Lorenz AG). July 8, 1941.

2264008 Magnetic Sound Recording Device. Arnold Stapelfeldt (C. Lorenz AG). November 25, 1941.

2351003 Recording and Reproduction of Vibrations. Marvin Camras and William Korzon. November 18, 1941.

2351007 Magnetic Recording Head. Marvin Camras. June 13, 1944.

2773120 Magnetic Recording of High Frequency Signals Earl E. Masterson (RCA). December 4, 1956.

2866012 Magnetic Tape Recording and Reproducing System. Charles P. Ginsburg and Shelby F. Henderson, Jr. (Ampex). December 23, 1958.

2900443 Magnetic Recorder and Reproducer for Video. Marvin Camras. August 18, 1959.

2900444 Means for Recording and Reproducing Video Signals. Marvin Camras. August 18, 1959.

2912517 Magnetic Tape Apparatus. Robert Fred Pfost (Ampex). November 10, 1959.

2912518 Magnetic Tape Apparatus. Alexander R. Maxey (Ampex). November 10, 1959.

2916546 Visual Image Recording and Reproducing System and Method. Charles P. Ginsburg and Ray M. Dolby (Ampex). December 8, 1959.

2916547 Recording and Reproducing System. Charles P. Ginsburg and Shelby F. Henderson, Jr. (Ampex). December 8, 1959.

British Patents

9961 Telegraphone. Valdemar Poulsen. 1899.

288680 Improved Means of Recording and Reproducing Pictures, Images and The Like. Boris Rtcheouloff. April 4, 1928.

297078 Improvements in or Relating to Television Systems. Ralph Vinton Lyon Hartley and Herbert Eugene Ives (Electrical Research Products). June 19, 1929.

386183 Improvements in Television Receiving Method and Apparatus. American Television Laboratories Incorporated. January 12, 1933.

German Patents

480288 Magnetic Recording Medium: Tobis AG. 1927.

500900 Magnetic Recording Media. Fritz Pfleumer. 1928.

541302 Magnetic Recording Media. Fritz Pfleumer. 1930.

647386 Magnetic Recording Apparatus. AEG. 1937.

700177 Magnetic Recording Head. AEG. 1940.

700178 Magnetic Recording and Reproducing Head. AEG. 1940.

Danish Patent

1260 Telegraphone. Valdemar Poulsen. 1898.

MANUSCRIPTS

Addeo, E.G. (n.d.). *The Ampex story.* Unpublished manuscript, Ampex Corporation.
Collection of David Sarnoff's speeches. (n.d.). Princeton, NJ: Sarnoff's RCA Research Laboratories.

FURTHER READING ON MAGNETIC/VIDEOTAPE RECORDING WITH EMPHASIS ON ENGINEERING DESIGNS

Baldwin, J.L.E. (1973). Digital television recording. *Institute of Electrical and Radio Engineers (U.K.) Conference Proceedings* (No. 26, pp. 67–70).
Cambi, E. (1948, January). Trigonometric components of a frequency-modulated wave. *Proceedings of the Institute of Radio Engineers,* pp. 42–49.
Chen, D. (1974, April). Magnetic materials for optical recording. *Applied Optics* (Vol. 13, No. 4).
Granum, F., & Nishimura, A. (1979, July). Modern developments in magnetic tape. *Proceedings of the Conference on Video Data Recording, IERE Conference Procedings* (43), pp. 49–60.
Iijima, S., Sugaya, H., Fujii, K., & Kano, M. (1977, September). Pleasing the consumer while playing to win. *IEEE Spectrum,* pp. 45–50.
Imamura, N., & Mimura, Y. (1976). Magnetic recording on Gd Fe amorphous alloy films in contact with some magnetic materials. (1976). *Japan Journal of Applied Physics,* 15(4).
Iwasaki, S., & Nokamura, Y. (1977, September). An analysis for the magnetization mode for high density magnetic recording. (1977, September). *Institute of Electrical and Electronics Engineers Transaction* MAG-13(5), pp. 1272–1277.
Kihara, N. (1971, February). Colour cassette system for the NTSC and Japanses colour-television standards. *European Broadcasting Union Review.*
Kono, T., & Kamai, T. (1983, August). Video recording and playback systems-beta hi-fi VCR. (1983, August). *IEEE Transaction on Consumer Electronics,* pp. 141–152.
Kihara, N., Kohno, N., & Ishigaki, Y. (1976, February). Development of a new system of cassette type consumer VTR. (Institute of Electronics and Electrical Engineers, Chicago Fall Conference on Consumer Electronic

Technical Digest, December 1975) in IEEE Transaction Consumer Electronic, pp. 26–36.

Kihara, N., Odagiri, Y., & Sato, T. (1983, June). High speed video replicator system using contact printing. Institute of Electrical and Electronics Engineers ICCE Technical Digest.

Machida, Y., Morio, M., & Kihara, N. (1979, February). Simplified television standards converter as a video tape reproducing system. (1979, February). IEEE Chicago Fall Conference on Consumer Electronics, pp. 45–49.

Morio, M., Matsumoto, Y., Machida, Y., Kubota, Y., & Kihara, N. (1981, August). Development of an extremely small video tape recorder. IEEE Tranaction on Consumer Electronics, CE-27(3), pp. 331–339.

Sato, S., Takeuchi, K., & Hoshida, M. (1983, August). Recording video camera in the beta format. IEEE Transaction on Consumer Electronics, pp. 365–375.

Shiraishi, Y., & Hirota, A. (1978, September). Magnetic recording at video cassette recorder for home use. IEEE Transaction MAG Mag-14, pp. 318–320.

Shiraishi, Y., & Hirota, A. (1978, August). Video cassette recorder development for consumers. Institute of Electronic and Electrical Engineers Transaction Consumer Electronic-24, pp. 468–472.

Sugaya, H. (1978, September). Recent advances in video tape recording. Transaction of the IEEE Mag-14(5), pp. 632–637.

The Philips video cassette recorder. (1979, November/December). Electronics Technology, 13.

Umeki, S. (1974, September). A new high coercive magnetic particle for recording tape. IEEE Transaction as Magnetic Recording, Mag-10(3), pp. 655–656.

Wallace, R.L. (1951, October). The reproduction of magnetically recorded signal. Bell System Technical Journal, Part II, 30(4), pp. 1145–1173.

Author Index

Subject Index